Questions & Answers

INTERNATIONAL LAW

QUESTIONS & Answers

Keeping you afloat through your exams

Ask anyone for exam advice and they'll tell you to *answer the question*. It's good advice but the Q&As go further by telling you how to answer the questions you'll face in your law exams.

Q&As will help you succeed by:

✓ identifying typical law exam questions

✓ demonstrating how to structure a good answer

✓ helping you to avoid common mistakes

✓ advising you on how to make your answer stand out from the crowd

✓ giving you model answers to up to 50 essay and problem-based questions

Every Q&A follows a trusted formula of question, commentary, answer plan, examiner's tips, and suggested answer. They're written by experienced law lecturers and experienced examiners to help you succeed in exams.

'What a brilliant revision aid! With summaries, tips, and easy-to-understand sample answers, Q&As really help with exam technique and how to structure answers. A great help not only during the revision process, but also throughout the course.'
Kim Sutton, Law student, Oxford Brookes University

LAW OF TORTS 2013 and 2014

PUBLIC LAW 2013 and 2014

LAND LAW 2013 and 2014

LAW OF CONTRACT 2013 and 2014

EU LAW 2013 and 2014

FAMILY LAW 2013 and 2014

Titles in the series cover all compulsory law subjects and major options.

Buy yours from your campus bookshop, online, or direct from OUP

www.oxfordtextbooks.co.uk/law/revision

Questions & Answers

INTERNATIONAL LAW

Third edition

Susan Breau

Professor of International Law, Flinders University

Adelaide, Australia

2013 and 2014

OXFORD
UNIVERSITY PRESS

OXFORD
UNIVERSITY PRESS

Great Clarendon Street, Oxford, OX2 6DP,
United Kingdom

Oxford University Press is a department of the University of Oxford.
It furthers the University's objective of excellence in research, scholarship,
and education by publishing worldwide. Oxford is a registered trade mark of
Oxford University Press in the UK and in certain other countries

© Oxford University Press 2013

The moral rights of the author have been asserted

First edition 2009
Second edition 2011
Impression. 4

Public sector information reproduced under the Open Government Licence v1.0
(http://www.nationalarchives.gov.uk/doc/open-government-licence/open-government-licence.htm)

Crown Copyright material reproduced with the permission of the
Controller, HMSO (under the terms of the Click Use licence)

British Library Cataloguing in Publication Data
Data available

ISBN 978-0-19-966196-1

Printed in Great Britain by
Ashford Colour Press Ltd, Gosport, Hampshire

CONTENTS

Key features

The Q&A series provides full coverage of key subjects in a clear and logical way. The book contains the following features:

- Questions
- Commentary
- Bullet-pointed answer plans
- Examiner's tips
- Suggested answers
- Further reading suggestions

 online resource centre

www.oxfordtextbooks.co.uk/orc/qanda/

Titles in the Q&A series are supported by additional online materials to aid study and revision.

Online resources for this title are hosted at the URL above, which is open access and free to use.

This is the third edition on public international law in this series. I extend my appreciation to my former doctoral student at the University of Surrey, Ashley Bowes, and my former student at Pepperdine University, Aly Challoner, for their research assistance. Any errors and omissions are my responsibility alone.

This book is intended as a student aid in structuring an answer to examination-type problems and in discussing some of the more difficult areas in the subject. It also contains reference to further reading, which should be of assistance in the preparation of coursework. There is the addition for this edition of Examiner's tips to make sure you address the essentials in your answers.

This edition has been updated to include recent developments in international law such as the pivotal decision on sovereign immunity by the International Court of Justice, the crisis in Syria, and the intervention in Libya. There is also an updated review of academic articles in each of the subjects canvassed in this edition as important scholarship is continuing to develop on each of these topics.

The law is stated as at 31 August 2012.

Susan Breau

TABLE OF CASES

TABLE OF LEGISLATION

1

Introduction

This questions-and-answers book has been written by a Professor of International Law with many years' experience teaching the subject in four universities and who has also served as an external examiner in the subject. The purpose of the book is to give guidance to students on what might be expected in the answers to typical examination questions on the various topics that together constitute the study of public international law.

A distinguishing factor in public international law is the tendency to rely not only on jurisprudence but also on opinions of distinguished academics which, after all, is one of the subsidiary sources of public international law. As a result, adequate preparation must include access to various texts, monographs, and articles on each one of these areas of discussion. It is not enough to rely on a standard textbook as, at best, the student might expect to receive a lower second class mark. Furthermore, this field, as with all areas of law, is developing rapidly and students will be well rewarded by sourcing recent articles for the topics that they are revising. The international law articles databases are replete with recent articles on a wide variety of international law subjects. There are more and more specialized law journals that are well worth reviewing and there may be a journal with articles right on point.

It is also important to note that individual lecturers will place emphasis on different parts of the course. Although this book has attempted to cover all of the areas of concern, it would be a foolish student who did not pay attention to the parts of the course that the lecturer pays particular attention to. It is also well worth exploring the publications of your lecturer to see what area he or she is particularly interested in.

Unlike some of the other areas in the study of law, examinations in public international law do not have a preponderance of problem questions. There may indeed be problem questions but essay questions are just as likely. Therefore, the questions in this book have tended to be balanced between the two types of question. I am often asked if there is a special skill to answering either type of question. There is not—both require extensive preparation of the jurisprudence and literature in the field. They both require a structured answer with a clear argument, even if the argument favours both sides of a controversy. However, it should be noted that there is a necessity in a problem question to refer to the facts in the problem and not just to launch into an academic discussion of the subject. The problem questions will often require the student to reach a conclusion with respect to the fact situation. It is very important in both types of question to read the question carefully and to draft a rough outline to the answer first.

The most important point in either type of question is to *answer the question that you are asked*, rather than embark on an answer to the question you wished you had been asked. Another temptation in public international law is to embark on an extensive analysis of the political situation rather than answering the legal question. Examination questions require a legal answer albeit with evidence of knowledge of the political and historical environment.

Also critical is that an examiner is not asking you to write all you know about a subject. Time management is crucial. You must divide the questions between the number of hours that you are allotted and stick to the correct amount of time for each question. It is common for students to run out of time on the last question because of poor time management.

It is not possible in such a vast subject to cover all of the possible topics that might be canvassed in an examination. These topics, however, will give you an opportunity to see how a proper examination answer in this subject might be written. Above all, memorizing this text is not a substitute for proper preparation and study of the topics contained in your syllabus.

Good reading and the best of luck in your examination preparation.

The nature of public international law

Introduction

This chapter will address important questions of the historical and philosophical development of public international law including the often-cited 'party question' of whether this discipline is law at all. Generally, a public international law examination will have one such general question on the nature of the subject.

This chapter contains four essay questions. The principles that apply to answering these questions are to draw up a plan in rough, including a proper introduction, a series of substantive points, and a conclusion. A danger with essays is to ramble in order to include everything you know—resist this temptation, as the marker is looking for an organized and coherent structure. Essay questions on theoretical topics require a specific style. They certainly require a base of academic opinion and plenty of examples on the points that you are making; but, for high marks, they also need a touch of original analysis. That would be your opinion on the topic based on your reading and reaction to the various opinions on the issue. It is quite acceptable to see both sides of a controversial issue, but then you must indicate clearly that you were persuaded by neither opinion and give reasons for so doing.

Therefore, success in answering these questions depends on a broad reading of the available literature and a historical and philosophical approach. Those students who spend the beginning of the course or perhaps even the vacation period generally reading on public international law and the history of (particularly) the twentieth century will be rewarded for their efforts.

These questions are difficult, as there is a temptation to engage in political arguments rather than develop an answer based on international law literature and cases. The three elements in any question must be the published work on the topic, any relevant international case law, and any relevant historical situations which support the existence of various rules of public international law. Therefore, the starting point for preparation of these essay questions is to spend some time in the library doing research, as if you were preparing for an assessed essay or piece of coursework.

This first chapter and the remainder of the book will contain suggestions of relevant literature, but these are suggestions only. The well-prepared student will impress by locating recent relevant literature on any of the topics in this book by conducting relevant online database searches. It is absolutely essential to name the sources that you use, whether in case law or in academic literature. Quotations are never required in an examination, but summarizing the substance of the various arguments is critical.

For this topic, suggested literature includes: Fitzmaurice *et al.* (2007); the chapters by Neff *et al.* in Evans (2010); the introductory chapters in Cassese (2004); Shaw (2008); and Harris (2010).

Question 1

'Modern international law has its origins in the Europe of the sixteenth and seventeenth centuries.'

Harris

Is this statement correct?

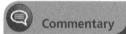
Commentary

It has often been argued that international law derives from Western philosophy and history. There are two equally correct approaches to this question. One avenue of discussion is to take a traditional approach and trace the development of international law from the European enlightenment and Hugo Grotius, who is often credited as the 'father' of international law. A second and perhaps more interesting approach would be to argue that from ancient times every culture has developed some sort of international law to deal with relations with other cultures. An excellent source for that account would be the chapter by Neff (one of only a handful of international law historians) in Evans (2010), as he traces the history of international law from ancient history. It is this second approach which will be addressed in this answer.

A fully developed answer will need to address both the historical and philosophical development of the subject and display knowledge of the key philosophical figures in international law theory from ancient times through to modernity. It must mention specifically those aspects of international law which existed in the various historical eras.

As with all essay questions, it is important to maintain a position on the answer. There are no right and wrong answers in this topic, just versions of opinions. However, it is important to support your opinion with knowledge of, and reference to, the relevant literature. Each answer should begin with an appropriately considered answer plan, so it is important to take a few minutes before beginning your writing to consider the content and structure of the answer.

Answer plan

- Developments in international law in other ancient cultures.
- Greek and Roman civilization and natural law.
- Continuation of natural law theories in the Middle Ages.
- The flowering of international law in the sixteenth and seventeenth centuries.
- The development of positivism in the eighteenth and nineteenth centuries.
- Modern international law theories.

Suggested answer

Professor Harris's statement is not entirely correct, as international law has many different historical and philosophical roots, other than those of the Europe of the sixteenth and seventeenth centuries, although this is the period when international law flowered. It can be argued that international law has developed historically and philosophically over many centuries, in many cultures and that a rudimentary system of international law existed even in ancient societies. To take issue with Professor Harris on his viewpoint one can refer to Neff's 'A short history of international law' in Evans (2010), which traces the development of international law in many historical traditions.

Neff persuasively contends that persons from even the most diverse historical cultures sought to relate to one another in a peaceful, predictable, and mutually beneficial way. His first historical example is Herodotus' description of '*silent trading*' between the Carthaginians and an unnamed North African tribe. He also points out that Mesopotamia, northern India, and classical Greece had three areas of international law: diplomatic relations, treaty-making, and rules governing the conduct of war. As these are still three major areas of international law, it establishes the view that international law has long historical roots. He also discusses: the Islamic empire of the seventh century AD, and the body of Islamic law that dealt with relations between states in the Islamic world and that body of the law regarding relations with the outside world.

Shaw (2008), however, argues that these systems were geographically and culturally restricted, as there was no conception of an international community of states. He does, however, admit that there was a powerful philosophical principle—the concept of natural law—which influenced the development of international law originating from Greek and Roman thought. This philosophy argued that a body of rules of universal relevance could be determined by human intelligence, and this constituted the roots of human rights. As Neff argues, one of the principal proponents of this philosophy was the Roman Cicero who argued that this law of nature would be '*spread through the whole human community, unchanging and eternal*'.

Neff and Shaw also discuss international law during the medieval period. Shaw points out that throughout Europe during this period maritime customs began to be accepted, founded on the Rhodian sea law and which was a Byzantine work. In addition, there was a 'continental law merchant', which was a series of regulations and practices governing trade. Neff asserts that the area of diplomatic relations developed in this period, with diplomats increasingly being accorded a broad degree of immunity. He also argues that, beginning in around the eleventh century, European states began to conclude bilateral treaties which spelled out reciprocal guarantees of fair treatment. During this historical period, 'just-war' theory also developed in the writings of St Augustine and St Thomas Aquinas, who continued the natural law theory with the modification that all laws originated with God.

Certainly, one has to agree with Harris that the sixteenth and seventeenth centuries constituted what Neff terms 'the classical age' of public international law. The major scholar of that era was Hugo Grotius whose main work was *On the Law of War and Peace*, published in 1625, and in which he further developed the just-war theory and argued that the law of nations was distinct from the law of nature. The purpose of the law of nations was to regulate the external conduct of rulers. Shaw also points out that the development of international law was further assisted by the Spanish writers Francisco Vitoria and Francisco Suárez and the Italian Gentile, but agrees that Grotius can be seen as the father of international law. His enduring contribution in Shaw's view is his proclamation of the freedom of the seas. All of these writers continued the natural law tradition first developed by ancient Greek and Roman philosophers and continued in the Middle Ages with St Augustine and St Thomas Aquinas. Another scholar in the seventeenth century who continued this work was Samuel Pufendorf, who was an exponent of this naturalist school.

Therefore, up to the nineteenth century, international law had developed over centuries, with its flowering in the classical age. Although Grotius might be known as the chief architect of our modern international legal philosophy, the roots of his scholarship are in the ancient natural law texts and developments of mercantile law in the Middle Ages. In the eighteenth and nineteenth centuries another philosophical tradition developed in contrast to Grotius' natural law theory which has also influenced modern international law: positivism. Such scholars as Zouche, Bynkershoek, and Emerich de Vattel emphasized the development of international law through consensual practice, the precursor to the theory of customary international law. Vattel introduced the doctrine of the equality of states. However, natural law did not disappear as it gave way to concepts of natural rights in the writings of Locke and Rousseau and their political theories which influenced the French and American revolutions.

It is important to note that modern international law has also been profoundly influenced by developments in the nineteenth and twentieth centuries; up until the end of the Second World War it was dominated by positivist thinking and the development of a plethora of bilateral and multilateral treaties, such as the treaties that constituted the results of the Hague Conferences, the establishment of the League of Nations, the Permanent Court of Justice, and, finally, the United Nations (UN). Neff argues that the instrumentalist approach gave positivism a moral ambivalence culminating perhaps in the Berlin conference in 1884 which resulted in the imperial partitioning of Africa. Among the writers influencing international theory were de Martens writing a treatise on state practice in 1785 and Wheaton, whose *Elements of International Law* in 1836 followed the same positivist pattern. However, by the middle of the twentieth century and the development of human rights conventions and concepts such as *jus cogens* and obligations *erga omnes* we see a return to natural law philosophy.

Recently in the late twentieth and early twenty-first centuries, in addition to the staggering developments in international legal instruments (multilateral law-making conventions) and international institutions (the UN, World Trade Organization (WTO), International Criminal Court) we have seen the rise of a diverse range of international law theories, even though, as Boyle and Chinkin (2007) argue, there is a continuation of natural law and positivism. One recent example is critical legal theory which challenges all of the language that is used in international law, as embodied by Martii Koskenniemi in his writings, including 'What is international law for?' (reproduced in Evans, 2006). This theory seeks to deconstruct the language used in international law and analyses the basic meaning, as Koskenniemi's famous book title indicates, of language which ranges from 'apology to utopia'. Juxtaposed with this philosophy are writers on liberal internationalism, such as Teson and Slaughter and the New Haven school which examines the process of international law-making as expounded by Myers McDougall and Michael Reisman. All of these theorists examine international law through the lens of philosophical thinking that might influence the development of international law into the future.

In this brief historical review, it can be seen that international law was developed over many centuries and that the classical age of Grotius and the Spanish philosophers might only be one stage in the continuing development of public international law that continues into the twenty-first century. There continue to be divergent theories of international law, which will inform future development of the subject.

 Examiner's tip

This question relates to the general issue of 'cultural relativism' canvassed later in this book. The background to the formation of international law might be primarily European but the only way to eliminate arguments about international law being a 'Western' construct is to trace the background back further. An excellent student in this area will also love history!

Question 2

It can be argued that international law does not exist in a world of power politics—a statement that is particularly true since the war in Iraq.

Discuss with supporting academic opinions whether you agree or disagree with this statement.

Commentary

Although this might be the 'party question' in international law, it is a particularly pertinent question given the international crisis that resulted over the war in Iraq in 2003 and the debate among international lawyers concerning the effectiveness of collective security particularly in the wake of the inaction concerning Syria. There has been a long-standing debate between international law and international relations scholars over the nature of the international system—is it governed by power politics or the international rule of law? A summary of the realist school of international relations is found in a chapter by Koskenniemi entitled 'Carl Schmitt, Hans Morgenthau, and the image of law in international relations' (in Byers, 1999). A relevant article to discuss here is 'Why the Security Council failed' (Glennon, 2003). The main tenor of this article is that the post-war collective security system has disintegrated in light of the division over the war in Iraq. Glennon is the first article that I give to my international law students in the first class to stimulate debate concerning international law.

Support for the existence of international law can be found in Jennings and Watts, *Oppenheim's International Law* (1992). This position is also expressed in academic arguments of an emerging international constitution. For this position, see: von Bogdandy (2006); Christian Tomushchat's two Hague Academy lectures: 'International law: ensuring the survival of mankind on the eve of a new century' (1999); 'Obligations arising for states without or against their will' (1993); and Jürgen Habermas (2006).

A student can choose to agree or disagree with the statement but should discuss the opposing views on the existence of rules of international law by reference to theoretical literature. It is important to set out the position early in the answer and support it throughout. This question also illustrates the importance of keeping up to date with current affairs!

Answer plan

- Discuss the theory of realism as embodied by Carr and Morgenthau.
- Discuss the support of later writers, including Glennon, in the wake of the war in Iraq.
- Introduce the idea of international constitutionalism and the opposing argument of Christian Tomushchat and Jürgen Habermas.
- Conclude with your view of this issue.

Suggested answer

The statement that international law does not exist in a world of power politics is indeed controversial. It has its roots in the post-war international relations school of realism but this view was revived in the wake of the crisis over the war in Iraq and now continues with the inactivity of the Security Council in the face of large loss of life in the conflict in Syria. It is correct that the invasion of Iraq can be seen as epitomizing power politics and unilateralism as the United States and its allies arguably disregarded the rules of international law. However, one can also assert that, if anything, the effort by the United States and the United Kingdom to support their action by international legal arguments and the reaction against the war in Iraq by a majority of states has strengthened the international rule of law. Furthermore, the reaction of the vast majority of states in the international community to the Russian and Chinese vetoes over resolutions concerning Syria can be seen as further support for the rule of international law. This answer will describe opposing views on power politics and arrive at conclusions on this statement.

First, Koskenniemi in 'Carl Schmitt, Hans Morgenthau, and the image of law in international relations' in Byers (1999) outlines the history of the realist school of international relations. Realists such as Carr and Morgenthau argued that states were self-interested actors engaged in a ruthless struggle for power, which can be defined as the ability of a state or states to control or influence directly how other states behave. Morgenthau (1954), was very influential in this field, and asserted that the international legal system was at the mercy of sovereign states. He stated that governments were *'anxious to shake off the restraining influence that international laws have upon their foreign policies'*. Another realist, Carr, proposed that international law could be changed at the will of states. Morgenthau supported his theory by arguing the serious weaknesses in the enforcement system of international law. His theory was later developed by a new generation of writers, such as Waltz (1979), who rejected international law as a structural element in the international system.

In the wake of the division over the Iraq war, the realist theory was revived. Glennon's (2003) provocative article argued that the division in the Security Council over the invasion of Iraq was the *'dramatic rupture'* that ended *'the grand attempt to subject the use of force to the rule of law'*. Glennon asserted that the Security Council would only be relevant if it dealt with matters not bearing directly on the upper hierarchy of world power. It has to be said that Glennon fails to take into account the efforts of both the United States and the United Kingdom within the Security Council to argue the legality of the intervention in Iraq as supporting previous Security Council resolutions. There is a clear disagreement about this argument within the international community but both sides argued international legality.

Although it may be argued that the realist theory is compelling, there is an equally persuasive opposite opinion. Jennings and Watts (1992) discuss the issue of the legal force of international law. They argue that the problem of whether international law is law properly so called, has been a problem of definition. Different definitions of what constitutes law can produce different answers to the question. For example, if a definition is drawn up based on municipal law it might be unnecessarily restrictive. Jennings and Watts propose that law was defined as a body of rules for human conduct within a community which by common consent of this community shall be enforced by external power. They acknowledge that in the past the weakness in international law was the lack of enforcement but in the past half century an emerging system for the enforcement of international law is discernible. This includes the existence of law-making treaties and certain aspects of the activities of international organizations. Other indicators of growing maturity of the international legal order is the recognition that certain rules have the character of peremptory norms known in international law as *jus cogens* and **Art. 103 UN Charter** which establishes for members the superior nature of obligations under the **UN Charter**.

This view is supported by von Bogdandy (2006) who refers to the German school of international constitutionalism. Two of its adherents are Tomushchat and the famous philosopher Habermas. Tomushchat (1993) in his two series of Hague Academy lectures traces developments in international law in the wake of the end of the cold war towards rules and principles which govern the international legal community. In his lectures Tomushchat argues that there is an international legal community guided by basic rules which are the norms of *jus cogens* and obligations *erga omnes* and thus there is an emerging international constitution based on an international rule of law.

In further support of his thesis, Tomushchat argues that there are a number of instruments which set out the rules of the international legal order. These instruments include: **Art. 2(1) UN Charter** that sets out the principle of the sovereign equality of states; **Art. 38(1) Statute of the International Court of Justice** which contains a list of the different categories of rules of international law, including customary law and treaty law; and **Art. 26 Vienna Convention on the Law of Treaties,** which declares that every treaty in force is binding on the parties to it and must be performed in good faith. This argument has been taken up more recently by Habermas (2006), in which he argues that the world dominated by nation states is in transition towards a global society. He addresses those sceptics such as Glennon (2003) who argue the end of collective security, as his main argument is that the international reaction against the war in Iraq, if anything, supports the idea of an international rule of law.

In examining the academic literature on this topic and indeed the international reaction concerning the war in Iraq as discussed by Habermas, one could agree with the view of Tomushchat. Since the advent of the **UN Charter,** there has been an emergence of an international legal community governed by the rules and principles of international law. These rules are embodied in law-making treaties and peremptory rules of public international law. The emergence of such a system can also be supported by the evidence of the debate over the legality of the invasion of Iraq as it can be seen that many states particularly in Security Council debates referred to a binding rule of international law, the prohibition against the use of force, in their arguments against the war. The British Chilcot inquiry regarding Iraq concentrated extensively on issues of legality with testimony from former Foreign Office legal advisers. Furthermore, debate over the situations in Libya and Syria focused on international criminal liability of the leaders of these nations. Based on these arguments, it can be argued that the statement that international law does not exist in a world of power politics is incorrect.

Examiner's tip

This question requires the student to be up to date on the current controversies in international law. The issue of Syria will merit closer study and mention of Libya and the consensual intervention there might be useful. However, environmental law students might also use the debate about climate change and the difficulty involved in developing binding carbon emissions controls.

Question 3

'Any enforcement of international law rules is based on consent.'
Do you agree with this statement?

Commentary

This is a question which begins the journey continued in the next chapter concerning the sources and enforceability of international law. One of the main critiques of international law is the lack of any clear enforcement mechanism which places its status as a legal system in jeopardy. This answer can address the theoretical debate and important new developments in the rise of international courts and tribunals and the more activist Security Council since the fall of the Berlin Wall.

Cassese (2004) discusses this issue in his first chapter and a key influential article on this subject is Sir Gerald Fitzmaurice, 'The foundations for the authority of international law and the problem of enforcement' (1956). In addition, the treatise by Jennings and Watts (1992) discusses the issue of international law enforcement.

Answer plan

- Describe how international law might be enforced domestically and internationally.
- Discuss the theory of reciprocity as the rudimentary theory of enforcement.
- Illustrate the enforcement system within the **UN Charter**.
- Discuss the International Court of Justice (ICJ) as a consensual tribunal.
- Mention the other international courts and tribunals.
- Discuss the nature of customary law and treaties as mechanisms of enforcement which might not be consensual.

Suggested answer

This essay addresses one of the leading critiques of international law as a legal system, the lack of an organized enforcement system. International law clearly does not have an organized system of courts and tribunals, such as that of a domestic system. However, it can be argued that there is a system of enforcement that has traditionally existed in international law based on bilateral treaty arrangements and customary international law. There has been a developing and more sophisticated formal system of enforcement in recent years.

As Cassese (2004) has argued, there is not a permanent power structure in the international community and relations between states remain horizontal. He identifies three functions within the international system: law-making, law determination, and law enforcement. However, he has pointed out that with respect to the third function, international law has developed systems of enforcement. The first way that international law is enforced is the obligation to incorporate the rules of international law within domestic laws in order that breaches of international law can be enforced domestically. This is increasingly the case and an excellent example of the incorporation of international legal obligations within domestic statutes are the national statutes adopting the International Criminal Court, which contain details of international criminal obligations, such as to refrain from committing the crimes of genocide, crimes against humanity, and war crimes.

A second way that international law is enforced is an international legal system based on reciprocity. The international system is based on those rules that all states would like to be applicable to them. An example is diplomatic immunity which allows international diplomacy to operate and is based on both states respecting and protecting each other's diplomats. The main reason that international law is respected is that countries develop and respect customary and treaty-based rules that they would like to see enforced against them.

Finally, Cassese introduces a unique notion to international relations, that of collective responsibility. Although he argues that in the present legal community traditional rules based on reciprocity will constitute the bulk of international law, there are new rules with different content and import. A number of treaties which came into being after the First and, most importantly, the Second World War contain obligations that are incumbent upon each state towards all other contracting parties and which are not reciprocal. Community obligations have the following features: (1) they are obligations protecting fundamental values, such as peace, human rights, self-determination, protection of the environment; (2) they are obligations *erga omnes*, obligations towards all other states; (3) they are attended by correlative right that belongs to any state; (4) this right may be exercised by any other state; (5) the right is exercised on behalf of the whole international community to safeguard these fundamental values of the community. These obligations are often incorporated in law-making treaties, such as the **International Covenant on Civil and Political Rights (1966) (ICCPR)** and the **International Covenant on Economic, Social and Cultural Rights (1966) (ICESCR)**. Unlike a domestic legal system where an individual who breaches the law must suffer the consequences, a breach of this type of international law by an official of a state means that the whole state community will have to suffer the consequences of the breach of an international obligation. However, Cassese cautions that enforcement of these community rights in still rare in international law, although one could take issue with this opinion by pointing to the rise in international criminal tribunals holding individuals to account for violations of these community obligations.

Fitzmaurice (1956) in his influential article argues that traditionally enforcement meant self-help usually epitomized by the use of force. However, with the advent of the **UN Charter** and its prohibition on the use of force in international relations, the question remains as to what recourses there are for collective enforcement of the rules of international law. Fitzmaurice points out that in the **UN Charter** both **Chap. VII** in the event of a breach of a particular rule of international law (breach of the peace) and **Chap. VI** providing for pacific settlement of disputes do not provide a developed enforcement system as they are directed against only one delict. Particularly in **Chap. VI** the measures are strictly voluntary. Once again, although this opinion supports Cassese in his pessimism on collective enforcement, it can be argued that in recent years there has been an increase in Security Council activity in such areas as the response to the Iraq invasion of Kuwait, peace enforcement missions in Africa, and in counter-terrorism initiatives.

However, as Fitzmaurice points out, there is another organ which might be very influential and that is the International Court of Justice (hereinafter ICJ). This is even more the case recently as, although the international legal system clearly does not have a developed judiciary, there are now several international courts and tribunals. However, the main judicial arm of the international legal system remains the ICJ. This court is a consent-based court, as contested matters heard have to be sent to the court on consent of the parties or by way of a referral from the Security Council which must have the consent of the permanent five members of the Security Council. Fitzmaurice argues that the authority of a decision of the ICJ is very great. Most countries accept the ruling of the court. Furthermore, under **Art. 94 UN Charter** a party may have recourse to the Security Council if the other party fails to adhere to the court's judgment. At the time Fitzmaurice was writing, states had not resorted to the ICJ on a very frequent basis and it can now be seen that the use of contested cases to resolve disputes has increased greatly in the past fifty years. Furthermore, advisory Opinions issued by the court have been influential in the development of international law. This is supported by Jennings and Watts (1992) who point out that in the *Military and Paramilitary Activities in Nicaragua* case the ICJ upheld the essential justiciability of even those disputes raising issues of the use of force and collective self-defence.

This argument could be extended even to such tribunals as the United Nations Human Rights Committee (UNHRC) which, although it issues recommendations only, practice has revealed that those recommendations are often followed by the states involved in the process. The ad hoc international criminal tribunals have done much to clarify and enforce rules of international criminal law against individuals. This promises to be the case for the International Criminal Court where, at the time of the writing, 121 states parties have agreed to the jurisdiction of the court for the most serious violators of international criminal law and which saw the indictment of the presidents and senior leaders in Sudan and Libya.

An important point made by Fitzmaurice is that even without a developed system of enforcement, international law rules are binding and that international law is enforced only because there exist legally binding rules. As Jennings and Watts argue, states not only recognize the rules of international law as legally binding in many treaties but they also affirm constantly that there is a law between them. An important part of that law is the rules of customary international law which are developed based on the consensual legally obligatory practice of states. Therefore, it can be seen that however rudimentary, there exists an active system of enforcement in international law.

 Examiner's tip

The issue of enforcement and international law is a continuing problem. An excellent student will be wise enough to see the gradations of enforcement that exist from international opinion through to international criminal courts. It is also important to examine not only what states do in violation of international law but also what they say, which often supports the international rule of law.

 Question 4

The United Nations is an embryonic world government.

Discuss.

 Commentary

This question is one version of the commonly asked international organizations question. Its purpose is to enable the student to display detailed knowledge of the structure and powers of the UN. It is critically important to describe the organization of the UN from the standpoint of the **UN Charter** and the practice of the UN since the Second World War. Included in the discussion of the UN must be the ICJ and the student should be familiar with the **Statute of the International Court of Justice (1945)**.

There may indeed be a separate topic in the course for the UN but generally a discussion of this important international organization is within the introductory part of the course.

Shaw (2008) has an excellent chapter on the UN in his textbook. Fassbender is a scholar who argues that the **UN Charter** is the constitution of the international community—see his article and books, especially: 'The meaning of international constitutional law', in MacDonald and Johnston (2005); 'The United Nations Charter as constitution of the international community' (1998); and *UN Security Council Reform and the Right of Veto: a Constitutional Perspective* (1998). See also Stefan Talmon's 2005 article in the *American Journal of International Law,* 'The Security Council as World Legislature'.

 Answer plan

- Introduce the three features of government: legislative, executive, and judiciary as part of a constitutional system of governance.
- Describe the structure and powers of the UN.
- Describe the key organs of the UN, including the ICJ and its possible influence on law-making, law determination, and law enforcement.
- Conclude with your reasoned opinion on the question.

 Suggested answer

In order to answer the question as to whether the UN is a world government, one first has to address the issue of what constitutes a government. From studying public or constitutional law, it is evident that any system of government has to have an executive, legislature, and judiciary. The powers of each three organs are set out in a constitution, which is either unwritten (examples are the United Kingdom, New Zealand) or written (examples are the United States, Canada). The UN, the major international organization set up under the 1945 **UN Charter,** has a unique and complex structure and specific powers. This essay will review the **UN Charter** powers and structure of the UN and argue that at this point neither the powers nor the structure are compatible with the domestic view of governance. The UN is a long way from what could be called a world government.

Fassbender discusses the **UN Charter** as the constitution of the international community. He argues (2005) that the principal reason for suggesting that the **UN Charter** is the constitution of the international community is that it is the one document which provides a statement of the fundamental rights and responsibilities of the members of the international community and sets out the values to which this community is committed. However, Shaw (2008) argues a contrasting opinion, that the **UN Charter** is simply the constitutive document of the UN itself and not a constitution for the Member States. However, in reviewing the **UN Charter,** the general statements concerning self-determination, sovereign equality, peace and security, and human rights certainly seem broader than the establishment of an international organization. By signing this treaty, these values are binding on all Member States.

Even though the **UN Charter** could arguably be seen as an international constitution that does not mean there is a world government. In reviewing the structure of the UN as set out in the **UN Charter,** there are six major organs: the Security Council, General Assembly, Secretariat, Trusteeship Council, Economic and Social Council, and the ICJ. At this point, the Trusteeship Council no longer operates, so it is necessary to examine the remaining organs to see if they constitute executive, legislative, or judicial arms. With respect to the executive arm, the Secretariat is the administrative arm of the UN with the Secretary-General at its head. The Secretary-General is elected by the General Assembly and Security Council but the executive arm in this case does not propose policy; rather, it is directed to perform the will of the Security Council or General Assembly.

In fact, Shaw argues that it was the Security Council that was intended to operate as an efficient executive organ and it was given primary responsibility for peace and security. The Security Council consists of 15 members, five of which are permanent (the United States, United Kingdom, Russia, China, and France), and these permanent members have a veto under **Art. 27 UN Charter**. However, Talmon (2005) has argued that the Security Council at various times has performed a legislative function, particularly in the counter-terrorism regime set out in **Security Council Resolution 1373**. As its decisions are binding on all Member States, this is more than an executive action. However, this legislative action is only in the field of international peace and security.

Shaw describes the General Assembly as the parliamentary body of the UN organization, as it consists of representatives of all of the Member States (currently 192). Yet Shaw acknowledges that it is not a legislature as, except for internal matters such as budgets, the Assembly cannot bind its members. Its resolutions are purely recommendatory. Shaw summarizes that the Assembly is essentially a debating chamber and a forum for the exchange of ideas and the discussion of international problems. Conversely, it can be argued that in certain circumstances these resolutions can evolve into binding effect if they become customary international law which is binding on all states. Sloan in his article 'General Assembly resolutions revisited (forty years later)' (1987) argued that in certain circumstances General Assembly resolutions can constitute customary international law.

The Economic and Social Council has no domestic equivalent, as it is a body to perform the work of the UN in the economic and social spheres. It has proposed a number of binding international treaties on various issues including the two international covenants on human rights but these do not take effect until they are ratified by domestic governments. Once again it is not legislative.

The major component of the judicial arm of the international legal system is the ICJ part of the UN system. The ICJ continued the work of the Permanent Court of International Justice (PCIJ) established in 1920 under the auspices of the League of Nations. The **Statute of the International Court of Justice (1945)** is attached to the **UN Charter**. It is not, however, a supreme court of the international system. By and large, states have to consent to have their disputes litigated in the international system. Its decisions are binding only on those states that are before the court and not on the world community of states, although its decisions may be very influential.

There have been courts established by the Security Council. These are the ad hoc criminal tribunals for the former Yugoslavia and for Rwanda. These courts have binding legal effect on those international criminals brought before them. The Security Council can also issue resolutions, such as the resolutions on terrorism, which can have binding legal effect. Another important source of judicial organs of binding legal effect is the appeals system in the World Trade Organization (WTO) and the Law of the Sea Tribunal. The world does not yet have an international human rights court and those states who allow their populations to bring their human rights violations before the international system only have views issued against them.

There are also a variety of regional systems such as the European Court of Justice and Human Rights, the Inter-American Court of Human Rights, and the newly established African Court of Human Rights which do or will issue binding decisions of international law but only on a regional basis.

It can be seen then that various organs can have executive and legislative functions and that the judicial system is not organized or generally binding on states. Furthermore, the legislative functions are only to constitute on occasion customary international law and binding resolutions in the field of international peace and security. One of the difficulties in this disorganized and non-hierarchical system is that various courts can issue conflicting rulings on the content and applicability of international rules. This phenomenon is known as the fragmentation of international law. In fact, the International Law Commission has established a working group to issue a report on this issue and its final report the 'Study on fragmentation of international law' was issued in 2006. It is clear that the ICJ is not a supreme court with powers to review decisions by the other organs and thus cannot constitute at this point an organized judicial arm of government.

Therefore this review of the structure and powers of the UN cannot support the proposition that it can be seen as an organized world government. It is a unique structure that has no equivalent in domestic law. It may well be in the future that the UN might evolve into a governmental structure, but not at this point in history.

 Examiner's tip

As the United Nations is so critical to the development of almost all areas of international law, knowledge of the Charter is vital. The student would be rewarded by examining an organizational chart of the United Nations and by thoroughly reviewing the various courts and tribunals that have been established internationally and regionally.

Further reading

Boyle, A. and Chinkin, C., *The Making of International Law* (Oxford: Oxford University Press, 2007).

Byers, M., *Custom, Power and the Power of Rules* (Cambridge: Cambridge University Press, 1999).

Cassese, A., *International Law*, 2nd edn (Oxford: Oxford University Press, 2004).

Evans, M., *International Law*, 3rd edn (Oxford: Oxford University Press, 2010).

Fassbender, B., 'The United Nations Charter as constitution of the international community' (1998) 36 *Columbia Journal of Transnational Law* 529.

Fassbender, B., *UN Security Council Reform and the Right of Veto: a Constitutional Perspective* (Leiden and Boston: Brill, 1998).

Fassbender, B., 'The meaning of international constitutional law', in R. MacDonald and D. Johnston (eds), *Towards World Constitutionalism: Issues in the Legal Ordering of the World Community* (Leiden and Boston: Martinus Nijhoff, 2005).

Fitzmaurice, G., Sir, 'The foundations for the authority of international law and the problem of enforcement' (1956) 19 MLR 1.

Fitzmaurice, M., Craven, M., and Vogiatzi, M., *Time, History and International Law* (Leiden and Boston: Martinus Nijhoff, 2007).

Glennon, M., 'Why the Security Council failed' *Foreign Affairs* (May/June 2003).

Habermas, J., *The Divided West* (Cambridge: Polity Press, 2006).

Harris, D. J., *Cases and Materials on International Law*, 7th edn (London: Sweet & Maxwell, 2010).

Jennings, R. and Watts, A., (eds), *Oppenheim's International Law*, 9th edn (London: Longman, 1992).

Morgenthau, H., *Politics among Nations* (New York: Alfred Knopf, 1954).

Shaw M., *International Law*, 6th edn (Cambridge: Cambridge University Press, 2008).

Sloan, B., 'General Assembly resolutions revisited (forty years later)', in the (1987) 58 (1) *British Yearbook of International Law* 39.

Talmon, S., 'The Security Council as World Legislature' (2005) 99 AJIL 175.

Tomushchat, C., 'Obligations arising for states without or against their will' (1993) 241 *Recueil des Cours* 195.

Tomushchat, C., 'International law: ensuring the survival of mankind on the eve of a new century' (1999) 281 *Recueil des Cours* 10.

von Bogdandy, A., 'Constitutionalism in international law: comment on a proposal from Germany' (2006) 47 *Harvard International Law Journal* 223.

Waltz, K., *Theory of International Politics* (New York: McGraw-Hill, 1979).

3

The sources of public international law

Introduction

It would be next to impossible for a public international law exam paper not to contain a question on sources. As international law is not derived from legislation or a precedential system of case law, its formation is unique and quite complex. There is no single legislative body creating the law, nor a system of courts with jurisdiction to interpret the laws. Sources are defined by Shaw (2008) as the provisions operating within the international law system on a technical level, the process whereby rules of international law are created. You must be familiar with this foundational part of the subject before proceeding to any other area. **Article 38 Statute of the International Court of Justice (1945)** describes the sources that the judges of the International Court of Justice (ICJ) rely upon when they determine what constitutes a rule of public international law. The two major sources are customary international law and treaties. This provision in the statute has now become the basis upon which all international law is determined. The major legal issues in this topic have to do with the formation of customary international law and the relationship between customary international law and treaty law. There is a separate chapter on specific treaty law (see Chapter 4, p. 34).

The conscientious student will be aware that **Art. 38** with its list of international conventions, international custom, general principles of law, the secondary sources of judicial decisions, and the teachings of the most highly qualified publicists, may not be comprehensive and there may be other emerging sources of public international law. Particularly, there is a growing area of debate surrounding the resolutions of both the General Assembly and the Security Council as potential sources of international law.

There are a number of academic articles and monographs on this subject. Furthermore, each textbook in international law has a chapter on this topic which contains discussion of the key issues. However, a very useful source that is often overlooked is the International Law Association's Committee on the Formation of Customary International Law which reported in 2000; its report is available on the International Law Association's website and provides an excellent summary of the critical issues and continues to resonate. Useful monographs on the subject are: d'Amato (1971), Danilenko (1993), Byers (1999); and often-cited articles are Akehurst, 'Custom as a source of international law', (1974–5) and Mendelson, 'The formation of customary international law' (1998). A particularly good chapter is that by Thirlway entitled 'The sources of international law' in Evans (2010).

In addition to the academic materials, it is particularly important that you are familiar with the key ICJ decisions and of those of its predecessor, the Permanent Court of International Justice (PCIJ), as this topic requires analysis of the key court decisions. Although ICJ cases are not precedents in the same way as cases within common law, these cases are highly influential and are cited repeatedly in subsequent decisions and in the academic debate about the nature of sources. Success in answering these questions will depend on an in-depth reading of these cases.

In this area, examiners are likely to ask questions on the controversial topics associated with the creation of international law which means that the answers can by no means be definitive. It is more important to support your answer by reference to international instruments, case law, and academic opinion than to find a correct answer. As with many legal disputes, there is justification to be found to argue either or both sides of an issue. If you attempt to analyse critically any of these topics and to render your own opinion, the marker will be impressed. However, you must support your opinion with relevant academic materials, including knowledge of the leading monographs, articles, and case law.

There are several complex questions associated with this topic which could be asked in an examination or in coursework. These could be asked by use of quotations from the leading case on the sources of public international law, or by essay questions. It is highly unlikely that a problem question would be asked, because of the complexity of the area. In this chapter there are four questions, three are essay questions and one is a quotation from a leading ICJ case.

There is one aspect of a question on sources that is common to all questions and that is the fact that any answer must start with a definition of what constitutes the sources of public international law. You may choose to quote **Art. 38** in detail or summarize the key sources. However, a mistake that is often made in these answers is to get off-track and to discuss in detail the meaning of each source without addressing the question that is asked. The majority of your answer should deal with the controversial issue rather than a repetition of textbook descriptions of the various sources. Furthermore, the cases in the ICJ are often long and complex—only a very brief description of the facts is needed, the critical part is the opinion of the court on the question that is being asked.

Question 1

'The Court does not consider that, for a rule to be established as customary, the corresponding practice must be in absolute rigorous conformity with the rule. In order to deduce the existence of customary rules, the Court deems it sufficient that the conduct of states should, in general, be consistent with such rules …'

Discuss this quotation from the *Nicaragua* case.

 Commentary

Probably the most difficult concept to grasp in the formation of public international law is the concept of custom. It does not relate to domestic sources of law, it harks back to an anthropological view of the development of law from traditional practices, which was also an early source of all domestic laws. As international law is still a relatively new legal system, it is not surprising that customary law might still exist.

This question will test your knowledge of the sources, the nature of custom, the relevant case law, and academic materials. It will also include your knowledge of the issue of whether a rule can become customary in the face of objector states. Although this quote is taken from the *Nicaragua* judgment in the ICJ, it is only one version of several dicta on how state practice influences the formation of customary international law.

The first issue will be to identify what actually is state practice, as there is also a debate as to what constitutes practice. Second, you should discuss the issue of quantity and quality with reference to the case law and academic materials. Finally, an excellent answer will review the further controversy of the effect on the formation of rule of customary law by the existence of persistent-objector states.

The major cases relating to this issue in the ICJ are the *Asylum* case, the *Anglo-Norwegian Fisheries* case, the *Fisheries Jurisdiction* case, the *North Sea Continental Shelf* case, the *Nicaragua* case, and the *Legality of Nuclear Weapons* advisory Opinion. You would be wise to consult the various international law texts on this issue and particularly consult the International Law Association's report on customary international law. Articles with particular relevance are Akehurst (1974–5), Charney, 'The persistent objector rule and the development of customary international law' (1985), and Roberts 'Traditional and modern approaches to customary international law' (2001).

 Answer plan

- Discussion of custom as one of the sources of public international law as per the definition provided in **Art. 38 Statute of the International Court of Justice**.
- The meaning and importance of state practice in the formation of custom.

- The role of the case law of the ICJ in the clarification of customary international law.
- A discussion of the various formulations of state practice contained in the case law.
- The role of the persistent-objector state and the controversy over what objection means, relying again on case law and academic sources.
- Summarize the various views and the lack of consensus on the topic.

 Suggested answer

This quotation highlights the disagreement in court opinions and academic literature over the definition of what constitutes state practice. **Article 38(1)(b) of the Statute of the International Court of Justice (1945)** states that: '*The Court, whose function it is to decide in accordance with international law such disputes as are submitted to it, shall apply: international custom, as evidence of a general practice accepted as law*'. There are two elements in the definition of international custom: the first is 'general practice' and the second element is that the practice is 'accepted as law'. It is the first part of the definition that this quotation from the *Nicaragua* case addresses. This is described by the International Law Association report on customary international law as the objective element in the formation of international law, whereas 'accepted as law' known as *opinio juris* is the subjective element.

State practice is the basis upon which a legal rule develops in international law which is not codified into a convention or treaty. As states are the principal subjects of international law it is logical that how a state might deal with a certain issue is in conformity with how other states might deal with a similar issue may well result in the emergence of a legal rule. Akehurst (1974–5) defines state practice as physical acts, claims, declarations, national laws, national judgments, and omissions. However, there is a controversy over whether inaction or omission can constitute customary law. This is the issue of the quality of state practice. D'Amato (1971) argued that only action can constitute state practice, whereas Byers (1999) argues that consent to rules is rarely given explicitly and silence can constitute acquiescence. Roberts (2001) supports a deductive approach to the development of customary international law and points out that custom can begin from a general statement of rules rather than specific instances of practice and that practice can emerge from statements in the General Assembly.

In addition, besides the qualitative issue there is also the issue of quantity. Various decisions of the ICJ have attempted to clarify the definition in the statute. As many of the disputes before the court concern the determination of what might constitute a rule of customary international law, the court's expansion of this definition is critical. The rather vague definition in the statute stems from the 1927 PCIJ ruling in the *Lotus* case, which defined customary international law as '*usages generally accepted as expressing principles of law and established in order to regulate the relations between those co-existing independent communities*'. It was the post-war ICJ that gave greater detail to a definition of customary international law in its two component parts: state practice and *opinio juris*. Regrettably, the cases are not consistent as to how much or what type of state practice is necessary.

Even the leading experts on public international law (a subsidiary source of public international law according to **Art. 38 Statute of the International Court of Justice (1945)**) do not agree on the issue of quantity. The division in the case law which this quotation from *Nicaragua* highlights means that there can be two distinct opinions on this answer. The first opinion is the view expressed in such cases as the *Asylum* case, the *Anglo-Norwegian Fisheries* case, and the *Fisheries Jurisdiction* case and supported by the International Law Association report that state practice should be virtually uniform. The second opinion, relying on the *Nicaragua* case and academic opinion, such as that of Byers, argues that the practice does not have to be uniform but general, which allows for objecting states. This version will also allow for practice from fewer states, such as maritime states with a particular interest in forming a rule of customary international law. This controversy is a continuing one particularly with almost 200 states in the international community, so neither opinion is incorrect.

The jurisprudence is not conclusive in any respect. In the *Asylum* case, the judgment stated that the rule invoked must be in accordance with '*the constant, and uniform usage practised by the states in question*'. In the *Anglo-Norwegian Fisheries* case, the court emphasized that custom could come into existence by '*constant and sufficiently long practice*'. The *North Sea Continental Shelf* cases added an extra dimension to the importance of state practice of the particularly interested states holding that '*state practice, including that of states whose interests are specially affected should... [be] both extensive and virtually uniform*'. In 1974, the *Fisheries Jurisdiction* judgment held that state practice must be '*common, consistent and concordant*'. This quotation from the more recent *Nicaragua* case seems to be a departure from this formula of an established, widespread, and consistent practice to a more generalized statement which allows general consistency. However, in the *Nuclear Weapons* case in 1996 the ICJ held that the fact that there was a small minority of nuclear weapons states objecting to the annual General Assembly resolutions declaring that nuclear weapons were illegal did result in there not being a rule of customary international law. This seems to hark back to the formula in the *Fisheries Jurisdiction* and *Asylum* cases.

Akehurst argued that the numbers of states participating in the practice is more important than the frequency or duration of the practice. He also argued that major inconsistencies in state practice would prevent the creation of custom. Byers on the other hand argued that the practice of the major powers may be more important than that of smaller states. Cassese (2004) accepted the *Nicaragua* formulation and argued that state practice did not need to be absolutely uniform and that individual deviations may not lead to the conclusion that no rule had crystallized. This is supported by Thirlway who argues that a rule of customary law need not be a practice of every single state but that it be widespread and consistent (in Evans, 2006). However, the International Law Association's report on the formation of customary international law argues for a return to the *Asylum/Fisheries* formula, by defining customary international law as being formed by the '*constant and uniform practice of states*'.

If the *Nicaragua* definition is to be accepted, a further issue arises with respect to those states who object to the practice. The quotation from the case went on to say that, if a state acts in a way inconsistent with the recognized rule but defends its conduct by appealing to exceptions or justifications contained within the rule, then that state's conduct confirms rather than weakens the rule. Notwithstanding this qualification, Charney (1985) argued that it is difficult to identify the role of a dissenting state in the development of customary international law. He asserted that a state which objects to an evolving rule of customary international law can be exempted from its application. He uses as support the *Anglo-Norwegian Fisheries* case with respect to Norway's persistent objection to a rule of coastline delimitation. His thesis was that there is no room for a persistent-objector rule in public international law and that even reluctant states eventually conform to the new norm—in other words, an objector becomes compliant. Charney addresses the issue of the practice of states indicating he supports the view that custom arises as a result of the views of the particularly interested states and any persistent objection from that type of state will prevent the rule from emerging but once the rule emerges, states are bound.

It has been argued by academics such as Shaw (2008) that the massive increase in the pace and variety of state activities has led to the role of custom being diminished. Put another way, it is extremely difficult with the numbers of states and practices to determine even a general trend. However, as this survey of case law and academic opinion reveals, there is a lack of consensus as to the quality and quantity of state practice needed. The views on quantity range from the virtually uniform advanced by a number of the cases or general practice as supported by academic opinion and *Nicaragua*. This lack of consensus will continue to make the quantity of state practice one of the most controversial issues in the development of public international law.

 Examiner's tip

The student will need to display an impressive knowledge of the case law in this area particularly the controversy concerning the *Nicaragua* decision. The student can well argue that the approach in the *North Sea Continental Shelf* case of 'extensive and virtually uniform' should be the way in which state practice is treated and that *Nicaragua* is not consistent with the other decisions. The other essential factor is to include academic discussion and the issue of what constitutes state practice is certainly not agreed upon.

 Question 2

Opinio juris as defined represents a circular argument and it should be abolished as a part of customary international law.

Discuss.

Commentary

Customary international law is argued to be based on the consent of sovereign states to their practices becoming law. The problem is how one determines whether a particular part of the behaviour of states reflects compliance with a legal rule. This is supposed to be addressed by the second subjective plank of customary international law, which is that the state practice is 'accepted as law'. This has resulted in the controversial concept of *opinio juris*.

This question will test students, and can only be answered if they are familiar with the academic debate on this issue. A key source would be the International Law Association's Report on customary international law, which recommended that the term *opinio juris* be abolished and replaced with a more general statement. Another excellent reference is Cassese (2004), which contains a new formulation for *opinio juris*.

Even formulating a definition of *opinio juris* is difficult, as the concept was not contained in **Art. 38 Statute of the International Court of Justice**; rather, there was a general statement of general practice being accepted as law. It is the phrase 'accepted as law' that has resulted in the phrase *opinio juris*. The concept has been developed in the case law of the ICJ, particularly in the seminal **North Sea Continental Shelf** case, and in relation to which you must be aware of the majority opinion and the dissenting opinion of Judge Tanaka.

You must explain in this answer why *opinio juris* could be a circular argument. The reason is quite logical. How can one argue that a practice is a legal practice before it has crystallized into a rule of public international law?

Answer plan

- Definition of customary international law particularly the subjective element, *opinio juris*.
- Discussion of the circularity of the definition of *opinio juris*.
- Discussion of the **North Sea Continental Shelf** case: majority, dissent, and the academic debate on this issue.
- Discussion of the recommendation of the International Law Association that *opinio juris* be abolished.
- Suggestion of how customary international law may be determined without *opinio juris*.
- Conclude with your opinion on the debate.

Suggested answer

One of the major sources of public international law is customary international law, which is defined by **Art. 38 Statute of the International Court of Justice** as having two elements: (1) a general practice; and (2) that the practice is accepted as law. This question concerns the second or what is known as the subjective element in the formation of customary international law; the belief in the rule's legality.

The PCIJ in the *Lotus* case introduced a general statement concerning the second of the two factors needed for the formation of customary international law, the general practice being accepted as law by stating '*only if such abstention were based on their being conscious of a duty to abstain would it be possible to speak of an international custom*'. This was further expanded upon in the famous dicta of the *North Sea Continental Shelf* judgment which defined this legal duty as *opinio juris* by stating:

> Not only must the acts concerned amount to a settled practice, but they must also be such, or be carried out in such a way, as to be evidence of a belief that this practice is rendered obligatory by the existence of a rule requiring it. The need for such a belief, i.e. the existence of a subjective element, is implicit in the very notion of the *opinio juris sive necessitatis*. The states concerned must therefore feel that they are conforming to what amounts to a legal obligation.

This was supported by the *Nicaragua* case—state practice had to be accompanied by the *opinio juris sive necessitatis*. In the *Continental Shelf (Libya v Malta)* case, the court stated that '*It is of course axiomatic that the material of customary international law is to be looked for primarily in the actual practice and* opinio juris *of states*'. As a result of this approach, Akehurst (1974–5) argues that *opinio juris* is necessary for the creation of customary rules. In a practical sense he illustrated that state practice must be accompanied by or consist of statements that certain conduct is permitted, required, or forbidden by international law. As Shaw (2008) argues, the court has maintained a high threshold with regard to the overt proving of the subjective element of customary law formation.

The problem with these definitions and the Akehurst position is the circularity of the arguments. How can an emerging rule of public international law be accompanied by a statement that it is already crystallized into a legal rule? Shaw further expands on this problem by questioning how a new customary rule can be created since it requires action different from or contrary to what is, until then, regarded as law. He gives the example of a three-mile territorial sea limit changing into a 12-mile limit requiring action that is contrary to existing law not as a practice 'accepted as law'.

Academic literature has attempted to grapple with this issue, as the case law has not adequately addressed the controversy. However, the opinion of the court is not unanimous on this issue. Judge Tanaka dissented in the *North Sea Continental Shelf* cases on the grounds that one way to discern the existence of *opinio juris* was the fact of external existence of a certain custom and the necessity felt in the international community, rather than to seek evidence as to the subjective motives for each example of state practice. Judge Sorensen in the same case argued that *opinio juris* could be presumed to exist if a uniform practice existed. Shaw seized on this statement and argued that there should be a more flexible approach to *opinio juris* by tying it more firmly with the overt manifestation of a custom, an action which contains the germ of a new law. D'Amato (1971) argued that *opinio juris* could be described as the 'articulation' of rules of customary international law. It is defined as the element that gives other states notice that a state's actions will have legal consequences. However, this does not address the issue of the emergence of a new rule of customary international law.

The *Nicaragua* case addressed the issue of the emergence of new custom by holding that reliance by a state on a novel right might, if shared by other states, tend towards a modification of customary international law. In a similar vein, Cassese proposed a sensible alteration to the requirement for *opinio juris*. He argued that the two elements need not be present from the outset. A practice could emerge from military, economic, or political demands (*opinio necessitatis*) but if it does receive strong and consistent objection from other states it can be held eventually that this practice is dictated by international law (*opinio juris*). The International Law Association Customary International Law Committee agreed with this position and argued that part of the confusion may be caused by a failure to distinguish between different stages in the life of a customary rule. Once a customary rule has become established, states will naturally have a belief in its existence; but this does not *necessarily* prove that the subjective element needs to be present during the *formation* of the rule. In their working definition of customary international law they stated that a rule of customary international law is one which is created and sustained by the constant and uniform practice of states and other subjects of international law in or impinging upon their international legal relations, in circumstances which give rise to a legitimate expectation of similar conduct in the future.

This definition of legitimate expectation and the formulation proposed by Cassese make infinite sense as it takes a gradualist approach to the formation of a rule and examines the belief in legality at different stages in the process. It is supported by the International Law Association definition and could resolve the issue of the circularity of the argument. Yet it should be emphasized that this is an academic opinion, not yet supported by the case law of the ICJ.

 Examiner's tip

The successful student will refer to the International Law Association report, one of the most important documents on customary international law and *opinio juris*. The definition of *opinio juris* from the **North Sea Continental Shelf** judgment is essential and if possible, quoted exactly. The excellent student will also engage with the academic literature on the subject which is constantly changing, an up-to-date article search will be essential.

 Question 3

Treaties are now the most important source of public international law.
Discuss.

Commentary

This question is deceptively simple. The purpose is to test the student on knowledge of the hierarchy of sources debate as identified in academic writings and the case law of the ICJ. International conventions, international custom, and the general principles of law are the three primary sources identified in **Art. 38 Statute of the International Court of Justice**. There is no indication in the provision of a hierarchy, although international conventions are listed as the first provision. However, this is not simply a question of where treaties stand within the statute but a debate within academic literature about the nature of international law itself. The issue is whether international law is based on a positivist level on the consent of states and that a natural law concept such as custom has no place as states should not be bound by international law without their consent. However, a competent student will know that treaties can also create or codify customary international law which can also be based on a consensual model of international relations.

The first step is to understand what exactly a treaty is. Treaties are a primary source of public international law as identified in **Art. 38 Statute of the International Court of Justice**. However, it should be noted that **Art. 38** describes international conventions, whether general or particular, as establishing rules expressly recognized by the contesting states. The most common term for conventions, covenants, or pacts is treaties. The treaty is an agreement between two states (bilateral) or a number of states (multilateral) which often sets out rules of public international law. This type of international legal instrument represents a high point in the positivist view of public international law as the law is based on the consent of sovereign states.

The answer should first contain an analysis of the various sources and a reasoned opinion on the relative weight of these sources. The particular importance of treaties in relation to customary international law is that it can codify already existing customary international law or lead to a creation of custom, binding states which are not parties to the treaty. The **North Sea Continental Shelf** cases judgment is of great assistance in this answer. Once again the Akehurst article and Cassese's text are particularly relevant to this issue, but especially helpful is the Thirlway chapter in Evans (2006) which has a section on this question.

Answer plan

- Definition of treaties as a source of public international law using **Art. 38 Statute of the International Court of Justice**.
- The differences between bilateral treaties and multilateral conventions and the growth in multilateral conventions as a tool of international law-making.
- The debate concerning positivism and international custom.
- How treaties can constitute customary international law with reference to the case law.
- The distinction between codification of existing customary law and the creation of customary law through treaties.
- The student's conclusion as to whether there is a hierarchy of sources.

Suggested answer

Treaties are not mentioned as such in **Art. 38 Statute of the International Court of Justice.** Article 38(1)(a) describes one of the primary sources of public international law as *'international conventions, whether general or particular, establishing rules expressly recognized by contesting states'*. International conventions is simply another term for treaties. Treaties constitute agreements between states and these can be between two states (bilateral) or groups of states (multilateral). Often treaties that establish regimes of public international law are multilateral conventions, an excellent example being the **UN Convention on the Law of the Sea (UNCLOS).** The ICJ has addressed the issue of interpretation of treaties in several of its judgments and advisory Opinions.

The second part of **Art. 38** mentions international custom, as evidence of a general practice accepted as law. The article does not set up a hierarchy in the definition, except to mention international conventions first but there is an active academic debate concerning whether indeed there is a hierarchy of sources. This represents a fundamental debate in international law. Positivist international lawyers would like to see all international law based on consent and thus international conventions would be preferable. The problem with custom is that new states and objecting states can potentially become bound by a rule of customary international law to which they did not consent. The positivists would like to see all international law negotiated as multilateral conventions which require ratification or accession by consenting states.

In spite of the positivist preference for treaties, treaties and custom interact together in the formation of public international law. It is indeed possible for a treaty to codify already existing customary international law or to result eventually in custom. An example of already codifying custom could be several provisions in the **International Convention on Civil and Political Rights (1966) (ICCPR),** which codified basic human rights guarantees that had been set out in the **Universal Declaration of Human Rights (1948) (UDHR).** An example of emerging custom would be the **UNCLOS,** which set out limits for territorial sea that now seem to be customary.

The main cases that discussed the relationship between these two areas are the *North Sea Continental Shelf* cases. These cases considered whether the relevant treaty, the **1958 Geneva Convention on the Continental Shelf** was declaratory of customary law. The judgment held that the convention was not in its origins or inception declaratory of customary international law (a rule of a principle of equidistance), nor had its subsequent effect been constitutive of the rule of customary international law. The judgment discussed three ways in which a treaty may relate to custom. It may be declaratory of custom, it may crystallize custom, or the provision within the treaty may come to be accepted and followed by states as custom in their practice. In the *Nicaragua* case, the court concluded that customary international law continues to exist separately from the treaty law, even where there is identical content. This is reflected in **Art. 43 Vienna Convention on the Law of Treaties,** which stipulates that an invalidity, termination, or denunciation of a treaty does not impair in any way the duty of any state to fulfil any obligation embodied in the treaty to which it would be subject under international law independently of the treaty.

Regrettably, other cases have not discussed this issue in detail. In the *Maritime Delimitation and Territorial Questions between Qatar and Bahrain* case, both parties agreed that the relevant articles of **UNCLOS** represented customary law. However, the way in which the treaty represented customary law was not analysed in the judgment.

Judge Lachs in his dissent to the *North Sea Continental Shelf* cases argued that the number of ratifications and accessions to a treaty could not be considered conclusive with regard to the general acceptance of a given instrument. He argued that you had to consider the types of states that were parties and not just the number and that the principles and rules in the convention had been accepted not only by the parties but those states which had subsequently followed it in agreements, or in their legislation, or followed it by acquiescence. This goes some way to arguing that a treaty can create customary law by inspiring subsequent practice.

Akehurst (1974–5) indicated his position that treaties were part of state practice and could create customary law if the requirement of *opinio juris* was met. That is, that the treaty or its *travaux préparatoires* contain a claim that the treaty is declaratory of pre-existing customary law. If the treaty does not contain this element it is the subsequent practice of accordance with the treaty provisions that creates the customary law and not the treaty itself. On the other hand, Cassese (2004) argues that most members of the international community tend to prefer treaties to custom, as the former is more certain and results from the willing participation of contracting parties. He also argued that custom is not the most suitable instrument for achieving change in the international legal system. Therefore, a number of states have turned to treaty-making for the codification or progressive development of international law. So too have representatives of civil society, with examples being the Ottawa process resulting in the **Convention on the Prohibition of the Use, Stockpiling, Production and Transfer of Anti-Personnel Mines and on their Destruction of 1997** and the Oslo Process resulting in the **Convention on Cluster Munitions of 2009**. However, it should be noted that Thirlway (in Evans, 2006) adds in another dimension by pointing out that when a rule of customary international law becomes accepted as *jus cogens* (a peremptory norm of public international law) it overrides a treaty provision according to **Art. 64 Vienna Convention on the Law of Treaties**.

Analysing the case law and academic opinion, it cannot be argued that treaties are the principal source of public international law; it is the interaction between these two sources which constitute the corpus of public international law. New states and those states not party to various treaties have to become part of an already existing legal system which includes rules of customary international law.

Examiner's tip

This answer takes one point of view on this issue of the relative importance of treaties and custom. It is equally valid to take the other view that as treaties are now codifying international law, they are more important. However, either view must be supported by the existing treaty, the **Vienna Convention on the Law of Treaties**, and academic literature.

Question 4

Certain rules of public international law are stated to be norms of *jus cogens* and others are stated to be obligations *erga omnes*.

Discuss the definition of both of these Latin terms and describe the relationship of these terms to customary international law and treaties.

Commentary

One of the most important yet difficult concepts to grasp in the terminology of public international law is *jus cogens*. This question requires first a definition of the term. The student must also trace the development of the concept. A caution is that there is no universal agreement on what are the exact rules that constitute *jus cogens*. The second term obligations *erga omnes* bears a close relationship to *jus cogens* and the two are often confused. It is vital to define each and distinguish between them.

Two excellent sources for reference are: Byers (1999) and Cassese (2004); an excellent article is Byers 'Conceptualizing the relationship between *jus cogens* and *erga omnes* rules' (1997); a textbook on human rights which discusses this concept is Steiner *et al*. (2007).

It is critical to have knowledge of the provisions in the **Vienna Convention on the Law of Treaties** on *jus cogens* and the limited references to both concepts in the jurisprudence of the ICJ.

Answer plan

- Define *jus cogens* and define the limitations on treaties imposed by *jus cogens* with reference to the **Vienna Convention on the Law of Treaties**.
- Define with reference to case law obligations *erga omnes*.
- Discuss the controversy as represented in the case law over the enumeration of the rules of *jus cogens*.
- Illustrate the relationship between *jus cogens* and other norms of customary international law and the concept of obligations *erga omnes*.

Suggested answer

Within the literature of customary international law are two important concepts, *jus cogens* and obligations *erga omnes*. The first in time chronologically is *jus cogens*. Byers (1997) argues that the concept originates from ancient writings and was discussed early in the twentieth century. He quotes a definition taken from the *Oppenheim's International Law* edition of 1905 which stated that a number of universally recognized principles of international law existed which rendered any conflicting treaty void and a principle of *jus cogens* was unanimously recognized as a customary rule of international law. Harris (2010) agrees that the concept of *jus cogens* originated in the law of treaties, in which there is a rule prohibiting states from making a treaty which seeks to conflict with a rule of *jus cogens*. Article 53 of the **Vienna Convention on the Law of Treaties** defines *jus cogens* as a norm that is accepted and recognized by the international community of states as a whole. Accordingly, **Art. 53** in itself is a norm of *jus cogens*. *Jus cogens* are also known as peremptory norms of public international law. According to Harris, this is a rule that proscribes conduct that if fundamentally immoral or anti-social. The other important provision in treaty law confirming the existence of *jus cogens* is **Art. 64**, of the **VCLT** which states that if a new peremptory norm of general international law emerges, and it conflicts with any treaty, then any such treaty becomes void and terminates.

Obligations *erga omnes* came to the forefront shortly after the concept of *jus cogens* was included in the **VCLT**. Then ICJ introduced another, related concept into the arena of international law. In the 1970 *Barcelona Traction* case the court referred to obligations *erga omnes*, which translated means 'as against all'. Enumerated in the case were the obligations derived from the outlawing of acts of aggression, and of genocide, and within the rules concerning the basic rights of persons, including protection from slavery and racial discrimination. Within the dictum it is made clear that these obligations involve the international community as a whole—a concern of all states. Obligations *erga omnes* were also referred to the *East Timor* case *(Portugal v Australia)* (the concept of self-determination) and in the *Application of the Convention on the Prevention and Punishment of the Crimes of Genocide, Preliminary Objections* ruling (the rights and obligations contained in the **Genocide Convention (1948)**). In the *Legal Consequences of the Construction of a Wall in the Occupied Palestinian Territory* case advisory Opinion, the ICJ stated that the right of peoples to self-determination was a right *erga omnes* and that there was an obligation for all states not to recognize the illegal situation resulting from the construction of the wall between Israel and the occupied territories and not to render aid or assistance maintaining the situation created by such construction.

Although there was an enumeration of obligations *erga omnes* in the *Barcelona Traction* case and later cases, peremptory rules—*jus cogens*—have not been authoritatively enumerated. Cassese (2004) proposes that the former **Art. 19 International Law Commission's Draft Articles on State Responsibility** enumerated that mention was made of

norms laying down international obligations so essential for the protection of fundamental interests of the international community that their breach was recognized by
the international community as a whole. Examples include the norms prohibiting
aggression, slavery, genocide, or apartheid. Byers (1997) agrees with these norms being
jus cogens but also includes torture in that list. Although **Art. 19** was not adopted in the
current rules of state responsibility, there is a concept of aggravated state responsibility
for violations of peremptory norms of international law. However, they are not listed
within the articles, but Crawford (2002) supports the addition of torture to the list and
also argues that self-determination ought to be included.

Jus cogens has also received little mention in the jurisprudence of the ICJ. According
to Byers (1997), the court mentioned the concept in its judgment in the 1969 ***North Sea
Continental Shelf*** cases and the 1986 ***Nicaragua (Merits)*** and held that the prohibition
on the use of force was a conspicuous example of an international rule having the character of *jus cogens*. Another important discussion was by ad hoc Judge Lauterpacht in
***Concerning Application of the Convention on the Punishment and Prevention of the
Crimes of Genocide***, in which he stated that *jus cogens* operates as a concept superior
to both customary international law and treaty. This may even include, according to
Byers (1997 and 1999), actions by the Security Council which would be invalid if they
conflict with *jus cogens*. Although in the case law there is agreement on the important
of the term, there is yet to be either a jurisprudential or treaty listing of these rules.

As to the relationship between the two terms in international law, Byers (1997) argues
that, although it is widely assumed that the concepts of *jus cogens* and *erga omnes* are
related, international lawyers have yet to agree on the character of that relationship.
Byers distinguishes them by arguing that *jus cogens* rules are non-derogable rules of
international public policy and that they render void other, non-peremptory rules which
are in conflict with them. On the other hand, *erga omnes* are rules which give a general
right of standing among all states subject to those rules to make claims. The distinction
according to Byers is that *jus cogens* rules as confirmed by the **VCLT** are created by
customary international law but that *erga omnes* rules can be created by custom or
treaty. *Erga omnes* rules thus could exist by treaty which are not of a *jus cogens*
character.

In conclusion to this brief overview, one could take issue with the Byers's view that it
is easily possible to distinguish these two concepts as both seem to take their content
from agreed primary rules of the international community. It is in fact difficult to distinguish between the two terms and until there is a complete enumeration of *jus cogens*
rules and obligations *erga omnes*, the confusion will continue to exist. In the same way,
it is difficult to argue that a rule has crystallized into a norm of public international law,
it is just as difficult to argue that a rule has become a peremptory norm.

Examiner's tip

A discussion of these two critical Latin terms, *jus cogens* and *erga omnes* must be accompanied by a thorough knowledge of the case law. The fact that the *'Wall'* case discussed *erga omnes* obligations is an essential part of this answer. Furthermore, the student will have to know the relevant provisions in the **Vienna Convention on the Law of Treaties** on this issue.

Further reading

Akehurst, M., 'Custom as a source of international law' (1974–5) 47 BYIL 1.

Byers, M., 'Conceptualizing the relationship between *jus cogens* and *erga omnes* rules', in (1997) 66 *Nordic Journal of International Law* 211.

Byers, M., *Custom, Power and the Power of Rules* (Cambridge: Cambridge University Press, 1999).

Cassese, A., *International Law*, 2nd edn (Oxford: Oxford University Press, 2004).

Charney, J., 'The persistent objector rule and the development of customary international law' (1985) 56 BYIL 1.

Crawford, J., *The International Law Commission's Articles on State Responsibility* (Cambridge: Cambridge University Press, 2002).

d'Amato, A. A., *The Concept of Custom in International Law* (Ithaca and London: Cornell University Press, 1971).

Danilenko, G. M., *Law Making in the International Community* (Dordrecht and London: Martinus Nijhoff Publishers, 1993).

Harris, D. J., *Cases and Materials on International Law*, 7th edn (London: Sweet & Maxwell, 2010).

Mendelson, M., 'The formation of customary international law' (1998) 272 *Receuil des Cours* 155.

Roberts, A., 'Traditional and modern approaches to customary international law' (2001) 95 AJIL 757.

Shaw, M., *International Law*, 6th edn (Cambridge: Cambridge University Press, 2008).

Steiner, H., Alston, P., and Goodman, R., *International Human Rights in Context*, 3rd edn (Oxford: Oxford University Press, 2007).

Thirlway, H., 'The sources of international law' in M. Evans, *International Law*, 3rd edn (Oxford: Oxford University Press, 2010).

4

The law of treaties

Introduction

Unlike customary international law which relies on state practice and *opinio juris*, a treaty is a formal method of international law creation governed by a series of rules codified in its own treaty, the **Vienna Convention on the Law of Treaties 1969** (in force 1980). A treaty is an agreement concluded between parties to the international system. It is generally between two or more states, but treaties can also be concluded between states and international organizations or between international organizations. International law-making treaties are usually entitled multilateral conventions, with an example being the **UN Convention on the Law of the Sea 1982**.

Examination questions in this area will focus on key provisions of the **Vienna Convention on the Law of Treaties** and will test the student's knowledge on the formation, enforcement, interpretation, and termination of treaties. This convention should be read and understood it its entirety. A treaty question will often deal with how treaties come into force domestically in your particular jurisdiction. There are also important questions arising concerning whether states can agree to a convention but make reservations with respect to all or part of the treaty. This is particularly the case in human rights conventions and one question in this chapter will concern the validity of reservations to human rights conventions. Reservations to treaties are a particularly difficult part of the subject but the student who wishes to excel in the exam would be well advised to attempt a question on this important and controversial topic. The second complex area is interpretation of treaties and the third area is how, if ever, a party can be released from treaty obligations. All require knowledge of the relevant international case law.

Two excellent monographs on this issue that are well worth referring to are: Aust (2007); and Klabbers (1996). The ninth edition of *Oppenheim's International Law* has a comprehensive chapter on the law of treaties with extensive examples of domestic practice on the ratification of treaties—see Jennings and Watts (1992).

This area requires knowledge of international and domestic case law and particularly knowledge of your own national law with respect to ratification of treaties. As with all international law questions, an excellent answer will reveal knowledge of relevant international and domestic case law, treaties, and academic literature. The added dimension in this subject is a thorough knowledge of the **Vienna Convention on the Law of Treaties.**

 Question 1

The international community convenes an international conference in New York to consider adopting a new arms trade treaty designed to regulate small arms trade.

Describe the process by which this treaty might come into existence? Second, address the issue of what states need to do to adopt legally this treaty.

 Commentary

This question allows students to display their detailed knowledge of the key provision on the formation of treaties to be found in the **Vienna Convention on the Law of Treaties**. It would also be necessary to examine the procedure by which multilateral conventions are negotiated, a good example being the process which resulted in the Rome Statute establishing the International Criminal Court.

The international community has been trying to negotiate a small arms trade treaty for some time and so the student will have the opportunity to study the actual treaty negotiating process.

There are four stages in the formation of a treaty which must be discussed in a complete answer. These are negotiation, adoption, expression of consent, and entry into force. At each stage there are legal controversies concerning the interpretation of the **Vienna Convention on the Law of Treaties**.

The coming into force of a treaty differs between jurisdictions and students will be expected to know the rules within their jurisdiction and perhaps other major countries, such as the United Kingdom and the United States. *Oppenheim's International Law*, ninth edition contains the practice of many states—see Jennings and Watts (1992).

 Answer plan

- Negotiation of a treaty—examples of practice and the provisions in the **Vienna Convention on the Law of Treaties**.

- Adoption of text of treaty—provisions in the **Vienna Convention on the Law of Treaties**.

- Expression of a state agreeing to be bound—provisions in the **Vienna Convention on the Law of Treaties**.

- Entry into force of the treaty—various states' domestic practice as to ratification of, or accession to, a treaty.

Suggested answer

The agreement on a treaty regulating the trade in small arms would be entitled a multilateral convention which is a law-making treaty negotiated between a number of states. These types of treaties are usually negotiated and adopted in a diplomatic conference convened for that purpose which in this case was held in New York in July of 2012. Three other examples of such processes were the Rome conference which adopted the **Rome Statute of the International Criminal Court 1998**, the Ottawa conference which adopted the 1997 **Convention on the Prohibition of the Use, Stockpiling, Production and Transfer of Anti-Personnel Mines and on their Destruction** (also known as the **Ottawa Convention**), and the Oslo Process which resulted in the **Convention on Cluster Munitions** in 2008. A unique recent innovation in treaty negotiation evidenced in all three of these Conventions and in the arms trade treaty process is the participation of civil society known as non-governmental organizations (NGOs). There are evidently four stages to the conclusion of a treaty which are common to multilateral and bilateral conventions.

The first phase is the negotiation phase. The negotiator must establish his credentials to represent a state by production of full powers which is defined in **Art. 2(1)(c) Vienna Convention on the Law of Treaties (VCLT)** as a document emanating from the competent authority of a state designating a person or person to represent the state for the purpose of negotiating, adopting or authenticating a treaty. **Art. 7(2) VCLT** contains exceptions to the necessity of producing full powers for heads of state, heads of government, and foreign ministries who are able to perform all acts with respect to conclusion of a treaty. Heads of diplomatic missions do not have to produce powers either, but do for the adoption of the text of the treaty. Finally, representatives accredited by states to an international conference, or to an international organization, or one of its organs, do not have to produce credentials for the purpose of adopting the text of a treaty, within that conference. If in the rare case a treaty is concluded by somebody who had no powers to represent the state, **Art. 8 VCLT** states that any such treaty has no legal effect unless it is afterwards confirmed by the state.

One example of state practice of the kind of situation that was not authorized was provided in the International Law Commission's Commentary on the **VCLT**. This occurred in Stresa in 1951 with respect to a convention relating to the naming of cheeses. It was signed by a delegate on behalf of both Sweden and Norway but it appeared that he only had authority from Norway. However, the agreement was later ratified by both parties and entered into effect, a procedure now codified by **Art. 8 VCLT**.

The second phase which in this case would also take place at the diplomatic conference occurring in New York is the adoption of the text of the proposed treaty by those authorized representatives of states. This is usually accomplished by the consent of two-thirds of states' delegates present at the conference. This procedure is confirmed by **Art. 9(2) VCLT**. This provision states that the adoption of the text of a treaty takes place by the consent of all the states participating *except* that at an international conference unless otherwise specified there shall be a vote of two-thirds of the states' delegates present and voting. In addition, an increasing number of treaties are now adopted and open for signature by means of the UN General Assembly (GA) resolutions such as the two **1966 International Covenants on Civil and Political Rights and Economic, Social and Cultural Rights** and the **1984 Convention Against Torture**. But these treaties follow a similar procedure by requiring a two-thirds' consent vote in the GA. This second phase *does not* result in a legal instrument and there are two more stages in this process.

The third phase is the expression of each state of consent to be bound by the proposed treaty. There are a number of ways that states may express consent to be bound by an international agreement. It may be signalled by signature or exchange of instruments. **Article 10 VCLT** states that, unless the treaty specifies otherwise, the signature or signature and referendum or the initialling by the representatives of those states present at the conference incorporating the text is the procedure by which states indicate their intention to be bound. However, that signature or exchange of instruments does not mean that the country is bound by the treaty—which is accomplished by the fourth stage: ratification or accession.

International law requires a fourth and final phase which is the entry into force of the treaty and that is ratification, acceptance, approval, or accession. These terms are defined in **Art. 2(1)(b) VCLT** as *'the international act so named whereby a state establishes on the international plane its consent to be bound by a treaty'*. The treaty itself specifies how many countries must ratify or accede to a treaty before it comes into force. Accession to a treaty is when a state was not part of the negotiating process or a new state which wants to become a party to the treaty. There are two conditions, one is that the treaty itself allows for accessions and the second is the domestic accession process which is normally the same as the ratification process.

The **VCLT** itself did not come into effect until 27 January 1980, the thirtieth day after the deposit of the thirty-fifth instrument of ratification. **Article 12 VCLT** states that in some minor agreements parties intend to be binding by signature alone but most treaties have to go through a ratification process. Although ratification or approval was originally the function of the ruler, it has in modern times made subject to constitutional approval. According to Shaw (2008), the advantage of waiting is twofold: internal and external. In the external case, it allows extra time for consideration, once the negotiating process has been completed. Internally, it reflects the change in politics and provides for much greater participation by a state's population in public affairs.

There are various domestic practices on the ratification of treaties. In the United States, **Art. VI, s. 2** of the **Constitution** provides that:

> All Treaties made or which shall be made with the authority of the United States, shall
> be the supreme law of the land and the Judges of every state shall be bound thereby;
> anything in the Constitution or laws of any state to the contrary notwithstanding.

Although treaties may require two-thirds of the senate, there is the concept of the executive agreement, made by the President on his own authority but which constitute treaties in international law. These, however, are reserved for the less important bilateral agreements.

In the United Kingdom, ratification of treaties is government by the Ponsonby rule whereby a treaty is laid before Parliament for twenty-one days before the actual ratification takes place.

Often the ratification process takes some time, although the Rome Statute for example entered into force one month after its sixtieth ratification on 1 July 2002, just four years after the treaty was concluded.

Once our multilateral convention on climate change has gone through these stages, the UN Secretary-General acts as a repository for ratifications and keeps track of when a treaty is to come into force. The UN also keeps an international database of treaties.

Examiner's tip

Be sure to mention the correct sections of the **Vienna Convention on the Law of Treaties**. Make sure you point out that a treaty does not come into force until ratification, acceptance, approval, or accession to the treaty (**Arts 14–16 VCLT**). It is also critical to point out the process of negotiation in chronological detail.

Question 2

The State of Narnia wishes to become a party to the Convention against Torture but wishes to enter into a reservation to this treaty to allow torture of terrorist suspects. The State of Oz is aware that Narnia is going to issue such a reservation and has serious objections.

Can Narnia become a party to the Convention in the face of the objection by the State of Oz?

Commentary

The legal effect of reservations is the most complicated part of treaty law (and one usually examined on). It requires extensive knowledge of the case law and an attempt to discuss a controversial area in international treaty law as the effect of reservations on the validity of a treaty has not been resolved, although the case law is of some assistance in human rights conventions.

First, the question must carefully define a reservation as there is a legal controversy between what constitutes a reservation and what constitutes a declaration. This answer should attempt, with reference to leading case law, to clarify what is meant by both terms.

Unlike domestic law, where a statute or bill is adopted as a complete text, international law allows for states to opt out of certain provisions of a treaty by means of what is called a reservation, defined in **Art. 2 VCLT**. However, there is a lack of clarity in international law as to the effect on the treaty itself of opting out of certain provisions, particularly with reference to human rights treaties.

This question will seek to elucidate an understanding of the nature of reservations generally and in specific with reference to human rights conventions. An excellent article particularly on reservations to human rights treaties is Goodman, 'Human rights treaties, invalid reservation and state consent' (2002). Aust (2007) also has a comprehensive section on reservations which deals with all types of treaties.

 Answer plan

- Discuss the general meaning of reservations with reference to the **VCLT**.
- Clarify the distinction between a declaration and a reservation.
- Discuss the particular situation of reservations to human rights conventions with reference to international and regional case law.

 Suggested answer

The issue with respect to the reservation proposed by Narnia and objected to by Oz has to be considered with reference to the **VCLT** but with an important caveat that reservations to human rights conventions are often treated differently. Reservations are defined in **Art. 2 VCLT** as a unilateral statement, however phrased or named, made by a state, when signing, ratifying, accepting, approving, or acceding to a treaty, where it purports to exclude or modify the legal effect of certain provisions of the treaty in their application to that state. Where a state is satisfied with most of the terms of a treaty, but is unhappy about particular provisions, it may, in certain circumstances, wish to refuse to accept or be bound by such provision, while consenting to the rest of the agreement. In this problem the State of Narnia is entering into just such a reservation allowing for the torture of terrorism suspects. Oz objects to this reservation and the question turns on the impact of that objection.

The use of reservations is argued by Shaw (2008) to be advantageous to the smooth functioning of the international system as it allows treaties to come into effect that would otherwise not be consented to. It also illustrates the principle of sovereignty of states, whereby a state may refuse its consent to particular provisions so that they do not become binding upon it. On the other hand, as Shaw asserts, a treaty that has many reservations from many different countries could jeopardize the nature and purpose of the treaty. It also leads to complicated relations between states with respect to their mutual international legal obligations.

The first legal issue in reservations is that they must be distinguished from other statements made with regard to a treaty that are not intended to have the legal effect, such as understandings, political statements, or interpretive declarations. These have no binding consequences to the treaty in question. However, the definition leads to complications as sometimes an interpretive declaration can constitute a reservation if the state indicates a certain interpretation which might change the sense of the treaty.

An example of relevant jurisprudence is the *Anglo-French Continental Shelf* case, where the Arbitration Tribunal emphasized that the French reservation to **Art. 6 Geneva Convention on the Continental Shelf 1958** which was challenged by the UK had to be construed in accordance with the natural meaning of their terms. The French had stated that the principle of equidistance was not applicable in areas of special circumstances, including the Bay of Granville. The UK argued that this was only an interpretive declaration. The tribunal held that although this reservation contained elements of interpretation it was a reservation as it constituted a specific condition imposed by France on its acceptance of the **Art. 6** delimitation regime. It therefore had the purpose of seeking to exclude or modify the legal effect of certain treaty provisions with regard to their application by the reserving state and therefore constituted a reservation.

In the *Belilos* case in 1988 the European Court of Human Rights (ECtHR) considered the effect of one particular interpretive declaration made by Switzerland on the right to a fair trial (the declaration had the effect of limiting rights of appeal). The court held one had to look behind the declaration and to determine its substantive content. The court held that Switzerland had indeed intended to avoid the consequences which a broad view of the right of access to the courts would have for the system of public administration and of justice in the cantons and held it to be a reservation incompatible with the purpose of the convention.

Therefore in order to determine whether a unilateral statement constitutes a reservation or an interpretive declaration, the statement will have to be interpreted in good faith and in accordance with the ordinary meaning to be given to its terms and within the context of the treaty in question. The intention of the state making the statement at that time will also need to be considered.

The second and more complex issue is the effect of reservations. The old general rule was that reservations could only be made with the consent of all other states involved in the process. This was to preserve as much unity of approach as possible to ensure the success of an international agreement and to minimize deviations from the text of a treaty. The League of Nations supported this concept. The effect of this was that a state wishing to make a reservation had to obtain the consent of all the other parties to the treaty. If this was not possible, that state could become a party minus the reservation, or not a party at all.

However, with the consideration of the issue by the International Court of Justice (ICJ) in the advisory Opinion *Reservations to the Convention on the Prevention and Punishment of the Crime of Genocide* **28 May 1951,** there is now a new rule. The advisory Opinion was sought by the GA in a resolution to the ICJ after some states made reservations to the **1948 Genocide Convention,** and a number of objections were made to these reservations. The court held that a state which has made and maintained a reservation which has been objected to by one or more parties to the convention but not by others, can be regarded as being a party to the convention if the reservation is compatible with the object and purpose of the convention. The reason for this, expressed by the court, was that there were special circumstances with regard to this convention which called for a more flexible approach. These circumstances included: the universal character of the UN; the extensive participation envisaged under the convention; the fact that the convention had been the product of a series of majority votes; the fact that the principles underlying the convention were general principles already binding upon states; that the convention was clearly intended by the UN and the parties to be definitely universal in scope and that it had been adopted for purely humanitarian purposes—that is, the importance of the treaty mandated a flexible approach.

The **VCLT** accepted the ICJ's interpretation in **Arts 19–21**. Therefore the general rule according to Cassese (2004: 174) is:

> A state can append reservations at the time of ratification or accession, unless such reservations: (a) are expressly prohibited by the treaty (because the treaty either prohibits any reservation (i.e. *Rome Statute of the International Criminal Court*) or only allows reservations to provisions other than the one that is the object of a reservation) or (b) prove incompatible with the object and purpose of the treaty.

However, it is still very difficult to determine if the object and purpose of the treaty have been offended. The question is also raised as to the authority able to make such a determination. At the moment, unless the treaty otherwise provides, whether a reservation is impermissible is up to the states themselves.

In this case Oz has an objection and is arguing that the reservation is not compatible with the object and purpose of the convention. However, a number of issues remain unresolved. It is unclear what effect an impermissible reservation has. One school of thought takes the view that such reservations are invalid and the other that the validity of any reservation is dependent upon acceptance by other states. While there is a presumption in favour of the permissibility of reservations, this may be displaced if the reservation is prohibited explicitly or implicitly by the treaty or is contrary to the object and purpose of the treaty. Will Oz continue to be a party to the treaty? Goodman in his article discusses the remedies available should the reservation be incompatible with the object and purpose of the treaty in human rights cases, which this treaty against torture clearly is. He indicates that there are three options:

Option 1: The state remains bound by the treaty except for the provision(s) to which the reservation is related.

Option 2: The invalidity of the reservation nullifies the instrument of ratification as a whole and thus a state is no longer a party to the agreement.

Option 3: An invalid reservation can be severed from the instrument of ratification such that the state remains bound to the treaty including the provision(s) to which the reservation related.

There is one clear trend present specifically in human rights treaties, which this treaty is, and that is to sever the impermissible reservation and view the treaty as still in effect. This option could apply in this case. An example is the *Loizidou* case in the ECtHR.

Turkey attempted to restrict operation of the **European Convention on Human Rights (ECHR)** in Northern Cyprus. The court held that in light of the special nature of the convention as a human rights treaty the reservation restricting applicability to Turkey was severable. Therefore, Turkey's acceptance of the jurisdiction of the commission and court remained in place, unrestricted by the terms of the invalid limitations attached to the declaration.

Another important source of the nature of human rights treaty reservations is **General Comment 24** issued by the Human Rights Committee (HRC) established pursuant to the **International Covenant on Civil and Political Rights (ICCPR)** which emphasized the special nature of human rights treaties. This comment stated that the provisions in the **VCLT** were inappropriate to address problems of reservations to human rights treaties. The committee stated that states would have a heavy onus to justify reservations. The committee also stated that the effect of an unacceptable reservation would normally be that the provision operated in full with regard to the party making such a reservation. The HRC regarded itself as the only body able to determine whether a specific reservation was or was not compatible with the object and purpose of the covenant. The International Law Commission disagreed, saying that the **VCLT** should apply and that states were the '*traditional modalities of control*'.

It seems that this issue is unresolved but it can be reasonably argued that, with respect to human rights treaties, the reservations can be severed from the treaty and the treaty can continue in full force and effect between Oz and Narnia.

In general, reservations are deemed to have been accepted by states that have raised no objection to them at the end of 12 months after notification of the reservation or the date on which consent to be bound by the treaty is expressed.

Examiner's tip

This problem is heavily dependent on case law. If the cases on reservations in the ICJ and ECtHR are not included the question cannot be answered. An excellent answer will also include **General Comment 24** to the **International Covenant on Civil and Political Rights**.

? Question 3

International case law does little to clarify the rules of treaty interpretation.
Discuss.

Commentary

Another area of controversy in treaty law is the issue of interpretation of a clause in a treaty which might be unclear or ambiguous. Although the **VCLT** has a number of provisions with respect to treaty interpretation, the case law reveals division in the approaches taken, which range from a strict textual approach to an approach based on a wider object and purpose of the treaty. This is particularly the case in human rights conventions for the same reason as discussed in the answer to the reservations question (see Question 2). This reason is that the interest in the international community is in having the widest possible participation in these conventions and thus a much broader theory of interpretation applies.

This question allows the student to engage in a discussion of various theories of treaty interpretation. It is essential that the student has knowledge of the various ICJ cases setting out theories of interpretations. Excellent sources are Fitzmaurice's article 'The law and procedure of the International Court of Justice: treaty interpretation and certain other treaty provisions' (1951), which sets out three theories of treaty interpretation, and more recent discussions in Aust (2007) and Malgosia Fitzmaurice in Evans (2010).

 Answer plan

- Set out the various theories of treaty interpretation as established in academic materials, cases, and the **Vienna Convention of Law of Treaties**.
- Discuss the controversy over the purposive approach, especially with respect to human rights conventions.

 Suggested answer

Any true interpretation of a treaty in international law has to take into account all aspects of the agreement, from the words employed to the intention of the parties and the aims of the particular document. As Aust (2007) has stated, there is no treaty which does not raise questions of interpretation.

There are three basic approaches to interpretation, as set out by Fitzmaurice (1951):

1 Examination of actual text of the agreement and analysis of the actual words used—the objective approach.

2 Look to the intention of the parties adopting the agreement—this may be termed the subjective approach.

3 Emphasizes the object and purpose of the treaty—which is the wider-perspective or object and purpose approach.

Articles 31–3 VCLT set out the rules of treaty interpretation which seem to be a compromise between all three of Fitzmaurice's categories. **Article 31** lays down the fundamental rules of interpretation and can be taken as reflecting customary international law. A treaty shall be interpreted in good faith in accordance with the ordinary meaning to be given to the terms of the treaty in their context and in light of its object and purpose. **Article 31** does little to clarify the actual method of interpretation. When the interpretation of a provision according to the provisions of **Art. 31** needs confirmation or determination since the meaning is ambiguous or obscure or leads to a manifestly absurd or unreasonable result, recourse may be had to supplementary means of interpretation under **Art. 32**. This may include the *travaux préparatoires* (preparatory works) of the treaty, and the circumstances of the conclusion of the treaty. This article sets out the treaty interpretation principle of effectiveness and will be used when terms of the treaty are ambiguous in order to give effect to provisions in accordance with the intention of the parties and in accordance with the rules of international law.

Finally, **Art. 33** provides that when a treaty has been authenticated in two or more languages, the text is equally authoritative in each language unless the treaty provides for which language will prevail.

However, from a review of the case law, the ICJ has determined that interpretation must be based above all upon the text of the treaty. There are several key cases on treaty interpretation. In the ***Competence of the General Assembly for the Admission of a State to the United Nations*** advisory Opinion of 3 March 1950 the ICJ held that the first duty of a tribunal called upon to interpret and apply the provisions of a treaty is to endeavour to give effect to them in their natural and ordinary meaning in the context in which they occur.

The Permanent Court of Arbitration in the ***Eritrea–Ethiopia Boundary*** case emphasized that the elements contained in **Art. 31(1) VCLT** were guides to establishing what the parties actually intended or their common will and in this process the principle of contemporaneity is relevant. This means that a treaty should be interpreted by reference to the circumstances prevailing at the time that the treaty was concluded. For instance, expressions and geographical names used in the instrument should be given the meaning that they would have possessed at that time. But this does not prevent the court or tribunal taking into account the present-day state of scientific knowledge as reflected in the documentary material submitted to it by the parties. Furthermore, as Malgosia Fitzmaurice (2010) argues in the ***Kasikili/Sedudu Island*** case decided by the ICJ, reference was made to the subsequent practice of the parties to a treaty as constituting elements to be taken into account in determining the treaty's meaning.

There are broader rules of interpretation applied in other cases. In ***Iran v United States*** decided by the Iran–US Claims Tribunal the provision whereby any relevant rules of international law applicable in the relations between the parties shall be taken into account was applied. The question was whether a dual US–Iranian citizen could bring a claim against Iran. The Full Tribunal held jurisdiction existed over claims by dual citizens when the dominant and effective nationality was US. The tribunal cited **Art. 31(3) VCLT** to state that the tribunal could use a large body of law and legal literature in the area in the context of interpreting the 1981 agreement setting up the claims. In the ECtHR, the *Lithgow* case held that the use of the phrase '*subject to the conditions provided for … by the general principles of international law*' in **Art. 1, Protocol I, ECHR** in the context of compensation for interference with property rights could not be interpreted as extending the general principles of international law in this field to establish standards of compensation for the nationalization of property of nationals as distinct from aliens (where there was a general principle). The word 'context' was held to include the preamble and annexes of the treaty as well as any agreement made by parties in connection with conclusion of treaty and any subsequent agreement.

Shaw (2008) concludes that the process of interpretation is a judicial function to find the meaning of a provision but not to change it. Any subsequent agreement or practice relating to the treaty must be considered together with the context. Subsequent practice may indeed have a dual role: it may act as an instrument of interpretation but it may also mark an alteration in the legal relations between the parties established by the treaty.

In two areas the principle of effectiveness is allied with the broader-purposes approach. In the case of treaties which also operate as the constitutional documents of an international organization, a more flexible method of interpretation would seem to be justified, since one is dealing with an instrument that is being used in order to accomplish the stated aims of that organization. This approach has been used as a way of inferring powers not expressly provided for in the relevant instrument but which are deemed necessary in the context of the purposes of the organization. This programmatic interpretation doctrine is now well established and particularly relevant to the UN which uses subsequent practice as a guide.

The more dynamic approach to interpretation is also evidenced in the context of human rights treaties, such as the **ECHR**, which created a system of implementation. It has been held that a particular legal order has been established involving objective obligations to protect human rights rather than subjective reciprocal rights. This means a more flexible and programmatic or purpose-oriented method of interpretation was adopted, emphasizing that the convention constituted a living instrument which had to be interpreted in light of present-day conditions. In addition, the object and purpose of the convention requires that its provisions be interpreted so as to make its safeguards practical and effective. In the *Licensing of Journalists* case the Inter-American Court of Human Rights held that the rule of interpretation most favourable to the individual must prevail in human rights treaties.

 Examiner's tip

This difficult area is greatly assisted by reference to both the Fitzmaurices and Aust. Liberal reference to these sources is a must. The other requirement is to understand the controversy concerning objective versus subjective approaches to treaty interpretation.

Question 4

Countries Alpha and Beta entered into a bilateral treaty agreeing to develop a joint nuclear power plant within the territory of Alpha but the power generated will be utilized by both countries. The treaty was concluded ten years ago but after work is well under way on the project the government of Alpha has decided to abandon the project firstly because of protests from citizens about the possible negative environmental impact of the project and secondly because of its spiralling costs. Alpha informs Beta that because of 'impossibility of performance' and 'fundamental changes in circumstances' it has decided to abandon the project.

You are the legal adviser to Beta. Advise your government on its legal position and whether there are any legal remedies that your country might pursue against Alpha.

 Commentary

This is a problem question highlighting the issue of one nation attempting to relieve itself of treaty obligations, in this case on the basis of fundamental changes in circumstances. This area of the law has been canvassed in case law—including the key case that must be referred to in this answer—which is the contested case in the ICJ, the *Gabčíkovo-Nagymaros Project (Hungary/Slovakia)* case which was decided in 1997 where Hungary raised both of these reasons to relieve it of its treaty obligations. There are also relevant provisions within the **Vienna Convention on the Law of Treaties** which must be discussed in this answer.

The second important area is the remedies that might be available for a breach of a treaty if the fundamental change in circumstance is not accepted. The concept of 'material breach' has to be considered, as well as the course of action that the wronged nation might adopt. Of particular assistance in answering this question is the chapter on termination of treaties in Aust (2007). This answer requires a step-by-step consideration of the issues highlighted in the problem.

 Answer plan

- Define fundamental change of circumstance according to the provisions in the **VCLT**.
- Apply the relevant case law to the problem question, particularly the *Gabčíkovo-Nagymaros Project (Hungary/Slovakia)* case.
- Define 'material breach'.
- Discuss the remedies that a country can pursue for breach of a treaty.

Suggested answer

This problem of the relationship between Alpha and Beta concerns the termination of treaties and the remedies available for breach of a treaty. **Part V VCLT**, specifically **Arts 42–5 and 54–64**, concerns how a country might relieve itself of its obligations under a treaty. In our problem, this is the case with Alpha which is attempting to relieve itself of its obligations under the treaty; as legal adviser for Beta, you must be aware of these provisions to respond to Alpha's position.

Although treaties are often for a fixed duration and specify when the obligations are at an end, in this case we can assume that Alpha is seeking to end the obligations before the expiration of the term of the treaty or the satisfaction of all of the obligations. This seems clear, as the plant is not completed. Alpha is seeking to argue two grounds, impossibility of performance and fundamental change in circumstances.

First of all, a treaty can be terminated or a party can withdraw from the treaty provided there is consent of all other parties. This is according to **Art. 54(b) VCLT**. In this case, Beta has not consented to the termination of the treaty.

Second, there is a principle in customary law that where there has been a fundamental change of circumstances since an agreement was concluded, a party to that agreement may withdraw from it or terminate it—in Latin the expression is *rebus sic stantibus*. This concept is similar to the English common law doctrine of frustration of contracts. Aust (2007) argues that **Art. 65 VCLT** was drawn in restrictive terms because the concept has been abused in the period particularly between the two world wars. **Article 62** defines the cumulative conditions, all of which must be met for acceptance that there has been a fundamental change in circumstances. These conditions summarized by Aust are:

(i)   the change is of circumstances existing at the time of the conclusion of the treaty;

(ii)   the change is 'fundamental';

(iii)   the change was not foreseen by the parties when they concluded the treaty;

(iv)   the existence of the circumstances constituted 'an essential basis of the consent of the parties to be bound by the treaty'; and

(v)   the effect of the change was 'radically to transform the extent of the obligation still to be performed under the treaty'.

In *Icelandic Fisheries Jurisdiction (United Kingdom v Iceland) (Merits)* the ICJ accepted that this strict approach was declaratory of customary international law. The case closest to the facts of the treaty between our countries Beta and Alpha are those which were involved in the *Gabčíkovo-Nagymaros Project (Hungary/Slovakia)* case decided by the ICJ in 1997. The court did not accept Hungary's argument that there were profound changes of a political nature, that the project had diminished economic viability and that the progress of environmental knowledge and the development of new norms and prescriptions of international environmental law constituted fundamental changes of circumstances. In the court's opinion the circumstances were not of a nature, either individually or collectively, that their effect would radically transform the extent of the obligations still to be performed. They declared that a fundamental change of circumstances must have been unforeseen and that changes of circumstances would only be granted in exceptional cases. Applying this ruling to the facts of Alpha's withdrawal from the project would mean that we could argue strongly that there has not been a fundamental change in circumstances and based on the mentioned case law we could argue that it is likely that the fundamental change in circumstances would not be accepted.

Aust has succinctly set out what is meant by impossibility of performance. **Article 61(1) VCLT** provides that if an object which is 'indispensable' for the execution of a treaty disappears permanently or is destroyed, thereby making the performance of the treaty impossible, a party can invoke this reason as grounds for termination of the treaty.

In the *Gabčíkovo-Nagymaros Project* case the ICJ determined that the object of the treaty had not ceased to exist. Examples given by the International Law Commission as quoted by Aust are the submergence of an island, drying up of a river, or the destruction of a dam by earthquake. Nothing of the kind has happened to the land in Alpha where the power plant is to be constructed.

If the fundamental change in circumstances or impossibility of performance are not accepted, the material breach of Alpha's treaty obligations entitles our country Beta to withdraw from the treaty or terminate it, or suspend its operation. This is set out in Art. **60 VCLT** as one of the remedies for a material breach which is defined in Art. 60(3) as a repudiation of the treaty not sanctioned by the convention, or the violation of a provision 'essential to the accomplishment of the object and purpose of the treaty'. Fitzmaurice (in Evans, 2006) argues that the *Gabčíkovo-Nagymaros Project* case also clarifies what constitutes a material breach. Hungary argued that the construction of a bypass canal known as 'Variant C' by Czechoslovakia which had not been authorized by their 1977 treaty was a material breach of the treaty. The court found that material breach had only occurred when the waters were actually diverted and thus Hungary's notification of termination in May 1992 before this had occurred was premature. This illustrates the fact that courts will again be very strict in determining what is a material breach. I would advise against our withdrawing from the treaty and to await the court's determination on the first two issues.

Given that the court is unlikely to accept the argument of Alpha on fundamental change of circumstances or impossibility of performance and might not accept our argument of material breach, are there remedies that Beta might pursue? It is likely that the treaty will be declared to be still in force and the first stage will be for Alpha to decide whether to continue with its treaty obligations. Alpha might decide to denounce its treaty obligations, which is a unilateral act where one party declares it will no longer participate. The **VCLT** is not very helpful in this regard. According to Aust, many treaties do not contain provisions on the consequences of termination and **Art. 70 VCLT** does not deal with any question of state responsibility for the consequences of the termination. **Article 70(1)** provides that parties are released from their obligations to further perform the treaty; but, importantly, this does not affect my right, obligation, or legal situation of the parties created through the execution of the treaty before its termination. Beta could therefore argue Alpha is liable for the financial loss created by lack of completion of the contract and rely particularly on the ***Gabčíkovo-Nagymaros Project*** case.

 Examiner's tip

This answer requires careful and detailed reading of one case, the ***Gabčíkovo-Nagymaros Project*** case. An examiner will be able to tell if just a text summary was used or whether the student actually read the judgment. It is a complex judgment but absolutely essential to answer this question as it is the only existing judgment that considers treaty obligations in such detail.

Further reading

Aust, A., *Modern Treaty Law and Practice*, 2nd edn (Cambridge: Cambridge University Press, 2007).

Cassese, A., *International Law*, 2nd edn (Oxford: Oxford University Press, 2004).

Fitzmaurice, G., Sir, 'The law and procedure of the International Court of Justice: treaty interpretation and certain other treaty provisions' (1951) 28 BYIL 1.

Fitzmaurice, M., 'The practical working of the law of treaties' in M. Evans, *International Law*, 3rd edn (Oxford: Oxford University Press, 2010).

Goodman, R., 'Human rights treaties, invalid reservation and state consent' (2002) 96 AJIL 531.

Jennings, R. and Watts, A., (eds), *Oppenheim's International Law*, 9th edn (London: Longman, 1992).

Klabbers, J., *The Concept of Treaty in International Law* (The Hague: Kluwer Law International, 1996).

Shaw, M., *International Law*, 6th edn (Cambridge: Cambridge University Press, 2008).

5 International law and municipal law

Surprisingly, a great deal of international law is considered within domestic legal systems, by executive, legislative, and judicial bodies. This area of study involves the reception by sovereign states of both customary international law and treaties. It is a vital area of examination as most public international law courses will include a discrete topic in this area and it is canvassed in most public international law textbooks. In addition, this topic often includes examination of the reception of municipal law in international courts and the relationship of the individual to the international legal system.

This chapter contains a question which calls for an examination of the two different theories on the incorporation of international law into domestic legal systems: monism and dualism. Second, there is a question on the role of the individual within the international legal system. Third, there is a question allowing students to introduce the latest cases that have considered international law within domestic courts—that is, those cases involving terrorism. Finally, there is a question of the reception of national law by international tribunals. The answers to these questions must incorporate key cases on international law decided in various jurisdictions, including the United Kingdom and the United States.

A source well worth reviewing for this topic is a chapter in Higgins (1995) entitled, 'The role of national courts in the international legal process' which makes a very complex topic clearer. Cassese (2004) also has a chapter entitled, 'The implementation of international rules within national systems'. All the classic texts also have chapters on this topic. The ninth edition of *Oppenheim's International Law* has a clear and comprehensive section on this topic, with the practice of many states discussed—see Jennings and Watts (1992). Finally, for up-to-date sources, the latest edition of Shaw (2008) contains recent case law on this issue.

As with other areas of international law, this is a rapidly changing area, as domestic courts are increasingly dealing with issues of public international law. It is worth reviewing your reading lists for additional cases and keeping up to date with the current jurisprudence. The diligent student will be rewarded by the marker for knowledge of current cases. In fact, this area has now assumed a heightened importance since the 11 September 2001 attacks in the

United States. There have been a number of cases in the United Kingdom, the United States, Canada, and in various European jurisdictions on terrorism that all deal with the effect of international human rights law on domestic authorities who seek to introduce measures to prevent further attacks. This is why there is often a specific question dealing with jurisprudence in domestic courts and the student will need to be aware of these cases. A hint is that these cases are often reported in the national media, and so reading newspapers or following the news channels is well worth the effort.

 Question 1

The way in which municipal courts approach arguments of international law differs between states.

With reference to case law, and international law theory, discuss how various states incorporate customary international law and treaties into their domestic legal system.

 Commentary

This question requires the student to be familiar with the two theories of incorporation of international law into the domestic system—monism and dualism. It will be necessary to discuss the theories in a general context but also to give specific examples of how countries receive both treaties and customary international law. It is necessary to illustrate the process by relevant case law from various jurisdictions. Each international law textbook has a section concerning this issue. Although this question is general, it may well be that the question your lecturer or professor drafts may involve how your specific jurisdiction receives international law and therefore knowledge of constitutional law is also essential.

Jennings and Watts (1992) give examples of the practice of many states, including all of the common law jurisdictions. An excellent article examining the US perspective is Cerone, 'The ATCA at the intersection of international law and US law' (2007–8). Another recent publication is Ellen Denza 'The relationship between international and national law' in Evans (2010).

 Answer plan

- Describe the two competing theories of incorporation of international law.
- Describe the dualist approach in the United Kingdom, the United States, and Commonwealth countries.
- Discuss the transformation theory.
- Review the monist approach in civilian law countries.
- Conclude with the notion that incorporation is changing in modern practice.

Suggested answer

The reception of international law, either customary international law or treaties, is not uniform among states. There are two competing theories of incorporation of international law into domestic law. The first is the theory of monism. Monists argue that there is one single system of law and that international law is an element of the domestic legal system along with all the other branches of law. Higgins (1995) illustrates this by arguing that international law is part of the law of the land, alongside labour law, employment law, and contract law. According to Cassese (2004), a supporter of this view was H. Kelsen, who asserted that there existed a unitary legal system. In contrast, the dualists assert that there are two different legal systems existing side by side but operating in different arenas. According to this theory of incorporation of international law there is the international arena and the domestic arena. Denza (2010) explains that under this theory international law has to be transformed into national law in order for there to be rights or obligations on individuals or entities. International law to be considered has to be domesticated. Various countries have adopted one or the other approach but generally many common law countries support the dualist view, whereas civilian systems subscribe to the monist view. However, it is not quite as simple as that, as it can be argued that there are elements of both views in the jurisprudence of many states.

However, generally, the United Kingdom and the United States employ the dualist approach according to Cassese (2004). He states that English case law and the US Constitution recognized the authority of international customary rules and ratified treaties only if they are approved by the competent constitutional authorities. In the United States and the United Kingdom there is no provision that accords customary international law a status higher than ordinary legislation. According to Cassese, if the United Kingdom Parliament were to pass a law conflicting with a rule of customary international law, the national law, being later in time, would prevail. Yet this may well not be the case if one reviews the two recent cases on terrorism in the United Kingdom (both named *A v UK*) in which Lord Bingham argued the authority of international customary law over UK anti-terrorism legislation or admission of evidence obtained by torture elsewhere.

This description of dualism however in the United States is supported by Cerone (2007–8), in which he argues that the US legal system would seem at first glance to be more monist than dualist. The US Constitution declares that treaties made under the authority of the United States, together with the Constitution and federal law '*shall be the supreme Law of the Land*'. In addition, the Supreme Court in *The Paquete Habana* case declared that customary international law was part of US law. However, Cerone argues that the practice of courts in the United States has diverged from this monist concept and maintains a dualist position requiring incorporation into domestic legislation.

There are specific provisions in both the United States and the United Kingdom on treaties. Shaw proposes that this is known as the doctrine of transformation. International law has to be transformed into municipal law by the appropriate constitutional machinery, such as by an act of Parliament. The general practice in the United Kingdom is that treaties do not bind national authorities unless they are translated into domestic legislation. Higgins gives the example of the *Arab Monetary Fund v Hashim* case **House of Lords [1988] 3 All ER 257**, at 275, which held that in the absence of a statutory instrument creating the Arab Monetary Fund, the fund did not exist as an international organization in the United Kingdom. It should be pointed out that Higgins argues that to an international lawyer this would be a 'departure from reality'. According to Shaw, treaties relating to the conduct of war, cession of territory, and the imposition of charges on the public purse do not need intervening acts of legislation before they are binding. However, it is the practice of the United Kingdom to lay before both Houses of Parliament treaties which the UK has signed and the text of any agreement requiring ratification, acceptance, approval, or accession is to be laid before Parliament at least 21 days before any of these actions is taken—this is called the 'Ponsonby rule'.

In the United States the Supreme Court case of *Boos v Barry* (1988) **121 ILR 551** held that the rules of international law were subject to the **US Constitution**. Under **Art. II US Constitution,** the President may only ratify treaties if he or she has the approval of two-thirds of the Senate. There is a method by which some international agreements do not need to go through this very time-consuming procedure and that is the executive agreement. These instruments can be made by the President alone, but these are generally for more minor agreements not affecting the rights of citizens. According to Cerone, there is a doctrine of self-execution. A treaty is to be regarded as equivalent to an act of legislature only when it operates of itself without the aid of any legislative provision. Cerone cites the Supreme Court of United States *Foster v Neilson* **1829 27 US 253** that when either of the parties engages to perform a particular act, the treaty addresses itself to the political, not the judicial department, and the legislature must execute the contract before it can become a rule for the court.

Canada, as with most Commonwealth countries, also subscribes to the dualist position. Customary law, however, is accepted as part of the law of the land as supported by the Canadian Supreme Court in the *Reference Re Secession of Quebec* judgment **(1998) 161 DLR 385**. This is also the case in New Zealand and Australia. Treaties, however, need incorporation by domestic legislation, as the provisions may alter the existing domestic law. For example, many jurisdictions have introduced legislation to incorporate the international obligations under the **Rome Statute of the International Criminal Court.**

There is a clear contrast with a monist country which according to Higgins will treat international legal obligations either from a treaty or customary international law as being part of the law to be given effect and directly applied. An example is French law, where all treaties once signed and ratified take precedence over domestic law. Cassese gives an example from 1991 when the French Council of State after many contrary decisions came to the right conclusion (in *Demizpence*) that **Art. 8 European Convention on Human Rights (ECHR)** is self-executing. In 1989 the Italian Court of Cassation held in *Polo Castro* that **Art. 5(1) ECHR** is self-executing. According to Cassese, in respect of customary international law in some monist states, such as Italy, Germany,

Japan, and Greece, constitutional provisions proclaim that international customary law overrides any inconsistent national legislation.

Nevertheless, understanding these two theories does not resolve the issue of reception of international law into domestic systems. Jennings and Watts (1992) argue that the difference in doctrine between monism and dualism is not resolved by the practice of states. International law developments, such as the increasing role of individuals as subjects of international law and the appearance of such legal orders as that of the European Communities have tended to make the distinction between municipal law and international law less clear. It can be argued that even in dualist states the current debate over customary law taking precedence is making a clear distinction between theories difficult.

 Examiner's tip

The student must have reference to the two theories of incorporation of international law regardless of which theory applies in their jurisdiction. The student should also be aware of the different ways in which custom and treaty are treated in domestic law and have reference to the burgeoning case law in this area.

 Question 2

'There are more and more international rules that address themselves directly to individuals, either by imposing obligations or by granting rights.' (A. Cassese)

Discuss.

 Commentary

This question relates to one of the major issues in the relationship between international law and municipal law—the issue of international rules being directly binding on individuals. Although this is discussed in more detail in international criminal law and international human rights law, more recent chapters on international law and municipal law make mention of this issue. This is a question that is probably less likely to be asked than the others covered in this chapter, but it is well worth preparing as it relates to the other two areas. This issue might be more relevant in the United States. An important example of practice is the litigation in the United States pursuant to the **Alien Torts Claim Act 1789 (ATCA)** where individuals are held financially accountable for violations of peremptory norms of customary international law in domestic courts. There are several cases pending in the United States courts on this issue and the student will need to keep up to date on the rulings in these cases.

This question would also give the student the opportunity to revisit the issue of the theories of receipt of international law—the monist and dualist theories. The argument against international law being binding in the dualist tradition is the necessity for domestic legislation, whereas in the monist tradition international law is part and parcel of the domestic legal system and thus automatically binding on an individual. The two leading sources are Cassese (2004) and Brownlie (2008). An excellent article on this issue is Cerone (2007–8).

Answer plan

- Discuss the theory of international rules reaching the individual directly.
- Discuss the individual criminal responsibility under rules of international criminal law.
- Describe the developing jurisprudence in the United States under the **ATCA**.
- Conclude with your theory of applicability of international law to the individual.

Suggested answer

This quote taken from Cassese argues that international law rules intend to, and do, reach individuals directly and not through the medium of the municipal rules of states. Cassese argues that there had been an increasing tendency since the First World War for many international rules to operate everywhere in the world. Although he does not specify them as such, these could be the rules of customary international law known as *jus cogens* or peremptory norms. There are two aspects to this argument. The first is that an individual derives rights directly from international law. The second and equally important is that individuals owe responsibility not just to a domestic legal order but to the international order. This argument is supported by Cerone (2008). He proposes that individuals have duties transcending the domestic sphere in addition to rights under international law. The thesis of his article supports the tenor of the question in that he argues that the structure of the positivist legal order has changed radically as a result of the Second World War after which the individual became universally recognized as a subject of international law.

Brownlie (2008) agrees with this position. He argues that national and international tribunals may try persons charged with crimes against international law, including war crimes and genocide. He supports this position by asserting that the International Military Tribunal at Nuremberg and many national tribunals did not admit pleas by accused persons charged with war crimes that they had acted in accordance with their national laws. In fact the International Military Tribunals did not accept as an excuse that these individuals were following superior orders. It seems clear that in international criminal justice at least an individual is subject to the rules of international law. Cases such as *Pinochet No. 3*, *Barbie*, and *Eichmann* from the United Kingdom, France, and Israel respectively, seem to confirm that an individual will be held to be criminally liable for violations of international criminal law. It could also be argued that this might also extend from criminal liability to liability for financial compensation.

This theory has been supported by the development of civil claims in one jurisdiction, the United States. Cerone (2008) highlights the current litigation brought by victims of the Bhopal disaster in India who have brought claims under international law, invoking as jurisdiction the **ATCA**. The **ATCA** provides that district courts have jurisdiction over any civil action brought by an alien for a tort, committed in violation of the law of nations or by a treaty of the United States. The first major case that considered this statute was the case of *Filártiga v Pena-Irala* in which Paraguayan citizens were successful in a lawsuit brought against another Paraguayan citizen for torture and murder of the plaintiff's family member. The key ruling was that torture was a violation of international law. This case, therefore, held an individual directly responsible for a violation of international law.

Cerone considers the US Supreme Court's interpretation of this statute in its 2004 judgment *Sosa v Alvarez Machain*. He criticizes the decision as it has not provided proper guidance to lower courts on the relationship between international law and the **ATCA**. Cerone argues that *Sosa* confirmed that customary international law was part of the United States law. Justice Souter held that for two centuries the domestic law of the United States recognized the law of nations citing, among others, *The Paquete Habana* case. The Supreme Court particularly recognized this to be the case with respect to international norms intended to protect individuals. However, it set a high bar for recognizing new causes of action derived from international law. According to Cerone, this corresponds to the general reluctance among US courts to apply international law. The court also indicated in this case that the common law recognized causes of action which entail personal liability of the perpetrator for acts deemed to be offences against the law of nations, such as piracy, assaults upon ambassadors, and violations of safe conducts.

However, Cerone criticizes this part of the ruling, arguing that domestic courts should not purport to find personal liability in international law where it does not exist. Instead, the court should look to international law only for a description of prohibited conduct and the common law should be left to create personal liability. Notwithstanding this criticism, it seems that the US Supreme Court opens the door in *Sosa v Alvarez Machain* to finding personal liability for violations of international law within domestic courts. This liability corresponds to international criminal liability in that it relates directly to the international prohibition, rather than taking its direction from domestic law. Therefore, this practice supports the argument that the person is a direct subject of public international law. Therefore, not only can the individual argue that his or her individual rights are violated but the victim can argue international responsibility, at least in the United States.

The **ATCA** had also been used to ensure corporate accountability for violations of human rights. These cases are now working their way through the United States judicial system. In July 2009, Royal Dutch Shell agreed to a $15.5m settlement in an **ATCA** case brought concerning the death of the poet Ken Saro Wiwa in Nigeria.

This practice, however, has not been extended to the United Kingdom in spite of the effort to do so in the case of *Jones v Saudi Arabia* decided by the House of Lords. In the absence of the **ATCA** a victim of torture in Saudi Arabia was not able to claim for compensation in the United Kingdom, as it was held that the citizen of Saudi Arabia had state immunity based on the **1978 State Immunity Act** on account of the fact that torture was an official and state act. This ruling confirmed the previous case of *Al-Adsani v Government of Kuwait* where the House of Lords had also held that torture was an official act and state immunity applied. This has caused concern particularly with human rights groups who argue that officials of the state should not be able to claim immunity for violation of a norm of *jus cogens*. However, it seems that, unlike the United States, individuals who act on behalf of their state will not be brought to account within a domestic system for compensation.

 Examiner's tip

Students should make sure and distinguish between criminal and civil liability as only the United States assigns civil liability for international wrongs. The *Alien Torts Claims Act* is an area of specific concern for students in law school in the United States and it is worth examining the cases before that court in detail. There is another case, *Esther Kiobel et al. v Royal Dutch Petroleum Co. et al.*, currently before the Supreme Court which will have a significant bearing on the law on this issue.

 Question 3

Case law in the House of Lords and the US Supreme Court on the issue of terrorism has discussed the binding nature of international law within domestic systems.

Consider the impact of these cases on domestic law.

 Commentary

This question gives the student the opportunity to conduct independent analysis of some of the leading domestic decisions that consider international law. There have been two leading cases in international law decided by the House of Lords both entitled *A v UK* and three leading cases decided by the US Supreme Court: *Rasul v Bush*, *Hamdan v Rumsfeld*, and *Boumedience et al. v Bush* (June 2008). All of these cases involve the detention of terrorist suspects and the conditions of their detention and the applicability of international human rights law.

The preparation to answer this question is to review these cases, but also to conduct a search of any more recent cases on this issue, as there are cases being decided constantly in this area.

It may also be necessary to review the case law from your own jurisdiction if it is not the United States or the United Kingdom. Considering the British cases is Breau, 'United Kingdom response to terrorism and the response of the courts to these measures' (2004–5); Nollkaemper in his article 'Internationally wrongful acts in domestic courts' (2007) discusses the ruling in **Hamdan v Rumsfeld**.

Answer plan

- Introduce the issue of the domestic cases on terrorism and their consideration of customary international law and treaty obligations.
- Review the two major House of Lords' decisions.
- Review the three US Supreme Court decisions.
- Conclude with an appraisal of the effect of international law on these decisions.

Suggested answer

In the context of cases which have considered measures against terrorism in the wake of 11 September 2001, courts have been required to consider the effect of international law on domestic law enactments and measures against terrorism. Although there are many cases on this issue, this answer will focus on leading cases in the House of Lords and the US Supreme Court. There is a contrast to the way in which each of these courts considers international law. In summary, it seems that the House of Lords is much more aware of international law and customary and treaty obligations than the US Supreme Court.

There are two major opinions of the House of Lords which consider the effect of domestic law on international obligations. The first was the *A. (FC) and others (FC) (Appellants) v Secretary of State for Home Department (Respondent)*, which was decided on 16 December 2004. The case concerned nine appellants, all of whom were detained under **s. 23 Anti-terrorism, Crime and Security Act 2001**. The legal issue was the argument that the detention was inconsistent with the obligations binding on the United Kingdom by the **ECHR** and given domestic effect by the **Human Rights Act 1998**. Lord Bingham, speaking for the majority, referred to a previous influential decision on detention, *Chahal v United Kingdom* in which the European Commission on Human Rights unanimously rejected qualification of the **Art. 3 ECHR** prohibition against torture for security reasons. The commission held that if a person could not be deported because of a risk of torture and there were no criminal charges pending, then he or she should not be detained.

Lord Bingham was prepared to accept that the emergency triggered by the September 11 attacks caused a public emergency which threatened the *'life of the nation'* and, therefore, derogation from the detention provisions in the **ECHR** might be justified. However, even though the derogation might be permissible, the actual measure of unlimited detention was not. Part of the material relied upon in making this decision was the Privy Counsellor Review Committee known as the Newton Committee's recommendation that the detention provisions be replaced. Lord Bingham held that even if there were a public emergency threatening the life of the nation, measures that derogate from **Art. 5 ECHR** were permissible only to the extent strictly required by the exigencies of the situation. Among his reasons were that in this case the state had not proved that the measures were proportional, as they had not explained why the measures were directed only to foreign nationals and why a terrorist, if a serious threat to the UK, ceases to be so elsewhere. He held later that these measures also violated **Art. 14 ECHR** (the discrimination provision). Thus, Lord Bingham considered the international legal obligations contained in the **ECHR**, an international treaty, to be binding on the United Kingdom.

The second leading case was *A. (FC) and others (FC) (Appellants) v Secretary of State for the Home Department (Respondent)*. Lord Bingham gave the majority decision on 8 December 2005. The question before the Lords was whether the Special Immigration Appeals Commission (SIAC), when hearing an appeal under **s. 25 Anti-terrorism, Crime and Security Act 2001** by a person certified and detained under **ss. 21** and **23** of the Act, that evidence would not be admissible which has or may have been procured by torture inflicted by officials of a foreign state without the complicity of the British authorities. This was a critical question in respect to terrorism, as the issue of obtaining probative evidence in these cases was a major concern for the executive branch.

Lord Bingham analysed this question from three perspectives: English common law; the **ECHR**; and international law. The third consideration was public international law and the proposition that the prohibition of torture enjoyed the highest normative force recognized by international law. Lord Bingham held that the prohibition against torture imposed on states certain obligations towards all other members of the international community and, therefore, there would be a claim to compliance on the part of all states (even if the torture took place elsewhere). Furthermore, torture had acquired the status of a peremptory norm of customary international law and thus one of the most fundamental standards of the international community. Lord Bingham held that there was reason to regard it as a duty of states to reject the results of torture inflicted in breach of international law. In this case, then, Lord Bingham discussed the binding nature of customary international law on domestic authorities.

The US Supreme Court in the past few years in three cases has had to consider the legality of detention of terrorist suspects at Guantanamo Bay and the possible trials of those suspects by military commissions. These cases are: *Rasul v Bush*, *Hamdan v Rumsfeld*, and *Boumedience et al. v Bush* (June 2008). It is particularly the case of *Hamdan v Rumsfeld* that should be examined, as it was this case which considered international legal obligations. Nollkaemper (2007) considers the ruling in *Hamdan v Rumsfeld* as supporting the argument that the strict separation between the international and the domestic spheres in unhelpful. The court's finding was that the Military Commissions to try terrorists were incompatible with the requirements of the **Geneva**

Conventions and that they also lacked a basis in domestic law. This was a rare occasion for the US Supreme Court to consider international treaty obligations and the extent to which they are binding. It should be noted that the **Geneva Conventions** had been incorporated into US law by legislation. It was clear from the ruling and those of *Rasul v Bush* and *Boumedience et al. v Bush* which considered terrorism measures from an American constitutional perspective that domestic terrorism legislation and procedures will be subject to scrutiny pursuant to the international rule of law.

However, particularly with respect to the United Kingdom cases, it seems clear that there will be a growing body of litigation with respect particularly to the threat of terrorism that will continue to test the relationship between domestic law and international law. It seems from this jurisprudence that domestic courts recognize the binding nature of international human rights obligations on the executive, legislature, and judiciary within their respective jurisdictions.

 Examiner's tip

The two leading jurisdictions considering this issue are the United Kingdom and the United States and knowledge of their case law is essential. Students from other jurisdictions would benefit from a search of their case law since mid-2012 (the time of writing this answer) to see if their courts have tested their terrorism legislation against international law.

 Question 4

International courts have to consider domestic law in their decisions.

With reference to international jurisprudence discuss the effect of domestic law in international courts and tribunals.

 Commentary

Reception of municipal law in international courts and tribunals is an important issue. The issue has been considered by international courts since the establishment of the Permanent Court of International Justice (PCIJ) in 1922. There have been two cases of note in the International Court of Justice (ICJ) considering the domestic legal system and the **Vienna Convention on Consular Relations**. The general rule on this issue is included in the **Vienna Convention on the Law of Treaties** and this provision should be memorized by the student.

Luckily for the student, both Shaw (2008) and Brownlie (2008) have sections on this topic which would be well worth relying on in preparation for this area.

Answer plan

- Describe the situations in which a court may consider municipal law.
- Discuss the relationship between domestic statutes and international legal obligations including the provision in the **Vienna Convention on the Law of Treaties**.
- Discuss the rules on reception of domestic law in international cases.
- As examples of consideration of domestic law, discuss the International Court of Justice cases in *Vienna Convention on Consular Relations (Paraguay v United States of America)*, *LaGrand (Federal Republic of Germany v United States of America)*, and *Avena (Mexico v United States of America)*.

 Suggested answer

Brownlie (2008) asserts that cases in which a tribunal dealing with issues of international law has to examine the municipal law of one or more states are by no means exceptional. A tribunal might have to examine municipal law relating to expropriation, fishing limits, nationality, or the guardianship and welfare of infants in order to decide whether particular nations are in breach of their international treaty or customary obligations. Furthermore, issues relating to human rights obligations, treatment of civilians during occupation, and the exhaustion of local remedies always involve consideration of domestic law.

The jurisprudence establishes that as a general rule (according to Shaw (2008)) a state which has broken a stipulation of international law cannot justify itself by referring to its domestic legal situation. It is not a defence to an international legal obligation to argue that a state was following its municipal law. **Article 27 Vienna Convention on the Law of Treaties 1969** sets out that a state cannot use the provisions of its internal law as justification for failure to carry out its international obligations. In the *Polish Nationals in Danzig* case (**PCIJ Series A/B, no. 44**) the court held that a state cannot argue its own constitution with a view to evading obligations under international law or treaties in force. Another example is the *Certain German Interests in Polish Upper Silesia* case (**PCIJ Series A, no. 7**) where the court held that there was nothing to prevent the court's giving judgment on the question whether or not, in applying municipal law, Poland was acting in conformity to its obligations to Germany as set out in the **Geneva Convention on Upper Silesia of 1922**.

Therefore, domestic law according to Shaw (2008) is neither irrelevant nor unnecessary. Often it is necessary to discover a state's position on international law by examining its domestic legislation. Brownlie proposes six different principles on the reception in international courts of municipal law as facts. First, municipal law may be evidence of conduct in violation of a rule of treaty or customary law, as just illustrated. Second, judicial notice does not apply to matters of municipal law. The tribunal will require proof of municipal law and hear evidence about it. The third principle is that interpretation of their own laws by national courts is binding on an international tribunal. This was confirmed in the *Serbian Loans* case in the PCIJ.

The fourth principle is that the dicta of international tribunals rest on the assumption that for any domestic issue for which an international tribunal is seized, there must always be some applicable rule of municipal law which is ascertainable in the same way as other facts of the case. As a matter of procedure, according to Jennings and Watts (1992) in proceedings in international courts a national law is generally regarded as a fact with reference to which rules of international law have to be applied, rather than as rule to be applied on the international plane as a rule of law. Insofar as the ICJ is called upon to express an opinion as to the effect of a rule of national law it will do so by treating the matter as a question of fact to be established as such rather than as a question of law to be decided by the court. The relevant case to support this view is the *Barcelona Traction (Second Phase)* (ICJ Reports 1970). Jennings and Watts assert that a national statute prescribing the treatment of aliens in a manner contrary to international law is simply one of the facts tending to establish the state's breach of international obligations and does not establish on the international plane the lawfulness of the state's action.

The fifth principle is that international tribunals cannot declare on the internal validity of rules of national law, since the international order must respect the reserved domain of domestic jurisdiction. However, this issue has come to the forefront in three ICJ cases considering the rules of the **Vienna Convention on Consular Relations**, which provided foreigners access to their embassy when they are arrested in another country. In the *Vienna Convention on Consular Relations (Paraguay v United States of America)* the ICJ issued a provisional order to ensure that a citizen of Paraguay, Breard, was not to be executed due to an allegation of a violation of **Art. 36(1)(b) Vienna Convention on Consular Relations** in that he had not been informed without delay that he had the right to have his consulate notified of his arrest and he had not been able to communicate with his consulate. In *LaGrand (Germany v United States)* (ICJ reports 2001) the court held that the United States could not adopt a procedural rule depriving the LaGrand brothers from accessing counsel from their embassy and that this rule was a violation of the US obligations under the **Vienna Convention on Consular Relations.** In *Avena (Mexico v United States)* (ICJ Reports 2004) the court held that the rights guaranteed under the same **Vienna Convention** were treaty rights which the United States had undertaken to comply with in relation to the individual concerned irrespective of the due process rights under the **US Constitution.** In the first two decisions the individuals were executed in spite of the order and in the third the United States finally agreed to review the case of 51 Mexican nationals covered by the *Avena* decision. These cases are examples of consideration of criminal rules and procedures adopted in a domestic context but are in violation of the international treaty regime. The international court will not allow these rules to interfere with their consideration of the international obligations of a state. Although they may not have specifically considered invalidity of domestic legislation, they certainly commented on the invalidity of rules and procedures denying inmates rights to consult their embassy officials.

The sixth principle as set out in the ***Application of the Convention of 1902 Governing the Guardianship of Infants (Netherlands v Sweden)*** decided by the ICJ in 1958 is that an international tribunal will not interpret national law as such. Brownlie (2008) disagrees with this final principle and indicates that there may be special agreements in international arbitral tribunals to interpret domestic law. Nevertheless, this principle seems to accord with the general rule that domestic law is to be considered as a fact. It seems logical that an international court will not try to interpret the various domestic statutes.

In conclusion, the general principle as confirmed by the **Vienna Convention on Consular Relations** cases discussed in this essay is that the practice in international tribunals confirms that domestic law will not be permitted to interfere with a state's international obligations.

 Examiner's tip

This question requires consideration of the various ways in which domestic law can be considered by an international court. The key cases in this question are those within the International Court of Justice considering the imposition of the death penalty in the United States. It is important to indicate to the examiner thorough knowledge of these few cases before the international courts that have considered death penalty and consular assistance.

Further reading

Breau, S., 'United Kingdom response to terrorism and the response of the courts to these measures' (2004–5) 11 *Yearbook of Islamic and Middle Eastern Law* 83.

Brownlie, I., *Principles of Public International Law*, 7th edn (Oxford: Oxford University Press, 2008).

Cassese, A., *International Law*, 2nd edn (Oxford: Oxford University Press, 2004).

Cerone, J., 'The ATCA at the intersection of international law and US law' (2008) 42 *New Eng. L. Rev.* 743.

Denza, E., 'The relationship between international and national law', in Evans, M., *International Law*, 3rd edn (Oxford: Oxford University Press, 2010).

Higgins, R., *Problems and Process* (Oxford: Oxford University Press, 1995).

Jennings, R. and Watts, A., (eds), *Oppenheim's International Law*, 9th edn (London: Longman, 1992).

Nollkaemper, A., 'Internationally wrongful acts in domestic courts' (2007) 101 AJIL 760.

Shaw, M., *International Law*, 6th edn (Cambridge: Cambridge University Press, 2008).

6

Legal personality and the creation of states

Introduction

This chapter contains questions that invite discussion of the principle of legal personality in the international legal system and issues of how a state is defined and recognized within international law, as the state is the key legal person in the international legal system. As Crawford (2007) argues in his important text on this issue, the emergence of so many new states since the end of the Second World War era represents one of the major political developments of the twentieth century. Therefore, this is an area that is often covered in examinations because there have been so many internal and international armed conflicts resulting from claims of self-determination and statehood. Groups such as the Kurds and Palestinians argue for self-determination and for historical claims over parts of the Middle East. This area's topicality remains undiminished and the fragmentations of the Soviet Union, Yugoslavia, and Czechoslovakia in the 1990s constitute key elements of state practice. Recently, Kosovo declared independence which resulted in a referral to ICJ for an advisory Opinion. The Court released its advisory Opinion on 22 July 2010 and confirmed the lawfulness of the Kosovar declaration of independence. The advisory Opinion is a must reference for those preparing this area. Finally, the international community has just seen a new State—South Sudan, which emerged after a long-standing armed conflict in Sudan.

There are a plethora of sources on this important topic. Along with the discussion in the classic texts, including Jennings and Watts (1992), an essential publication for this topic is Crawford's new edition of *The Creation of States in International Law* (2007). Higgins (1994) has an excellent chapter on self-determination. Each time a new political unit makes a claim for statehood or there is an armed conflict on self-determination a number of academic articles are published on this subject. It is well worth a search on the online databases.

Questions in this area will ask the student to discuss the definition of legal personality, the criteria for statehood, and the declarative and constitutive theories of recognition of states within international law. There may also be a question which discusses the role of self-determination in the creation and recognition of states, a question often asked in examinations due to the importance of the concept within international human rights law and the fact that many internal armed conflicts are due to claims for independence.

The issue of the independence of Kosovo will continue to result in a host of academic articles written on Kosovo and self-determination and the ICJ advisory Opinion will be hugely influential particularly on other independence movements. Furthermore, after an armed conflict between Russia and Georgia, Russia recognized the two breakaway portions of Georgia—South Ossetia and Abkhazia—although this was not accepted by most of the rest of the international community.

 Question 1

1. What is meant by international legal personality?
2. To what extent are the following subjects of international law:
   (a) Palestine;
   (b) the United Nations;
   (c) Radovan Karadžić, former President of the Serbian state within Bosnia;
   (d) the Kurdish people;
   (e) Shell International Oil plc; and
   (f) Human Rights Watch.

 Commentary

The purpose of this question is to elicit discussion of various entities which might possess rights, duties, and powers within the international legal system. This area is replete with examples of state and international organization practice and case law discussing the notion of personality. There is a key International Court of Justice (ICJ) advisory Opinion on this issue: *Reparation for Injuries Suffered in the Service of the United Nations* **(11 April 1949)**.

The classic view was that only states had international legal personality in international law, but that view radically changed in the twentieth century with the advent of international organizations and international criminal law which included international governmental organizations and individuals as international legal persons. However, there are still territories and groups of people who have not yet achieved statehood and yet have some sort of hybrid legal personality. More recently there is an emerging debate concerning the role of civil society and corporations within international law. This answer will need to distinguish between those entities which are subjects and those which are objects of public international law.

The answer to this question will require knowledge of the classic definitions of legal personality and up-to-date information on current debates, particularly with respect to the legal personality of corporations. An excellent source for part of this discussion on peoples is McCorquodale's chapter in Evans (2006) entitled 'The individual and the international legal system'; Shaw (2008) also has a good discussion on legal personality.

 Answer plan

- Discussion of the idea of international legal personality.
- Discussion of the notion of a subject within the international legal system.
- Discussion of the various participants within international law as listed and giving an opinion on whether or not they have international legal personality.

 Suggested answer

O'Connell (1970) argued that legal personality is only shorthand for the proposition that an entity is endowed by international law with legal capacity. Jennings and Watts (1992) introduce the concept of international person as one who possesses legal personality in international law and enjoys rights, duties, or powers as established in international law and has the capacity to act on the international plane either directly or indirectly. Personality is a requirement to bring legal claims in the various international enforcement tribunals. This means that this international person would be a subject of international law defined by Brownlie (2008: 57) as: '*an entity of the type recognized by customary law as capable of having these capacities (rights duties and powers to bring a legal claim) is a legal person*'. This is a crucial concept in public international law, as institutions and groups need it to operate within the international legal arena. This can be contrasted with entities that are objects of the law; these are entities that might have legal rules to protect them (such as rules protecting animals and young children) but they do not in themselves have the legal rights and duties to enforce these rights in a court system.

The classic position was that states were the principal (and sometimes argued to be only) subjects of public international law, but as Lowe (2007) argues this was not the case even a century ago as states concluded agreements with principalities, cities, indigenous peoples, and others who would not have fitted into the concept of a state. However, Warbrick ('States and recognition in international law' in Evans, 2010) maintains the position that international law is *mainly* to do with states as it is states which create or acknowledge the other entities. One could take issue with Warbrick and agree with Shaw (2008) that the Holy See, insurgents and belligerents, international organizations, chartered companies, and various territorial entities such as the League of Cities were at one time or another treated as possessing the capacity to become international persons.

Perhaps a compromise position would be that there are entities within the international legal system with personality but perhaps that personality might be limited according to the context in which the subject operates. Therefore, the second part of this question seeks to determine whether these various entities have international legal personality and are thus subjects of international law.

(a) Palestine represents other entities that are somewhat like states such as the: Free City of Danzig, Internationalized Territories (Kosovo until it declared independence), exile governments, federations, associations of states, protectorates and protected states and the usual cases such as the Sovereign Order of Malta, and the Holy See (often referred to as the Vatican).

Palestine is particularly pertinent due to the Israel–PLO Declaration of Principles on Interim Self-Government Arrangements which gave the Palestinian territory some of the attributes of a state. One could conclude that Palestine has international legal personality in some circumstances, for example, it was permitted to file materials in the International Court of Justice for the advisory Opinion in *Legal Consequences of the Construction of a Wall in the Occupied Palestinian Territory* and is permitted to have a non-voting seat in the UN. A recent development is the consideration by the Prosecutor of the International Criminal Court, subsequent to the Gaza conflict, as to whether Palestine can be considered a state for purposes of international criminal prosecutions. A decision has not yet been announced on this issue.

(b) The UN—the personality of the United Nations was considered in *Reparations for Injuries Suffered in the Service of the United Nations* ICJ Rep. 1949. This case was considering compensation for a UN employee, Count Bernadotte, who was killed in Israel. The ICJ in its advisory Opinion declared that the UN has an international legal personality and this is for all purposes including bringing legal claims and concluding international treaties.

(c) Individuals—in *Danzig Railways Officials*, the Permanent Court of International Justice (PCIJ) discussed individual criminal responsibility at the international level. This is supported by the decision of the Nuremberg Tribunal and the International Military Tribunal in Japan and the subsequent International Military Commission trials and within treaty law, such as the **1949 Geneva Conventions** and their **1977 Additional Protocols**. The ad hoc tribunals for Yugoslavia and Rwanda and the development of the International Criminal Court (ICC) confirm individual criminal responsibility within international law and the ICC also includes rights for victims as well as perpetrators. It might have been argued previously that individuals were only objects of international law, as they were protected by human rights instruments but as they can bring claims in human rights tribunals and are criminally responsible they are now subjects and objects in international law. As McCorquodale (in Evans, 2006) concludes, individuals have considerable rights and responsibilities independent of the state but they do not as yet have the same degree of participation as states.

(d) The Kurdish peoples—peoples constitute ethnic and cultural groups which claim the right of self-determination. This norm is confirmed in **Resolution 1514 (XV) on the Declaration on the Granting of Independence to Colonial Countries and Peoples.** Cases in the ICJ include the 1960 *South West Africa* cases, the *Western Sahara* case, and the *East Timor* case, and accept there is an international right of self-determination. However, at best, it could be argued that peoples have some status as their rights as groups are considered by some of the human rights mechanisms and within deliberations at the General Assembly and Security Council. They do not as yet have full international legal personality as they cannot bring or respond to international litigation.

(e) Shell Oil plc—transnational corporations: this is very topical because of the introduction of corporate norms of social responsibility in human rights law. There are allegations that Shell Oil for example has been responsible for environmental and human damage within the Niger Delta region. It cannot be argued that corporations have international legal personality, as such, as they are subject to the particular national jurisdiction in which they are incorporated. There is a movement within human rights to bring corporations within international legal responsibility by the draft norms of corporate social responsibility, but they have been adopted by neither the Human Rights Council nor any sovereign states. Corporations have been brought into the international arena only voluntarily within such mechanisms as the global compact but it cannot be argued that they have full international legal personality.

(f) Human Rights Watch—this entity is part of what is now known as international civil society often called non-governmental organizations (NGOs). Other examples of such groups include Amnesty International and Greenpeace. These groups have become participants in treaty negotiations such as the **Statute for the International Criminal Court and the Landmines and Cluster Munitions Conventions** and recently as parties in human rights cases in the African and Inter-American system. They also file independent reports when human rights records of states are reviewed by the human rights treaty enforcement bodies in the United Nations system. However, it cannot yet be argued that they have international legal personality as they have no capacity to enforce their rights within international tribunals.

 Examiner's tip

The successful student will start with a definition of legal personality. It is important to give specific examples for each category as how these entities are dealt with in international law. This is an active area of development as NGOs in particular are winning more and more rights within the international community.

Question 2

The sovereign State of Napanee, a member of the UN and located in Africa, is composed of three provinces made up of diverse ethnic groups, Odessa, Kingston, and Brockville. The state had been ruled for the past twenty years by a dictator known as 'Big Daddy' who recently passed away. The federal government is now composed of a ruling council of leaders from the three separate provinces.

The province of Odessa has the largest area and ethnic group, the Odessans. The second province in size is Kingston and its ethnic group is the Kingstonians. This province has always been unhappy under Big Daddy and now that he is dead has announced its intention to separate. Thirty per cent of Kingston is also Odessan and this group refused to vote in the recent independence referendum which was passed by 90 per cent of those who voted. The day after the referendum, an elected group of Kingstonians declared a separate state of Kingston.

Does customary international law or any existing treaty law, including human rights covenants, recognize within the right of self-determination the right to secede? How are new states created in public international law?

Commentary

This is an example of a problem question with very similar facts to the break-up of the Socialist Federal Republic of Yugoslavia (SFRY). The question seeks to elucidate the student's knowledge of the classic legal formula for creation of a state and the debate as to whether self-determination should be an additional criterion. The role of self-determination is very controversial, as it is not one of the traditional accepted criteria for statehood.

This problem question calls for an answer which contains a combination of recent state practice, including the important work done by the Badinter Commission concerning the Federal Republic of Yugoslavia (whose findings are neatly set out in Harris (2010)) and academic discourse and international case law. A pertinent opinion is the ICJ's advisory Opinion in *Legal Consequences of the Construction of a Wall in the Occupied Palestinian Territory* **9 July 2004**. An excellent theoretical analysis of this topic is the chapter on self-determination in Higgins (1994).

Answer plan

- Discussion of criteria for statehood as set out in the **Montevideo Convention**.
- Application of the criteria to this problem question.
- Discussion of self-determination and whether this allows for secession from an existing state and the creation of a new state.

Suggested answer

Article 1 Montevideo Convention on the Rights and Duties of States 1933 sets out the criteria for statehood:

> The State as a person of international law should possess the following qualifications: (a) a permanent population; (b) a defined territory; (c) government (d) capacity to enter into relations with other states.

This set of criteria has now passed into customary international law. There are now 192 members of the UN, and Kosovo has recently declared independence. As new states are coming into existence all the time, these criteria are very important. It is this standard that the independence of Kingston must be assessed against.

For each criterion there are examples of state practice and case law.

(a) Permanent population—as Shaw (2008) and Warbrick (in Evans, 2006) argue, although the existence of a permanent population is required, there is no minimum number of people specified. Examples of state practice are the recognition of Nauru and Tuvalu which have 10,000 and 12,000 people respectively. In this case, Kingston has a clear recognized population but with a significant cultural minority.

(b) Territory—the case of *Deutsche Continental Gas-Gesellschaft v Polish State (1929)* is pertinent. The German–Polish mixed arbitration panel held that in order for a state to exist and be recognized as such, it is enough that its territory has a sufficient consistency, even though its boundaries have not been accurately delimited. Another example is obviously Israel which to this day still does not have settled borders. In this case, the province of Kingston has had long-standing provincial boundaries which can constitute national boundaries under the long-standing doctrine of *uti possidetis*. A recent example of state practice could be Bosnia, which was constituted a state during an armed conflict when its territory and population were not properly delimited.

(c) Government—there are several examples of state practice concerning the necessity for a stable government. A pertinent example of state practice is the *Aaland Islands* case. In this situation the International Committee of Jurists prepared a report which considered the situation of Finland in 1917–18, and declared that as of May 1918 a stable political organization existed. An example of failed state—an entity that does not have a government—is the case of Somalia which continues to this day in a state of constant civil war after the disastrous UN intervention. However, according to Warbrick, Somalia still exists as a state even though there is not an effective formal government. Shaw argues that recent practice of the recognition of Croatia and Bosnia-Herzegovina when significant parts of their territories were controlled by other forces modifies the criterion of effective control of a government.

In the case of Kingston there is an independent government elected by the people in spite of 30 per cent of the population failing to take part. This is a similar situation again to Bosnia and Croatia in the break-up of the former Yugoslavia and the recognition given to the break-up by the Badinter Commission.

(d) Independence—capacity to enter into relations with other states requires factual as well as legal independence from other states. So this means that puppet states can lose independence. An example was Manchukuo which came into existence after Japan invaded Manchuria, a province of China in 1931. The League of Nations sent a commission which reported and the League of Nations decided that sovereignty over Manchuria belonged to China.

An excellent case example is the *Austro-German Customs Union* case, in the (PCIJ) in 1931. Austria and Germany created a customs union in 1931. The court had to consider whether Austria was still independent. The court held that according to the **Treaty of Saint-Germain** Austria had to continue as a separate state. The court held Austria was still independent. Different aspects of independence were that the state had the sole right of decision in all matters economic, political, and financial. Independence is the normal condition of states according to international law and can also be described as sovereignty which means that the state has no authority over it other than that of international law.

Other examples are the cases of the Transkei and other South African homelands. In 1976 South Africa established satellite homelands and transferred sovereignty to an African government over Transkei. The UN General Assembly condemned the establishment of these homelands, as they were to continue apartheid and destroy the territorial integrity of South Africa and called on other governments not to recognize the existence of the territory.

Another example is the area of northern Cyprus. The Turkish government invaded northern Cyprus in 1974 and controlled 36 per cent of Cyprus. Turkey declared the Turkish Republic of Northern Cyprus with its own constitution. The Security Council declared that Turkey's intervention was illegal and therefore it is not a state.

In the case of Kingston, the issues of independence and capacity to enter into relations with others are not resolved. As with Bosnia and Croatia, the state of independence and ability to enter into relations with other nations will depend on recognition by other nations or entities such as the European Union (EU).

The problem of the Kingstonians also poses the question as to whether self-determination should be a criterion is the creation of states as the country has declared independence on the basis of self-determination. This principle of self-determination is very controversial. However, since the end of the cold war, this is how most new states are being created. In the post Second World War, it became a critical part of UN practice on account of the policy of decolonization. A key international instrument is the *Declaration on the Granting of Independence to Colonial Territories and Peoples UN General Assembly* **Resolution 1514 of 1960** under which self-determination is a right where peoples freely determine their political status and freely pursue their economic, social, and cultural development. The most recent case to consider this issue is the advisory Opinion in *Legal Consequences of the Construction of a Wall in the Occupied Palestinian Territory* in the ICJ. The court assessed the impact of the construction of the wall on right of the Palestinian people to self-determination. The court stated that the right of peoples to self-determination was a right *erga omnes* (binding on the international community as a whole). This followed the dicta in the *Western Sahara* case **ICJ Rep. 1975**, at 12 where the court held that the principle of self-determination was paramount and a principle of customary international law. See also the *East Timor* case **ICJ Rep. 1995**, at 90.

However, there are recent examples of state practice that have nothing to do with a post-colonial situation including the situation in the former Yugoslavia and the recent declaration of independence by Kosovo. In the early 1990s the disintegration of the former Yugoslavia resulted in turmoil over which portions constituted states. The EU had a great interest in the situation and appointed a commission known as the Badinter Commission to investigate. In its **Opinion No. 2** it addressed the question of whether the Serbian people in Croatia and Bosnia-Herzegovina had a right to self-determination. The commission declared that all the implications of self-determination were not spelled out in international law. Would it involve changes to existing frontiers? The Commission did not grant the Serbian population the right to a separate state.

However, after the NATO campaign in 1999, part of Serbia, the province of Kosovo, became a territory administered under the auspices of the UN. In 2007 the provincial government declared its independence from Serbia recognized by the United States and the EU but strongly opposed by Russia. It remains to be seen whether Kosovo becomes a fully functioning state within the international community. The International Court of Justice released its advisory Opinion on 22 July 2010 and the majority of the court accepted the lawfulness of the declaration of independence. However, it did not rule on the more thorny issue of whether there is a right of external self-determination.

In the various instruments in the UN, self-determination is tempered by caution against violation of territorial integrity—acceptance of colonial boundaries were not to be challenged after independence under the principle of *uti possidetis*—therefore, self-determination is carefully balanced with the importance of national unity and territorial integrity.

According to Higgins (2004: 123) '*the right of self-determination continues beyond the moment of decolonization and allows choice as to political and economic systems within the existing boundaries of the state*'. However, even though Higgins does not believe that self-determination is a right which authorizes minorities to break away, one could argue that state practice in the 1990s may be supporting just such a practice.

However, based on the international case law and academic opinion, including Higgins, it can be argued that minorities are to be protected—through the guarantee of human rights, including **Article 27 International Covenant on Civil and Political Rights** and when a particular problems arises, for example, Iraq and the Kurds, internal autonomy may provide the best guarantee for the realization of these rights. However, autonomy is not independence. The right of self-determination is interlocked with the proper protection of human rights, but these are discrete rights not to be confused with each other. Therefore, at this stage, one cannot argue that Kingston is entitled to be a separate state based on self-determination.

Examiner's tip

The important facet in this question is for the student to recognize that there is external and internal self-determination. The issue of independence for Kingston has to be contrasted with possible autonomy. The key for the examiner is the use of actual examples in international relations, the case law, and the unique Badinter Commission reports.

 Question 3

The crisis caused by the break-up of the Socialist Federal Republic of Yugoslavia did much to clarify the law of state recognition.

Do you agree?

 Commentary

This question is one which elicits discussion of the theories of recognition in international law. Students should be warned that these aspects of statehood and recognition could well be combined in one question but for the purposes of this chapter this question will be treated separately, as there is plenty to discuss in this answer without the criteria for statehood. Shaw (2008) divides this topic into two separate chapters and devotes a chapter to recognition. The element of self-determination can also be brought into this answer, as it might be part of the constitutive theory of recognition. This question can be answered by either agreement or disagreement with either or both of the two theories of recognition, and allows students to reveal their analytical skills in viewing the two contested theories of recognition.

The question also calls for detailed knowledge of the activities of the Badinter Commission which issued opinions that relate to the issue of recognition. Harris (2010) contains the relevant excerpts from the Badinter Commission as well as the European Commission statements on Yugoslavia and Russia. Three excellent articles on this topic are: Rich, 'Recognition of states: the collapse of Yugoslavia and the Soviet Union' (1993); and two shorter articles on recognition by Warbrick (1992 and 1993).

 Answer plan

- What is the significance of recognition in international law?
- Discuss the two theories of recognition: constitutive and declaratory.
- Apply the Badinter Commission rulings and the SFRY to the theories.
- Conclude with your own opinion on which is the most likely theory.

Suggested answer

The break-up of the SFRY did little to clarify the controversy surrounding recognition in international law. In this context, recognition is the act of accepting the existence of a state and that the state has the consequent rights and responsibilities within the international community. There is confusion in international law between recognition of states and government but for this question we are speaking of recognition of states as countries such as the United States and the United Kingdom no longer recognize governments.

There are two theories of recognition in international law. The first is the constitutive theory. This theory maintains that it is the act of recognition by other states that creates a new state and endows it with legal personality and not the process by which it actually obtained independence. New states are established in the international community as fully-fledged subjects of international law by virtue of the will and consent of already established states. The disadvantage to this approach is that an unrecognized state may not be subject to the obligations imposed by international law and may accordingly be free from such restraints.

The second theory is the declaratory theory. This theory maintains that recognition is merely an acceptance by states of an already existing situation and applies the criteria of the **Montevideo Convention**. A new state will acquire capacity in international law not by virtue of the consent by others but by virtue of a particular factual situation. It will be legally constituted by its own efforts and circumstances and will not have to await the procedure of recognition by other states.

The international law of recognition has been left in limbo as a result of the activities of the international community of states, particularly with respect to the states making up the European Union as a result of the activities of the Badinter Commission established to consider the legal implications of the disintegration of Yugoslavia. According to Shaw (2008), actual practice leads to a middle position between these two theories. The act of recognition by one state of another indicates that the former regards the latter as having conformed to the basic requirements in international law as to the creation of the state. However, Harris (2010) argues that the declaratory theory is adopted by most modern writers and by arbitral practice.

A key case supporting the Harris view is *Tinoco Arbitration (Great Britain v Costa Rica)* where William Taft, the sole arbitrator, held that recognition is simply evidence that the international law requirements have been met and thus this case clearly supports the declaratory theory. However, this case was decided in 1923 and there have been examples of state practice that threw this theory into considerable doubt.

In fact it could be argued that in state practice the constitutive theory might be of more importance. Rich (1993) argues that recognition is more of a discretionary and political act than it was earlier. He gives examples, the first being the situation with respect to Russia and the break-up of the USSR. The **European Commission Guidelines on the Recognition of New States in Eastern Europe and in the Soviet Union (1991)** imposed additional requirements from those of the **Montevideo Convention**. These were:

1   respect for the provisions of the **UN Charter** and **Helsinki Accords;**

2   guarantees for the rights of ethnic and national groups and minorities;

3   respect for the inviolability of all frontiers;

4   acceptance of all disarmament commitments; and

5   commitment to settle by arbitration all issues of state secession.

Applying these guidelines, the EC and Member States recognized as states 11 out of the 15 republics of the former USSR, and then also the three Baltic states and Russia as continuing the Soviet Union. Rich argued that these guidelines added new requirements and supplanted the previous accepted criteria for statehood.

The EC declaration on Yugoslavia imposed the same guidelines as in Russia to the former Yugoslav republics. In this case there resulted a bloody civil war and then international armed conflict when Serbia and Montenegro did not want to accept the various declarations of independence of the other republics. In this case a further requirement was that a Yugoslav republic had to confirm that it had no territorial claims on neighbouring community states. Warbrick argued in his short article 'Recognition of states' (1992) that political conditioning of recognition of statehood was new to UK practice.

The constitutive theory can be further supported by the opinions of the Badinter Commission. The Arbitration Commission of the Conference on Yugoslavia (commonly known as the Badinter Arbitration Committee) was a commission set up by the Council of Ministers of the European Economic Community on 27 August 1991 to provide the Conference on Yugoslavia with legal advice concerning the international law issues arising from the dissolution of the SFRY. In its *Opinion No. 1* the Badinter Commission gave its legal opinion that recognition was purely declaratory in effect.

Nevertheless, it is the rest of the Badinter Commission statements on this issue that contradicts their first opinion and might well support the constitutive theory. These are opinions numbers 4, 5, and 7 which discussed the independence of Bosnia-Herzegovina, Croatia, and Slovenia. In *Opinion No. 4* the Commission stated that Bosnia had fulfilled the European Commission criteria except for a referendum to determine the will of the people. The referendum was subsequently held and the EC counties and the United States recognized Bosnia-Herzegovina. *Opinion No. 5* also supports the constitutive theory in which it called for Croatia to amend its **Constitutional Act** to include provisions protecting minorities which again was an additional requirement for recognition from the traditional **Montevideo** criteria. In the cases of Bosnia and Croatia at the time there were armed conflicts which meant that the new states did not have control over large portions of their territory in contravention of the **Montevideo Convention** and yet the Badinter Commission discussed their independence.

One might argue that in certain contexts the recognition of Bosnia and Croatia might have been premature. This is typified in the case of Biafra when five states recognized the state before it had won its civil war and then it lost. This again may also be the case in Croatia when it did not control one-third of its territory for several years. Similarly, Bosnia controlled less than one-half its territory at the time it was recognized by the EU and many states. This again might support the argument for the constitutive theory.

Another important example of state practice supporting the constitutive theory is the issue of another former Yugoslav republic, Macedonia. There was a year's delay in recognition on account of the Greek objection with respect to the name and the necessity for a compromise, naming Macedonia the Former Yugoslav Republic of Macedonia, even thought Macedonia met all of the **Montevideo** requirements a year prior to recognition. As Rich concluded, a country (Bosnia) torn by violence and headed by a government sadly reduced to calls for outside intervention, was widely recognized by the members of the international community, while a neighbouring republic which met all the traditional criteria for statehood was having its calls for recognition ignored.

Examining state practice one can agree with Rich's conclusion that all of these recent events—and additional elements of recognition of the Baltic States and Ukraine—point towards a trend to constitute states through the process of recognition.

 Examiner's tip

The student has to display knowledge of the importance of recognition to the creation of a state. The two theories of recognition must be discussed. The student should also support their discussion with actual examples of recognition or the lack of recognition of states.

 Question 4

The State of Lovely splits into two separate states, Lovelier and Loveliest.

What is the effect on the entity that was the State of Lovely? What will be the international obligations of the new states of Lovelier and Loveliest?

 Commentary

This question is probably not as common as the first three but the issue of state secession is critical in international law as the situation of the SFRY revealed. Since the fall of the Berlin Wall, there have been many new states created, particularly from the former Soviet Union and by and large, except for the tragedy in the SFRY, the extinction of old states and the secession of new states has taken place harmoniously.

This question might not be a usual one in an examination but it is well worth engaging in some preparation of this area if your professor or lecturer emphasized this issue in his or her lectures. It calls for knowledge of the two **Vienna Conventions** on this topic and relevant examples of state practice.

Answer plan

- Define the notion of extinction of states with reference to state practice.
- Define the idea of secession to the rights and duties of the former state with reference to state practice and with particular emphasis on the Badinter Commission.
- Discuss the relevant international instruments.
- Discuss the consequence of the dissolution of a state on the existing territorial boundaries.

Suggested answer

The State of Lovely is now becoming extinct and two states, Lovelier and Loveliest, are coming into existence. Harris defines the extinction of states with reference to several examples. He contends that a state may cease to be an international person when it ceases to exist in the following:

(a) when one state merges into another it becomes merely a part of it;

(b) when (like the situation above) a state breaks up so that its whole territory henceforth comprises two or more states;

(c) when a state breaks up into parts all of which become part of another usually surrounding state; and

(d) formerly when a state was subjugated (although this is no longer lawful according to **Art. 2(4) UN Charter**).

A state that becomes extinct is replaced by other political and territorial entities and that involves the second principle of state secession. According to the Badinter Commission, *Opinion No. 1*, the expression 'state secession' means the replacement of one state by another in terms of the responsibility for the international relations of a territory. It occurs wherever there is a change in the territory of the state. The outcome of such a secession should be equity and the states concerned are free to settle the terms and conditions by agreement. However, according to the Badinter Commission, the peremptory norms of general international law and, in particular, respect for the fundamental rights of the individual and the rights of peoples and minorities, are binding on the parties to the secession.

In practice, extinction and secession often go hand in hand, recent examples being the dissolution of the Soviet Union, the break-up of Yugoslavia, the break-up of Czechoslovakia, the unification of Germany, and the creation of the State of Eritrea separate from the State of Ethiopia.

An important example of state practice is the European Commission Peace Conference on Yugoslavia which was convened following the eruption of civil war in SFRY. The conference asked the five members of the Badinter Commission to act as an arbitration panel and as such they handed down *Opinions 1–10*, three of which are relevant to the situation of extinction and secession of states, and represent important examples of state practice in this complex area. *Opinion No. 1* stated that the SFRY was in the process of dissolution and that the various constituent republics had an obligation to settle problems of state secession in keeping with the principles and rules of international law in particular with regard to human rights and rights of minorities. *Opinion No. 8* indicated that the dissolution of a state meant that it no longer had legal personality, and in this case the SFRY no longer existed.

Finally, in *Opinion No. 3*, the commission dealt with the territorial repercussions of the break-up of the SFRY. In this case, the commission found that all external frontiers had to be respected and that the former internal boundaries between Croatia and Serbia and Bosnia-Herzegovina and Serbia now became international frontiers in compliance with the principle of *uti possidetis* which was now recognized as a principle outside of the colonial context.

There are examples of contractual dissolutions of states, such as the break-up of the Former Soviet Union which instead of an extinction of a state was treated as a partial secession with the Russian Federation, by agreement becoming the successor to the rights and obligations of the USSR, including its retaining the permanent seat on the UN Security Council. The **European Commission Guidelines on the Recognition of the New States in Eastern Europe and the Soviet Union** also confirmed respect for existing frontiers. This practice confirms that respect for the former provincial boundaries is an important part of state secession.

Two other examples of state practice are found in the extinction of the Democratic Republic of Germany and its merger into the unified state of the Federal Republic of Germany. The unified state assumed all the international rights and responsibilities of the former state. The second is the consensual break-up of Czechoslovakia into the two states of the Czech Republic and Slovakia. In keeping with the peaceful nature of the 'Velvet Revolution' this dissolution was peaceful and the territorial boundaries of the former parts of the republic were respected. In addition, the two new states agreed on issues such as treaty obligations and division of public property and debts.

If there is no contractual agreement, there are two treaties governing the secession of states, the **Vienna Convention on Secession of States in respect of Treaties** and the **Vienna Convention on Secession of States in respect of State Property, Archives and Debts**. The provisions are long and complex but Lowe (2007) neatly summarizes the law in this area. He argues that states are not automatically bound by the treaties of their predecessor states, except in the case of provisions defining borders; in this case for Lovelier and Loveliest, their provincial boundaries would now become international boundaries under the principle of *uti possidetis*. Lowe also argues that there is a broad principle of secession to public property and debts which means that Lovelier and Loveliest would have to agree to apportion the public property and debts of Lovely.

As for membership of an international organization, Jennings and Watts (1992), state that membership of an international organization will cease upon the dissolution of the old state unless there is an agreement (like Russia) for the new state to continue the membership. This was very controversial with respect to Yugoslavia as Serbia-Montenegro attempted to keep the SFRY seat in the UN. The situation remained unresolved until a new government took over in Serbia-Montenegro and applied for UN membership. Montenegro also separated from Serbia in 2006 and now has its own seat in the UN. It is clear, therefore, that Lovelier and Loveliest will have to apply for UN membership and for membership to other international organizations.

 Examiner's tip

The extinction of states is perhaps a rarer event in international relations but it is important to have a detailed understanding of the break-up of the Yugoslav federation. The Badinter Commission reports are also necessary to refer to in this answer. The student who also discusses the break-up of Czechoslovakia and the Soviet Union will be well rewarded.

Further reading

Brownlie, I., *Principles of Public International Law*, 7th edn (Oxford: Oxford University Press, 2008).

Crawford, J., *The Creation of States in International Law* (Oxford: Oxford University Press, 2007).

Evans, M., *International Law*, 3rd edn (Oxford: Oxford University Press, 2010).

Harris, D. J., *Cases and Materials on International Law*, 7th edn (London: Sweet & Maxwell, 2010).

Higgins R., *Problems and Process* (Oxford: Oxford University Press, 1994).

Jennings, R. and Watts, A., (eds), *Oppenheim's International Law*, 9th edn (London: Longman, 1992).

Lowe, V., *International Law* (Oxford: Oxford University Press, 2007).

McCorquodale, R., 'The individual and the international legal system' in M. Evans, *International Law*, 2nd edn (Oxford: Oxford University Press, 2006).

O'Connell, D. P., *International Law*, 2nd edn (London: Stevens & Sons, 1970).

Rich, R., 'Recognition of states: the collapse of Yugoslavia and the Soviet Union' 4 EJIL (1993) 36.

Shaw, M., *International Law*, 6th edn (Cambridge: Cambridge University Press, 2008).

Warbrick, C., 'Recognition of states' (1992) 41(2) ICLQ 473.

Warbrick, C., 'Recognition of states part 2 (1993) 42(2) ICLQ 433.

Warbrick, C., 'States and recognition in international law' in M. Evans, *International Law*, 2nd edn (Oxford: Oxford University Press, 2006).

7

Territory

Introduction

The major actor with international legal personality is the state, and part of the **Montevideo** criteria of statehood, is a defined territory. The concept of statehood is also directly related to the notion of sovereignty. Sovereignty is founded on the fact of exclusive control over territory. Respect for territorial sovereignty is one of the key principles of international law. Contests over acquisition of territory occupy a majority of the jurisprudence emerging from the International Court of Justice (ICJ). Regrettably, territorial disputes occasionally result in armed conflict. Therefore, this is one of the key international law topics that students are examined on.

The problem and essay questions within this chapter canvass a few of the controversial topics within the subject of territory and the examination could contain one or more of these topic areas. A warning to be given is that some of the key international decisions may not be included in your usual textbooks, as there are frequent decisions on territory—it is up to the student to stay current on the jurisprudence from the ICJ. This is an area particularly dense with international jurisprudence and necessitates reading of long and complex international decisions.

The questions in an examination will likely include problem questions, as territorial disputes lend themselves to interesting fact situations—and it can be amusing to see the fictional names that lecturers come up with for the disputed territories! Often, these problems will relate to the fact situations of famous territorial disputes, so a background in these historical conflicts is essential. The problems and essay questions also expect the student to be familiar with methods of resolving territorial disputes. These questions will test the student's knowledge of theories of territorial acquisition, including conquest, occupation, and prescription. It is important to prepare a proper outline in problem questions, so that the answer not only addresses the legal issues but also answers the question that the problem poses. Too often, the answer will convert into an essay topic discussing the issue involved without answering the question that the examiner posed. A suggestion is to use a diagram outlining the parties to the territorial dispute and their respective claims, so that the student will not confuse the names involved.

Recommended publications in this area are: Sharma (1997) and chapter 5 in Jennings and Watts (1992). In the traditional textbooks, the chapter in Brownlie (2008) is particularly comprehensive. An upcoming book which will be well worth obtaining (it is to be published shortly) is Malcolm Shaw, *The International Law of Territory* to be published by Oxford University Press.

 Question 1

Fantasia is an island located in the Atlantic Ocean a thousand miles away from the coast of South America. In 1700, the island was claimed by Portugal as it had been discovered by a Portuguese naval captain. At that time the island was uninhabited. A few years previously, the Portuguese had also settled the colony of Lisboa in South America, which is the nearest land mass to Fantasia. However, neither the Portuguese captain nor any of his crew remained on Fantasia and no settlers were landed.

In 1795 the European state of Colonia made a claim on the island, as one of their naval ships landed and discharged settlers. The settlers planted a flag and established a small settlement which included a governor, but the settlers and their descendants only remained for a period of 50 years on account of a lack of water and vegetation. Since that time, there has not been a colony on the island. However, since about 1850, there has been regular fishing in the waters of Fantasia by Colonian fishing boats, and their sailors land on the island to process their catch before returning to Colonia.

Between 1795 and 1955 there have been no landings by Lisboans on the island. However, in 1955, the state of Lisboa obtained its independence from Portugal and as part of the treaty the Portuguese stated that Fantasia was part of the Lisboan territory and it was incorporated into maps of the newly independent Lisboa.

Since 1960, when the Colonia foreign office was alerted to Lisboa's claim, both countries have asserted that Fantasia is part of their territory and there have been minor skirmishes between the natives of Lisboa and Colonia in the waters off the island.

In a compromise filed with the court, both states have agreed to submit the dispute to the ICJ. How should the ICJ determine the dispute between these two states?

 Commentary

This problem question deals directly with the situation of long-standing disputes over territory which arose both in the Falkland Islands dispute and the fact situations in the *Island of Palmas* arbitration, the *Clipperton Island* arbitration, and the *Minquiers and Ecrehos* judgment in the ICJ.

This is an answer which will be heavily reliant on the relevant case law. Another important source is the *Report on the Falkland Islands* prepared by the Foreign Affairs Committee of the United Kingdom House of Commons (excerpts are included in Harris (2010)). This report contains excellent discussion on the issue of acquisition of territory and the concept of inter-temporal law as a method of resolving territorial disputes. It should be noted that this dispute continues particularly on the part of the Argentinians who have never relinquished their claim on the territory despite losing an armed conflict.

The student must in this case discuss the various methods of acquisition of territory and be familiar with the relevant cases on title to territory. A danger is to spend too long on the various methods and not deal with the problem at hand. The student should quickly dismiss inapplicable methods of acquisition, such as accretion, but it is wise to define all of the methods of obtaining territory. The key to success is to apply the method of analysis in the case law mentioned earlier to the fact situation in this problem.

 Answer plan

- Discuss significance in international law concerning title to territory.
- Discuss methods by which title is acquired.
- Define the concept of *terra nullius*.
- Provide relevant case law examples on territorial disputes and discuss the factors used to decide sovereignty.
- Discuss the Falkland Islands case and the report by the Foreign Affairs Committee.

 Suggested answer

The dispute between Lisboa and Colonia over the island of Fantasia concerns title to territory. As the arbitrator, Judge Huber stated in **Island of Palmas (Netherlands v US) Permanent Court of Arbitration, 1928**, '*sovereignty in relation to a portion of the surface of the globe is the legal condition necessary for the inclusion of such portion in the territory of any particular state*'. He also stated that the principle of exclusive competence of the state in regard to its own territory is the point of departure in settling most questions which concern international relations. Therefore, it is vital for both of these nations to settle the title to the territory of Fantasia.

The function of the ICJ in the dispute between Lisboa and Colonia according to **Island of Palmas** is to examine which of the states claiming sovereignty possesses a title by cessation, conquest, or occupation and which is superior to that which the other state might have. The timing is critical, as, at the time of the claim of sovereignty, the state must show continuous and peaceful display of state authority up to the time the legal dispute arose in 1960 which in international law is the critical date when the dispute is crystallized. Any sovereign activity after that time is irrelevant.

According to Jennings and Watts (1992), there are five modes of acquiring territory: cession, occupation, accretion, subjugation, and prescription. One of the concepts not relevant here is accretion, as it means the increase of land through new formations, such as an island arising from a river. There is another concept that can be discussed briefly, subjugation, defined by Oppenheim—see Jennings and Watts (1992)—as the acquisition of territory by conquest. We shall see later that title to territory by conquest is very different from subjugation. In the case of Fantasia there is no evidence of persons living on the island before its discovery and no evidence that any colony was conquered. This is in contrast to the Falkland Islands situation where at one stage of the conflict the Argentinians took the island by force and the United Kingdom used force to take it back. The determination is that since the statements in the Kellog–Briand Pact and the judgment by the International Military Tribunal at Nuremberg, subjugation is illegal. Only after a war is concluded can title to territory be determined. An excellent example of the reaction to subjugation is the Stimson Doctrine of non-recognition which was a note from the US secretary of state to the Japanese and Chinese governments refusing to recognize the puppet state of Manchukuo. Other examples are Northern Cyprus and East Timor where the international community refused to recognize Turkey or Indonesia's claim to those territories after a military takeover. Another example was the **Security Council Resolution 242** on the Middle East of 22 November 1967. This resolution called for withdrawal of Israel from recently occupied territories. The key provision confirming the illegality of acquisition of territory by force is **Art. 2(4) UN Charter**.

There are three methods of acquisition of territory which are important in this case. First, there is cession defined in Oppenheim as the transfer of sovereignty over state territory by the owner state to another state. This is often accomplished in a peace treaty after a war or by gift or purchase of land, such as the Alaska purchase by the United States from the Russian empire in 1867. This concept may be partially relevant as the state of Portugal has ceded sovereignty over the island to Lisboa but as established in *Island of Palmas* you can only cede ownership over land which you actually have title to in the first place.

Second, there is the concept of prescription defined in Shaw (2008) as the establishment of continuous and *peaceful* governmental possession. The principle is that occupation must be effective even if there is an existing treaty or similar granting title to this or another state. In *Island of Palmas* the island was part of the Philippines the whole of which had been ceded to the United States but this island was flying the Dutch flag. In this case the Netherlands title was acquired by continuous and peaceful display of state authority, going back beyond 1700 and therefore it was held to be good title.

Third, there is the concept of occupation. The difference between prescription and occupation is that prescription is the acquisition of territory which belonged to another state, whereas occupation is of territory that is *terra nullius*. There are few territories in the world that have not been inhabited by an indigenous group which is why in

Western Sahara the ICJ was prepared to consider Mauritania and Morocco's pre-colonial claims, as there were persons present in the disputed area and therefore it was a case of determination of prescriptive title. However, in the case of Fantasia there is no evidence of persons having lived there. Therefore another relevant case is the ***Clipperton Island*** arbitration which declared that the island in dispute was *territorium nullius* and therefore susceptible to occupation. France claimed this island for itself in 1858 and yet exercised no positive or apparent act of sovereignty but did not abandon it either. No other country had proclaimed sovereignty and even though France did not do anything with it, the arbitrator pronounced it to belong to France. This is a particularly relevant case to this fact situation, as it seems that Colonia had claimed the island and this claim had not been opposed until the 1950s.

Another relevant case is ***Minquiers and Ecrehos (France v UK)*** decided by the ICJ in 1953. This was a case of sovereignty over the islets and rocks of the Minquiers and Ecrehos group. The court held that the title had been established by treaty at the beginning of the thirteenth century to the English and that the British authorities had exercised state functions during the greater part of the nineteenth and twentieth centuries. In ***Eastern Greenland,*** Norway and Denmark contested ownership of Greenland. The Permanent Court of International Justice (PCIJ) in 1933 declared that even though Denmark had not colonized eastern Greenland the court found sufficient evidence of state authority over the area. The two factors were the intention and will to act as sovereign and some actual exercise or display of such authority.

In ***Kasikili/Sedudu Island (Botswana/Namibia)*** in 1999 in the ICJ, the Huber concept in the ***Island of Palmas*** arbitration of continuous and peaceful display was further developed. The court held that there were four conditions for prescriptive title:

1   the possession must be exercised *à titre de souverain*—exercising functions of state authority;
2   possession must be peaceful and uninterrupted;
3   possession must be public; and
4   possession must endure for a certain length of time.

This is the basis upon which territorial disputes are decided.

In addition there could be added that there is a lack of protest from the other claimant. Another example of the disputes that arise under this area is the dispute between Argentina and the UK over the Falkland Islands as to who acquired the islands due to abandonment of territory. The question was: did the Argentinians exercise effective control? The Foreign Affairs Committee *Report on the Falkland Islands* examined historical title and was unable to establish either party's claim to the islands, as, although there were British settlers, Argentina had filed continuous protests. Title by prescription or occupation according to *Island of Palmas* arbitration arises out of a long, continued possession even if wrongful if the original proprietor has neglected to assert its right. Effective control over a thinly populated or an unsettled country is difficult to determine, as is evident from the Falkland Islands situation.

A relevant case on lack of protest over one state's exercise of sovereignty is the recent case *Sovereignty over Pedra Branca/Pulau Batu Puteh, Middle Rocks and South Ledge (Malaysia/Singapore)* 23 May 2008. The court held that in certain circumstances, sovereignty over territory might pass as a result of a failure of the state which has sovereignty to respond to conduct *à titre de souverain* (exercise of sovereignty) of the other state. If these displays of sovereignty call for a response, the absence of reaction could be held to be acquiescence of the other state.

In applying the case law to Fantasia, it is necessary to examine the evidence of continued peaceful possession or effective control over the island by either claimant. Although the island was ceded to Lisboa, there was no evidence of long, continued possession or effective control by Lisboa. It was Colonia that could establish long possession and evidence of tacit acquiescence by Lisboa and its colonial predecessor, as there were no actual protests until the territorial dispute arose in 1960. It seems almost certain that in spite of the island being ceded to Lisboa, actual title by occupation of this *terra nullius* belongs to Colonia.

 Examiner's tip

Ensure you define *all* of the ways territory may be obtained in international law, even if it is not relevant to this question. It is also important to render a reasoned legal opinion either in favour of Lisboa or Colonia as the court would rule in favour of one party. The student who refers in detail to the Foreign Affairs Committee report on the Falkland Islands will impress the examiner!

 Question 2

'[T]he continuous and peaceful display of territorial sovereignty…is as good as title.' (*Island of Palmas Case*, 1928)

Critically evaluate this statement in light of the contemporary law of title to territory.

 Commentary

This question allows the student to display knowledge of the case law on territorial disputes. This draft answer will utilize some recent case law, but the student should be aware that there might even be more recent cases to rely on and continuous checking of the ICJ website is critical. Although **Island of Palmas** gives a statement of the criteria of continuous and peaceful display of territorial sovereignty, later cases have given content to that statement and these newer cases must be discussed.

An excellent source for an answer to this question is the section on historic titles, critical date, and self-determination in chapter 5 of Jennings and Watts (1992).

Answer plan

- Discuss the quotation in the case together with the notion of balancing of displays of state functions.
- Discuss the significance of the critical date.
- Define inter-temporal law.
- Define the doctrine of *effectivités* (elements of governance).
- Discuss the recent case law with respect to displays of territorial sovereignty.

Suggested answer

According to Harris (2010), the arbitral award by Judge Huber in *Island of Palmas* is of outstanding importance in the law on the acquisition of territory for two reasons: its full and scholarly treatment of the nature of territorial acquisition; and for the quotation in this question, as it established the method by which territorial disputes can be resolved. This quotation should be discussed together with another dictum from Huber in the case. He held that '*it cannot be sufficient to establish the title by which territorial sovereignty was validly acquired at a certain moment; it must also be shown that territorial sovereignty has continued to exist and did exist at the moment which for the decision of the dispute must be considered as critical*'. Both of these statements establish that in the event of a dispute over territory it is vital to establish a time line of continuous and peaceful display of the functions of a state. According to Jennings and Watts (1992) in a contention between two states it may not be a question of finding an absolute title, as the decision might turn upon the relative strength of the titles invoked by either party. Moreover, as pointed out in *Island of Palmas*, state authority need not be displayed at every moment, on every point of a territory. Huber argued that there could be gaps in the exercise of territorial sovereignty and that the fact that a state could not prove display of sovereignty in a portion of the territory could not be interpreted that sovereignty did not exist. Therefore, one can conclude that each case has to be assessed by its particular circumstances.

Important dicta concerning continuous and peaceful display of sovereignty can also be found in *Legal Status of Eastern Greenland (Norway v Denmark)*, a judgment of the PCIJ in 1933 which states that a claim to sovereignty which is based not upon some particular act or title, such as a treaty of cession but merely upon continued display of authority, involves two elements each of which must be shown to exist: the intention and will to act as sovereign; and some actual exercise or display of such authority.

In *Kasikili/Sedudu Island (Botswana/Namibia)*, an ICJ judgment of 1999, the Huber concept of continuous and peaceful display was further refined. The court held that there were four conditions for prescriptive title:

1   the possession must be exercised *à titre de souverain*—exercising functions of state authority;

2   possession must be peaceful and uninterrupted;

3   possession must be public; and

4   possession must endure for a certain length of time.

This is the basis upon which territorial disputes can be decided.

There is another term that is relevant in the discussion of peaceful and continuous display of sovereignty introduced in *Island of Palmas* and that is the critical date which is the date when the territorial dispute is crystallized. Jennings and Watts (1992) assert that there is an important difference of opinion about what is to be regarded as the critical moment or critical period in relation to a particular dispute. Sir Gerald Fitzmaurice in his speech in *Minquiers and Ecrehos* argues that the whole point of the critical date is that time is deemed to stop at that date, and the rights of the parties are determined based on the situation that exists at that date and therefore that would be the cut-off date in examining peaceful and continuous displays of sovereignty. However, this doctrine might not be definitive, as Jennings and Watts, in examining the case law, argue that courts are reluctant to exclude consideration of subsequent acts of the parties. Brownlie (2008) also argues that the difficulty is determining which date might be the critical date. He states that there are several types of critical date, and it is difficult and probably misleading to formulate general definitions. He states that there may be several dates of varying significance.

There are several cases discussing the critical-date theory. In *Eastern Greenland* in the ICJ the court stated that the critical date was 10 July 1931, the date of the Norwegian proclamation announcing occupation of the area. Therefore, Denmark had to establish title prior to the occupation. In *Island of Palmas* the United States was named as the successor to Spain in the treaty of cession dated 10 December 1898 and the case turned on the Spanish rights to the island at that time. The court decided that the Netherlands had title at that critical date. In *Nicaragua v Honduras* there was also a discussion of the critical date. The ICJ held that in the context of a maritime delimitation dispute or of a dispute related to sovereignty over land, the significance of a critical date lies in distinguishing between those acts performed *à titre de souverain* which are in principle relevant for the purpose of assessing and validating *effectivités*, and those acts occurring after such critical date, which are in general meaningless for that purpose, having been carried out by a state which, already having claims to assert in a legal dispute, could have taken those actions strictly with the aim of buttressing those claims. Thus a critical date will be the dividing line after which the parties' acts become irrelevant for the purposes of assessing the value of *effectivités*. As the court explained in *Sovereignty over Pulau Ligitan and Pulau Sipadan (Indonesia/Malaysia)* in 2002, it could not take into consideration acts having taken place after the date on which the dispute between the parties crystallized, unless such acts are a normal continuation of the prior acts and are not taken for the purpose of improving the legal position of the party which relies on them.

Another critically important doctrine limiting the consideration of peaceful and continuous display of sovereignty is the doctrine of inter-temporal law, which is the requirement that title must be valid in accordance with the law in force at the time at which it is claimed to have been established. Brownlie argues that this can now be regarded as an established principle of international law. This means that the situation must be appraised and the treaty interpreted in light of the rules of international law as they existed at the time. This could also mean that although acquiring territory through subjugation is now unlawful it would have been lawful at the time the territory was acquired and that is the relevant time period under consideration. This was yet another important concept developed by Huber in *Island of Palmas*. However, he distinguished the law in effect when the territorial rights were created and the law evolving to support the existence of the rights at the time of the dispute. Brownlie criticizes this extension as it might lead to the title having to be maintained at every moment of time which could threaten many titles and lead to instability. Brownlie concludes that one should be cautious in the application of the rule.

Therefore, although the Huber dictum of peaceful and continuous display of sovereignty has been further refined in later case law—and joined by such important terms as inter-temporal law, critical date, and sovereign *effectivités*—it continues to remain the key factor in the determination of territorial disputes. The court must examine up to the critical date and in accordance with inter-temporal law the exercise of sovereign power by either claimant to territorial title.

☆ **Examiner's tip**

The only way in which to respond to this answer correctly is to read the *Island of Palmas* decision. It is also important to stay up to date on the case law as there are always territorial disputes before the International Court of Justice. It is important to summarize only briefly the facts of the case as the emphasis has to be on the conditions for prescriptive title.

 Question 3

The states of Bestia and Cilla share a common boundary which was set when both obtained independence in the 1960s. However, they now cannot agree on the boundary between their states. The first issue is that part of the boundary is a river which middle point constituted the boundary between the two territories. The river has changed course over the past 100 years and part of the river now runs two miles into the territory of Cilla. The second issue is that there is an island in the river which was given to Cilla upon independence, but ethnic Bestians have always occupied the island and Bestia claims title to this island.

Discuss with reference to case law how the dispute over the river boundary and the island in the river might be settled.

In addition to disputes over maritime areas, the most common area of international litigation concerns disputes over border areas. Even though the doctrine of *uti possidetis* should resolve many border disputes, the territory may either shift by accretion or there may be areas of territorial control that remain unresolved, dating from colonial administration. There can be disagreements on the delimitation on maps or actual exercise of sovereignty.

Once again there have been a series of relevant cases in the ICJ and by arbitration that are relevant to answering this problem. A thorough review of these decisions is mandatory.

Answer plan

- Define the concept of accretion and examine the change in river boundaries.
- Define the concept of *uti possidetis*.
- Discuss the concepts of colonial and post-colonial sovereign *effectivités*.
- Apply the relevant case law concerning boundary disputes to this fact situation.

Suggested answer

This case concerns the competing claims over the new territory emerging from a river and the island in the river given to Cilla on independence but which is also claimed by Bestia. Boundary disputes are relatively common and often result in international litigation. The location of a land boundary line is a matter of a correct interpretation of a legal instrument; the most common of these instruments is a boundary treaty. Boundary and territorial disputes are distinguished, as these disputes are not about the fact and mode of acquisition but about the important doctrine of *uti possidetis* and the exercise of colonial and post-colonial sovereign *effectivités*.

The first part of this problem question concerns the issue of accretion on the border between Cilla and Bestia. Accretion is defined in Oppenheim—Jennings and Watts (1992)—as the name for an increase in land through new formations. This is the case of enlargement of a territory through modification of existing state territory. In this case although the boundary ran through the centre of the river, it has now changed course and if the territory is accepted then Bestia will secure more territory. There is a relevant case right on point. In *Chamizal Arbitration* the Rio Grande by 1911 changed its course and a tract of land of some 600 acres—the Chamizal Tract—had opened up and both sides claimed sovereignty. In this case as it was new land the previous treaty did not apply and there was no prescriptive title. Brownlie controversially argues that accretion may not be the root of title in this case. In this type of case, even in the absence of applicable agreements, sudden, forcible, and significant changes in river courses known as avulsion will not be considered to have changed the frontier line. In international boundary rivers there is a special rule. In general, where there is a navigable channel the boundary follows the middle line of the channel. Where there is no such channel the boundary line will, in general, be the middle line of the river itself, or its principal arm. This line might shift if the river changes course as a result of gradual accretion on one bank or degradation of the other bank. If the river course changed suddenly and left its original bed for a new channel, the international boundary would continue to be the middle of the deserted river bank. This means that Bestia cannot claim the movement in the river into Cilla results in its border moving into Cillan territory.

The second issue concerning this island involves a traditional boundary dispute common to the former colonies in Africa, Asia, and South America. The key to the determination of post-colonial boundary disputes is the important concept of *uti possidetis*. In *Continental Shelf (Libya/Malta)* and the *Frontier Dispute (Burkina Faso v Republic of Mali)* the court held that the concept means respect for the territorial boundaries that existed at the moment independence was achieved. Such territorial boundaries might be no more than delimitations between different administrative divisions or colonies, all subject to the same sovereign. *Uti possidetis* results in administrative boundaries being transformed into international boundaries. This is true of the states of South America that were part of the Spanish colonies. In Africa there has been a challenging of traditional international law, where the successive attainment of independence and the emergence of new states bring about claims of self-determination of cultural or ethnic groups intersecting these colonial boundaries. The court held in this case that the wisest course was to preserve the territorial status quo to avoid a disruption which would deprive the continent of the gains achieved.

The Organization of African Unity passed a resolution in 1964 declaring that colonial frontiers existing as at the date of independence constituted a tangible reality and that all members pledged themselves to respect such boundaries. This doctrine has continued in the widespread disapproval of secessionist states in Nigeria (Biafra) and Sudan (Darfur). The Badinter Commission also made declarations about the concept. In *Opinion No. 2* the commission declared that 'whatever the circumstances the right to self-determination must not involve changes to existing frontiers at the time of independence except where the parties concerned agree otherwise'. In *Opinion No. 3* the former boundaries became frontiers protected by international law. Therefore, even internal boundaries can become international frontiers as was the case for Bosnia, Croatia, Slovenia, Macedonia, Montenegro, and Serbia, all former provinces of the Socialist Federal Republic of Yugoslavia (SFRY).

However, this does not always resolve the issue, as it may be the case, as is evident in this dispute between Cilla and Bestia, that in spite of the boundary being drawn in a certain way there is a portion of territory that has always been within the other nation's control. There are recent cases in the ICJ which have gone beyond *uti possidetis* to examine sovereign *effectivités*. A relevant case is *Land, Island and Maritime Frontier Dispute (El Salvador v Honduras)* decided in 1992. In this case the court held that the principle of *uti possidetis* can be altered by a boundary treaty or adjudication creating another critical date. This meant that the boundary set by the **General Treaty of Peace of 1980 between El Salvador and Honduras** was now critical.

In *Land and Maritime Boundary between Cameroon and Nigeria* of 2002 the court held that even thought Nigeria had exercised some *effectivités* (elements of governance) over areas of dried-up land on the Cameroon side of Lake Chad this did not diminish the legal title that had been established by the Anglo-French treaty. The reason for this is that the boundary might not have been completely resolved, especially the maritime areas on independence. The court did acknowledge that there could also be post-independence practice that land is controlled by the other state by acquiescence but this was not the case in this dispute.

Another influential case on this issue is *Territorial and Maritime Dispute between Nicaragua and Honduras in the Caribbean Sea (Nicaragua v Honduras)* of October 2007. This case expands on *Cameroon and Nigeria* for those cases where the doctrine of *uti possidetis* could not resolve the dispute. The court held the dispute over sovereignty of the islands could not be resolved by the doctrine of *uti possidetis* and the court had to ascertain whether there were relevant *effectivités* during the colonial period. This test of 'colonial *effectivités*' has been defined in *Frontier Dispute (Burkina Faso/Republic of Mali)* as '*the conduct of the administrative authorities as proof of the effective exercise of territorial jurisdiction in the region during the colonial period*'. In *Nicaragua and Honduras* this could not be accomplished because of the lack of trustworthy information during colonial times as much of the territory was unexplored and therefore the boundaries had not been fixed with precision. In this case the court then had to turn to post-colonial *effectivités* and sovereignty over the disputed islands. The categories of post-colonial *effectivités* considered were: legislative and administrative control; application and enforcement of criminal and civil law; regulation of immigration; regulation of fisheries activities; naval patrols; and public works.

In the case of Bestia and Cilla the first question would be to examine the evidence of colonial *effectivités*. However, if the evidence is not available, then the court will turn to consider the post-colonial situation and the evidence of the factors already mentioned. The court will have to examine the exercise of sovereignty during colonial times and if that is not possible then to turn to the exercise of sovereign *effectivités* since the date of independence. In this case it might be argued that both colonial and post-colonial actions supported the title of Bestia to the island, but it would depend on the availability of that evidence. Unless actions in sovereignty can be proven, title based on *uti possidetis* will remain with Cilla.

 Examiner's tip

The first thing the examiner will look for is knowledge of disputes over river courses and accretion, particularly in light of the impact of the ***Chamizal Arbitration***. The other factor is the importance of the doctrine of *uti possidetis* in territorial disputes. There are a number of territorial disputes in the International Court of Justice that consider the concept and it is also important to discuss post-colonial *effectivités*.

? Question 4

Discuss the international law concept of 'common heritage of mankind'.

Commentary

This is a very important part of the law of territory, the discussion of those areas that are not subject to territorial dispute, but which belong to the whole of humankind. It is important in this area not only to discuss the areas to which this concept applies, but also the treaty regime that governs these areas. This is also an important customary rule that applies particularly with regard to the high seas and outer space. However, it is also relevant to territorial disputes, as the sea and planets can also be subject to territorial claims because of the resources that are contained within these entities.

It is also important to discuss the fact that, although some argue that the Arctic Circle and Antarctica are part of the common heritage of humankind, there are also serious territorial disputes surrounding both regions, particularly in regard to the melting of the polar ice cap due to climate change. In addition to the discussion in the various textbooks, there is also an excellent article which discusses the origin of the definition of the concept: 'The concept of "common heritage of mankind": a political, moral or legal innovation?' by Gorove (1971–2).

Answer plan

- Define the notion of common heritage of humankind.
- Discuss the areas to which this might apply, including the Arctic, Antarctica, high seas, and outer space.
- Distinguish between airspace and outer space.
- Outline the various treaties that specify certain areas that are part of the common heritage of humankind and the legal implications of such a designation.

Suggested answer

According to Gorove (1971–2), it was Malta's representative Ambassador Pardo who first suggested to the General Assembly in 1967 that it declare the seabed and ocean floor and its resources as the 'common heritage of mankind'. Indeed, the General Assembly passed a resolution in 1968 to the effect that exploitation of the resources of the seabed and ocean floor be carried out 'for the benefit of mankind as a whole'. There had been an earlier concept of *res communis* which according to Shaw (2008) is territory not being capable of being reduced to sovereign control. The two terms can be distinguished, as some territory referred to as the common heritage of humankind could indeed at some point be subject to territorial control.

There are several geographical regions argued to be part of the 'common heritage of mankind'. The first is the international seabed area. In 1970 the General Assembly passed a resolution entitled **Declaration of Principles Governing the Sea Bed and Ocean Floor, and the Subsoil Thereof, beyond the limits of National Jurisdiction (Resolution 2749)**, which declared that the seabed and ocean floor and the subsoil thereof, beyond the limits of national jurisdiction, are the common heritage of humankind. This meant that the area was not to be subject to appropriation by any means by states or persons. This was later modified by **Part XI Law of the Sea Convention** which sets out an International Seabed Authority which does provide for access to seabed mine rights but also contains a confirmation in **Art. 136** that this area is part of the common heritage of humankind.

The second area is outer space. Gorove argues that the **Treaty on the Principles Governing the Activities of States in the Exploration and use of Outer Space including the Moon and other Celestial Bodies (1967)** stipulates that the exploration and use of outer space shall be carried out for the benefit and interest of all countries and shall be the 'province of humankind'. The treaty also provides that astronauts are envoys of humankind. According to Shaw, there was a rule entitled *usque ad coelum* which indicated sovereignty over airspace to an unlimited height. That has been altered by the regime for outer space. This means that the sovereignty of states over their airspace is limited in height at most to the point where the airspace meets space itself. Figures between 50 to 100 miles have been proposed. Outer space includes the moon and other celestial bodies, and these objects are not subject to national appropriation by any sovereign state. This treaty is the one example given of instant customary law. Although the territory of outer space is not subject to sovereignty, satellites for spying purposes are not outlawed. However, the passage of ballistic missiles through space is prohibited.

The third area of the planet which could arguably be part of the common heritage of humankind is the polar regions but regrettably this is not the case. In Antarctica, for example, New Zealand made claim to *terra nullius* in the Ross Dependency on the basis of discovery of the territory. This is a portion of Antarctica. Several states have made claim to the Antarctic region including Argentina, Australia, Chile, France, New Zealand, Norway, and the United Kingdom. It is an ice-covered land mass in the form of an island. Claims have been based on a variety of grounds, ranging from mere discovery to the sector principle employed by South American states. However, the United States has refused to recognize any of the claims and although US Admiral Byrd discovered and claimed Marie Byrd land for his country, the United States refrained from adopting the claim.

In 1959 the **Antarctic Treaty** was signed by all states concerned with territorial claims or scientific exploration in the region. Its major effect, apart from demilitarization of

Antarctica, was to suspend, but not eliminate, territorial claims for the life of the treaty. As the treaty does not provide for termination, an ongoing regime has been created and there are 43 parties to the treaty and of those 28 have consultative status. The original parties have full participation in the meetings which take place annually.

In 1988 there was a **Convention on the Regulation of Antarctic Minerals Resource Activities**. This creates a regime to regulate three stages of mineral activity—prospecting, exploration, and development. The convention did not come into force because of opposition by environmentalists and in 1991 there was a **Protocol on Environmental Protection** to the original **Antarctic Treaty**. This prohibits activity relating to mineral resources, unless there is in force a binding legal regime. There is therefore a comprehensive integrated environmental regime.

According to Shaw (2008), the Arctic region is of some strategic importance given the fact that it connects North America and Russia. It consists to a large extent of ice packs beneath which submarines can operate. Denmark possesses Greenland and its associated islands within the region, whereas Norway has asserted sovereign rights over Spitsbergen and other islands. The Norwegian claim is based on occupation and exploitation of minerals.

More controversial are the respective claims made by Canada and Russia over the Arctic. Use has been made of the concept of contiguity to assert claims over areas forming geographical units with those already occupied, the so-called sector principle. This is based on meridians of longitude as they converge on the North Pole and as they are placed on the coastlines of the particular nations, thus producing a series of triangular sectors with the coasts of the Arctic states as their baselines. The other Arctic states of Norway, Finland, Denmark, and the United States have abstained from this assertion. Shaw states that it is doubtful that this claim would be accepted as anything other than a political claim. The other issue is that large parts of the region are on moving packs of ice. These would be part of the high seas open to all. This controversy will only grow in intensity as global warming continues and the lands of the Arctic and Antarctic become inhabitable and the oceans become navigable. It will be critically important to assert that the natural resources existing in these territories, as with the deep seabed, are part of the common heritage of humankind.

As Gorove points out in his article, there remain difficulties in defining the term common heritage and what might represent humankind. It seems clear that there will have to be some type of multilateral administration of such areas and the Law of the Sea Convention's International Seabed Authority and the regime established over Antarctica might be excellent examples. The Seabed's resources are also going to be used to assist developing nations, so that the assets are distributed equitably. In Antarctica it can be argued that the scientific exploration is for the benefit of humankind as a whole. Humankind is represented not only by states but perhaps by international civil society. In a more cosmopolitan outlook, states and civil society will have to cooperate to develop these areas for the benefit of all the world's citizens.

Examiner's tip

The examiner will be looking for knowledge of the activity in the United Nations concerning this concept, particularly the General Assembly resolution and the Law of the Sea Convention. A student will also benefit from discussing debate concerning sovereignty over the Arctic and Antarctica. Knowledge of the treaty governing Antarctica will be sure to impress.

Further reading

Brownlie, I., *Principles of Public International Law*, 7th edn (Oxford: Oxford University Press, 2008), pt III.

Gorove, S., 'The concept of "common heritage of mankind": a political, moral or legal innovation?' (1971–2) 9 *San Diego Law Review* 390.

Harris, D. J., *Cases and Materials on International Law*, 7th edn (London: Sweet & Maxwell, 2010).

Jennings, R. and Watts, A., (eds), *Oppenheim's International Law*, 9th edn (London: Longman, 1992), chapter 5.

Sharma, S. P., *Territorial Acquisitions, Disputes and International Law* (The Hague: Brill, 1997).

Shaw, M., *International Law*, 6th edn (Cambridge: Cambridge University Press, 2008).

8

Law of the sea

Introduction

A distinct and interesting area of international law is the discussion of those legal rules that govern the law of the sea. As the sea has, since time immemorial, been a source of both transit of ships and exploitation of resources it was one of the first areas that saw the development of international law. Hugo Grotius developed the doctrine of the open seas as *res communis* where the oceans were to be available to the ships of all nations but not as part of their sovereign territory. However, in spite of this doctrine there are various portions of seas that are not high seas and thus capable of some sort of territorial control from sovereign states. This area is of particular concern to maritime powers such as the United States, the United Kingdom, Canada, New Zealand, and Australia but even land-locked states can be financially involved in maritime exploration and merchant navies.

This chapter will focus on the particular complications in determining the various legal regimes governing the sea. These questions will focus on the important treaty in this area, the **United Nations Convention on the Law of the Sea 1982** with its definitions of the various types of seas, including the territorial sea, continental shelf, exclusive economic zones, and the high seas.

Once again this chapter will contain a combination of problem questions and essay topics, as this area lends itself to both. Although there is an established treaty regime, this does not mean that all issues are settled between states, as there are disagreements in treaty interpretation and the customary law of the sea. The essays and problem questions will cover four of those areas of controversy. It is important to study the various parts of the **United Nations Convention on the Law of the Sea** and to understand the history of the delimitation of the various areas of the sea.

Two helpful publications to refer to in addition to the chapters in the standard public international law texts are Freestone *et al.* (2007) and Churchill and Lowe (1999). This is also an area which benefits from a thorough search of the rich vein of international law of the sea articles in the various online databases. The proposed answers contain references to only a fraction of the articles available on the various issues of controversy. This is a field that is rapidly developing because of the international concern with the environmental impacts of deep-sea resource extraction and the transportation by merchant ships of dangerous substances. Some law schools also have specific topics on the law of the sea.

Once again a particular warning must be issued to students with respect to the problem questions: *read the problem carefully*! It is a complex area and confusing the parts of the sea asked about will lead the student into choppy waters.

There is also a growing jurisprudence in the International Tribunal for the Law of the Sea (ITLOS) and students should check for recent cases prior to revising any of these areas. Furthermore, in recent years the International Court of Justice has delivered a relevant decision: see *Case Concerning Maritime Delimitation in the Black Sea (Romania v Ukraine)* Judgment 3 February 2009.

 Question 1

Natalia is a coastal state with a long coastline on the Atlantic Ocean. The southern boundary of the state is shared with Freedonia which has a small section of the coastline but is mostly landlocked. Freedonia has a large fishing fleet and a merchant fleet which transports nuclear waste and a navy which uses nuclear fuels for power.

The government of Natalia has made the following statements:

1   No ships carrying nuclear waste or using nuclear fuels for power will be allowed to enter into waters within 200 miles of Natalia. All such ships will be detained by and boarded by Natalia's navy.

2   Only ships of Natalia's fishing fleet can fish in the waters within 200 miles of Natalia.

Freedonia has become aware of the statements and seeks advice from its Foreign Affairs Office on whether its ships which carry nuclear waste, or its nuclear submarines, can transit Natalian water. Freedonia also wishes to determine whether its fishing vessels can fish in the waters within 200 miles of Natalia.

As the legal adviser to Freedonia, discuss the legitimacy and effect of the two statements with reference to the **Law of the Sea Convention** to which both Natalia and Freedonia are parties.

 Commentary

This problem question highlights three of the controversial aspects of the law of the sea. There are three elements that must be discussed within this problem: the legal status of the 200-mile economic zone; the regime of legal control over passage of nuclear fuels; and the regime of control over natural resources within the 200-mile zone. Each area of the sea has a specific regime set out in the **UN Law of the Sea Convention** and students must be aware of the provisions within the convention that govern the Exclusive Economic Zone (EEZ). Furthermore, there are decided cases within international jurisprudence concerning disputes over areas of the oceans. The 200-mile EEZ has been particularly controversial and the well-prepared student will review the areas of dispute concerning this zone.

In addition to the books cited in the introduction, relevant articles (among many) concerning this topic are: Bardin, 'Coastal state's jurisdiction over foreign vessels' (2002); and Galdorisi and Kaufman, 'Military activities in the exclusive economic zone: preventing uncertainty and defusing conflict' (2001–2). Churchill and Lowe included a specific chapter on pollution that is well worth reading.

 Answer plan

- Identify the areas of dispute between Natalia and Freedonia.
- Discuss the 200-mile EEZ within the **UN Convention on the Law of the Sea** and the disputes of countries not parties to the convention.
- Discuss the issue of free passage of ships and nuclear waste/fuels.
- Discuss the issue of fisheries.
- Summarize your opinions as the legal adviser to Freedonia.

 Suggested answer

The government of Natalia is attempting to limit access to the waters adjacent to its territory in the following fashion:

1   limitation of free passage of ships; and

2   limitation of use of the 200-mile EEZ for fishing.

As legal adviser to Freedonia, I have consulted the text by Lowe and Churchill which indicates that the **UN Convention on the Law of the Sea 1982 (UNCLOS)** provides a framework within which most uses of the seas are located. Currently, there are 162 ratifications of the treaty that has often been called the constitution of the seas. I can advise that Freedonia and Natalia have deposited instruments of ratification with the United Nations and therefore both states are bound by this treaty.

This dispute between Natalia and Freedonia concerns the issue of the use of the 200-mile EEZ. Churchill and Lowe define this as a zone extending up to 200 miles from the baseline, within which the coastal state enjoys extensive rights in relation to natural resources and related jurisdictional rights, but a zone in which third-party states enjoy the freedoms of navigation, overflight by aircraft, and the laying of cables and pipelines. The EEZ is a recent claim first put forward by Kenya in 1971 and supported by Asian,

African, and Latin American countries. According to Churchill and Lowe (1999), this reflected the aspiration of the developing countries to economic development and to gain control over the resources off their coasts. This position began to attract the support of the developed states and **Part V UNCLOS** establishes a specific legal regime for the EEZ.

The first issue to be dealt with is the definition of the EEZ. **Article 55 UNCLOS** provides that the EEZ is an area beyond and adjacent to the territorial sea, which shall not extend beyond 200 nautical miles from the baselines from which the breadth of the territorial sea is measured. This zone subject to the specific legal regime is established in **Part V UNCLOS**. Galdorisi and Kaufman (2001–2) describe the delimitation of this zone as a relatively new juridical concept. **Article 56** establishes the right of the coastal state to sovereign rights for the purpose of exploring and exploiting, conserving and managing the natural resources, and, with regard to other activities, for economic exploitation and exploration of the zone—such as: the production of energy from the water, currents, and wind; for maritime scientific research; and the protection and preservation of the marine environment. **Article 58**, however, sets out the rights and duties of other states in the EEZ, including being granted the freedoms referred to in the part concerning the high seas, particularly **Art. 87** freedom to lay submarine cable and pipelines. However, the EEZ allows the coastal state to regulate the fishing within the zone. Foreign ships have free passage but are subject to the coastal state's enforcement in respect of illegal fishing and the control of pollution. The coastal state has a duty to preserve the fishing and to allow landlocked and other states access to surplus. Some states like the UK only claim this area as an exclusive fishing zone. The exclusive fishing zone is a zone of the sea adjacent to a coastal state's territorial sea within which the coastal state has exclusive jurisdiction over fishing.

However, Freedonia must understand that Natalia's EEZ is more than an exclusive fishing zone and that it has ratified **UNCLOS** and has accepted the regime concerning pollution and resource development. Although the convention does not obligate states to claim such a zone, 111 states now claim 200-mile EEZs. It is the case that some states are unable to claim such a distance due to geographical restrictions. The concept is so important that it has now also become part of customary law. The reasons for the customary practice, as argued by Churchill and Lowe (1999), are the number of states making the claim for such a zone and the complete absence of protest by other states. This customary status was confirmed by the International Court of Justice (ICJ) in *Libya/Malta Continental Shelf* (1985). This means that Natalia would be able to claim this zone even if it were not a party to the convention and it is too late for Freedonia to object at this point.

Natalia's first specific claim is to prevent the passage of ships with nuclear waste or if powered by nuclear fuels. It seems likely that Natalia will be able to control but not restrict the passage of ships containing nuclear waste. Although **Arts 58 and 87 UNCLOS** describe the customary rule of free passage of ships, there is the power to regulate nuclear waste and fuels in the EEZ as **Art. 56(1)(b)(ii)** is the power to protect and preserve the marine environment which nuclear fuels could clearly impact negatively. However, there is also **Art. 23** which governs the territorial sea but is also pertinent here. It states that foreign nuclear-powered ships and ships carrying nuclear or other inherently dangerous or noxious substances shall, when exercising the right of innocent passage through the territorial sea, carry documents and observe special precautionary measures established for such ships by international agreements. This means that Natalia will have to allow passage subject to strict controls. Freedonia must ensure that the ships carrying nuclear material comply with these safety regulations.

There are also specific powers within **UNCLOS** to control fishing in the EEZ. **Art. 56(1)(a)** specifies control of natural resources, living and non-living and **Art. 61** allows the coastal state to determine the allowable catch, including capping fishing levels to produce a 'maximum sustainable yield'. Under **Art. 62(3)**, where there is no capacity to harvest the entire allowable catch, the coastal state is under a duty to share its catch with other states. This must be done by giving priority to landlocked states (**Art. 69**) and geographically disadvantaged states (**Art. 70**). The coastal state can charge for allowing fishing as set out in **Art. 62(3)**. Freedonia may argue that because of its small coastline it is geographically disadvantaged and will have to negotiate with Natalia to be allowed to fish in its waters.

The conclusion of my legal advice to the government of Freedonia is that Natalia does, under **UNCLOS** and customary international law, have the power to control both fishing and the passage of nuclear fuels and waste in its EEZ. As Galdorisi and Kaufman assert, the EEZ is a zone of shared rights and responsibilities. Coastal states have the primary rights over natural resources in the zone, whereas foreign states retain the freedom of navigation through the zone. Therefore, my legal advice is that: (a) Freedonia's fishing vessels will probably not be able to fish—unless Natalia specifically agrees; and (b) the nuclear vessels will be able to pass, subject to safety regulations. It can be argued that neither of the statements of Natalia is in accordance with **UNCLOS**, as Natalia may well not be able to control all of the fishing, nor disrupt the free passage of ships.

Examiner's tip

The examiner will want to ensure that you cite the correct sections of **UNCLOS** so make sure you know the relevant sections. The examiner will also want to confirm that you have correctly defined the exclusive economic zone.

Question 2

UNCLOS has established coastal state jurisdiction over various areas of the sea.

Discuss with reference to the convention the various territorial limits imposed over different areas of the sea and whether these limits also constitute customary international law.

Commentary

This essay question allows you to display your knowledge concerning the various areas of the sea, but it is deceptively simple. There are of course controversies concerning each area and the complete answer will refer to these controversies. **UNCLOS** establishes a regime over each area and the provisions are detailed. There are two main issues to be discussed: the geographical delimitation of these zones and the rights of vessels from foreign states within these zones. There is not time in this answer to go into every aspect, but a concise summary of the various areas is needed. The answer would be greatly assisted by the summary of these areas provided in Shaw (2003) and the more detailed descriptions in Lowe and Churchill (1999).

Answer plan

- Territorial sea.
- International straits.
- Continental shelf.
- EEZ.
- High seas.

Suggested answer

UNCLOS establishes a specific legal regime over each area of the seas. This essay will briefly describe the treaty regime and whether the general legal regime for each area constitutes customary international law.

The first and most directly related to the coast is the territorial sea. **Article 2** states that the territorial sea includes the airspace over the territorial sea and its seabed and subsoil. **Article 3** specifies that the territorial sea has a limit not exceeding *12 nautical miles* and Harris (2010) argues that this reflects customary international law in spite of a few states claiming a 200-mile territorial sea. In the past the claim had been for three miles, as it was easier to patrol. This was because the territorial sea involves responsibilities as well as rights, such as policing and maintaining order; buoying and marking channels and reefs, sandbanks, and other obstacles; keeping navigable channels clear; and giving notice of dangers to navigation and providing rescue services.

The width of the territorial sea is defined from the low-watermark around the coasts of the state. In the majority of cases it will not be very difficult to locate the low-waterline which is to act as a baseline for measuring the width of the territorial sea. According to the conventions this will be the low-waterline of the low-tide elevation which may be used as a baseline for measuring the breath of the territorial sea. Sometimes, however, the geography of the state's coasts will be such as to cause problems, such as where there are numerous islands or where there are bays cutting into the coastline. Special rules have evolved to deal with this issue which is of importance to coastal states, particularly where foreign vessels fish close to the limits of the sea. This was discussed in *Anglo-Norwegian Fisheries*. This case concerned a Norwegian decree delimiting the territorial sea along some 1,000 miles off its coastline by using straight baselines linking the outer-most parts of the land. As a result it took in more of the high seas than if a traditional method had been used. The UK disputed the territorial sea but the court held that the Norwegians had used this method for many years and it had not been disputed in the past. The court decided that the drawing of the baselines had not to depart from the general directions of the coast, in view of the close dependence of the territorial sea upon the land domain. The baselines had to be drawn so that the sea area lying within them had to be sufficiently closely linked to the land domain to be subject to the regime of internal waters, and it was permissible to consider 'certain economic interests peculiar to a region, the reality and importance of which are evidenced by long usage'. These prin-ciples were codified in the **Geneva Convention 1958** and **UNCLOS**.

Some states take advantage of this alteration when it is not necessary. For example, one should examine *Maritime Delimitation and Territorial Questions between Qatar and Bahrain (Qatar v Bahrain)*. Bahrain was not considered to have a cluster of islands or an island system allowing for straight-baseline determination.

Another problem of territorial seas is bays which can include several states such as the Gulf of Aqaba in the Red Sea bordered by Egypt, Israel, Jordan, and Saudi Arabia. The conventions do not cover such a bay. In several cases the court has dealt with it on a case-by-case basis, as there can be historic regimes over these areas.

Another controversy is over archipelagos. The waters may be stated to be within the sovereignty of the archipelagic state but are subject to rights of innocent passage.

Internal waters are not part of the territorial sea but are classed as waters appertaining to the land territory of the coastal state. These can be harbours, lakes, rivers and they are to be found on the landward side of the baselines from which the territorial or other zones are measured. Unlike the territorial sea, there is no right of innocent passage.

The second area that is present in some areas is international straits. In the *Corfu Channel* case the ships were actually passing through international straits which again have a slightly different regime to that of the territorial sea. In **UNCLOS** a new right of transit passage is posited with respect to straits used for international navigation between one part of the high seas or an EEZ and another part of the high seas or an EEZ. It involves the exercise of the freedom of navigation and overflight solely for the purpose of continuous and expeditious transit of the strait. States bordering the straits in question are not to hamper or suspend transit passage.

The continental shelf is a geological expression referring to the ledges that project from the continental landmass into the seas and which are covered with only a rela-tively shallow layer of water and which eventually fall away into the ocean depths. These ledges take up some 7 to 8 per cent of the total area of the ocean. They are rich in oil and gas resources and quite often host to extensive fishing grounds.

There is a separate regime for the continental shelf. The first claim was the **Truman Proclamation on the Continental Shelf 1945**. It argued that the continental shelf is a continuation of the land mass of the territory and the coastal state could have access to the subsoil and seabed. The issue here is the exploration of natural resources. Many states made claims and the **Convention on the Continental Shelf 1958** attempted to resolve the issue and *North Sea Continental Shelf* in the ICJ attempted to resolve the issue of delineation of the shelf, but the court held that it was not yet part of customary international law.

UNCLOS in 1982 resolved this issue. According to **UNCLOS,** no continental shelf may extend more than 350 miles from the territorial sea baseline or, beyond that, 2,500 metres deep plus 100 miles. This is not sovereignty but the rights to living and mineral resources and the related rights to exploit them. This definition in **Art. 76** has caused problems and there is a Commission on the Limits of the Continental Shelf, with 21 experts elected by states parties. This is an additional claim to the EEZ. The rights and duties of coastal states are to explore and exploit natural resources and include living organisms belonging to sedentary species but not fish. Wrecks lying on the shelf are also excluded. Where the shelf extends beyond the 200-mile limit, the coastal state must make payments or contributions in kind in respect of the exploitation of the non-living resources up to 7 per cent. This shall be distributed on the basis of equitable sharing taking into account the needs of the developing and landlocked states.

The EEZ marked a compromise between those states seeking a 200-mile territorial sea and those wishing a more restricted regime of coastal state power. A major reason was the controversy over fishing zones. **Article 56 UNCLOS** states that the coastal state in the economic zone had sovereign rights for the purpose of exploring and exploiting, conserving, and managing the natural resources whether living or non-living. The convention treats the zone as an intermediate area of sea between the high seas and the territorial sea with a distinct regime of its own.

Some states like the UK only claim this as an exclusive fishing zone. The exclusive fishing zone is a zone of the sea adjacent to a coastal state's territorial sea within which the coastal state has exclusive jurisdiction over fishing.

However, the EEZ is more than fishing and has to do with concern over pollution and resource development. In 2002, 111 states were claiming 200-mile EEZs. It is actually 188 miles as the territorial sea comes first. In *Libya/Malta Continental Shelf*, the ICJ stated that the EEZ is part of customary international law. For a case that considers delimitation on both the continental shelf and EEZ see the *Case Concerning Maritime Delimitation in the Black Sea (Romania v Ukraine)* Judgment 3 February 2009 in which the court applied equitable principles to the delimitation.

The area common to all is the high seas defined in **Art. 1 Geneva Convention on the High Seas 1958** as all parts of the sea not included in the territorial sea or in the internal waters of a state. This reflected customary international law. In **UNCLOS** the definition was expanded to all parts of the sea which are not included in the EEZ, in the territorial sea, or in the archipelagic waters of an archipelagic zone.

Article **87 UNCLOS** provides that the high seas are open to all states and that the freedom of the high seas is exercised under the conditions laid down in the convention and by other rules of international law. It includes the freedom of navigation, over-flight, the laying of submarine cables and pipelines, the construction of artificial islands and other installations permitted under international law, fishing, and the conduct of scientific research. Such freedoms are to be exercised with due regard of the interests of other states in their exercise of the freedom of the high seas.

 Examiner's tip

The key element of this answer is knowledge of the various areas of the sea and particularly, the legal definition of those areas.

 Question 3

You are the commanding officer of a British naval warship and are en route to an official visit to the Russian city of St Petersburg. On the way to St Petersburg you went through 'The Sound' which is an international strait between Denmark and Sweden connecting the North and Baltic Seas.

During your passage through The Sound, you observe ships of many nations apparently in routine transit, including warships of Russia, Denmark, Sweden, and Germany. On entering the Baltic Sea and continuing towards Russia your ship was at its closest point to the Swedish coastline and you receive a message from Swedish naval control that your ship is in Swedish territorial waters and that you are to leave the waters.

Sweden, upon signing UNCLOS, took exception to the right of innocent passage for warships in territorial seas and required notification prior to entry into their territorial waters.

As the commanding officer are you going to remove your warship from the passage between Denmark and Sweden?

 Commentary

This problem question highlights one of the remaining controversies in the law of the sea—the right of warships to unhindered passage through territorial seas. There is, unsurprisingly, a difference in opinion between those nations that do not have navies and those that do. One pivotal relevant case is **Corfu Channel**, one of the first cases decided by the ICJ. However, there is a twist, as the case decided the issue of passage over international straits, not territorial seas.

In addition to the original material contained in Harris (2010), relevant articles are: David Froman, 'Uncharted waters: non-innocent passage of warships in the territorial sea' (1984); and Bardin, 'Coastal state's jurisdiction over foreign vessels' (2002).

Answer plan

- Regime for passage of foreign ships through territorial sea or international straits.
- Controversy between various nations on warships.
- Discussion of **Corfu Channel**.
- Discussion of the *USS Pueblo* incident and other state practice.
- Discussion of the joint UK and US statement on warships.

Suggested answer

As Churchill and Lowe (1999) argue, the right of warships to engage in innocent passage has long been one of the most controversial aspects of the law of the sea.

David Froman (1984) poses the questions that are still unanswered: who decides whether passage of a foreign warship in the territorial sea is innocent? By what criteria? What enforcement and appeal mechanisms, if any, exist? What factors may shape such decisions?

The right of foreign merchant ships to pass unhindered through the territorial sea of a coast has long been an accepted principle in customary international law. It is established in **Art. 17 UNCLOS** which states that ships of all states, whether coastal or landlocked, enjoy the right of innocent passage through the territorial sea. However, **Art. 19 UNCLOS** defines innocent passage as innocent so long as it is not prejudicial to the peace, good order, or security of the coastal state. This provision gives examples of activities which are not peaceful and which may be relevant to warships:

1 any threat or use of force against the sovereignty, territorial integrity, or political independence of the coastal state, or in any other manner in violation of the principles of international law embodied in the **UN Charter;**

2 any exercise or practice with weapons of any kind;

3 any act aimed at collecting information to the prejudice of the defence or security of the coastal state;

4 any act of propaganda aimed at affecting the defence or security of the coastal state;

5 the launching, landing, or taking onboard of any aircraft; and

6 the launching, landing, or taking onboard of any military device.

Therefore, it would seem that a warship not engaged in any of these activities would be able to pass through territorial seas. A key case in support of this proposition is *Corfu Channel*, one of the first cases decided by the ICJ, even though the issue there was the issue of passage over straits. The British government had sent their warships through the North Corfu Strait. The court ruled that, in accordance with international custom, states in a time of peace have a right to send their warships through straits used for international navigation between the high seas without the previous authorization of a coastal state, provided the passage is innocent. The minesweeping done by the British ships was not considered an exercise in safe passage. The British argued that the minesweeping was necessary, as the explosions were suspicious and raised an issue of responsibility. Therefore, they needed to take possession of the evidence. The court did not accept this argument and stated that although Albania had failed to carry out its duties after the explosion the action of the British navy violated Albanian sovereignty.

David Froman argues that subsequent writers have confused the limited and special customary rule on the exercise of passage of warships through straits used for international navigation between two parts of the high seas with the general principle regarding passage of warships through territorial seas. In fact David Froman argues that the court was '*conspicuously silent*' on this issue. Therefore, one has to turn to state practice.

In practice, coastal states have attempted to regulate the passage of warships by requiring notice. Although this was not included in **UNCLOS**, according to David Froman, 30 states at the time of the negotiation put on record their displeasure at the lack of inclusion of such a provision. According to Harris and David Froman, 40 coastal states, including Sweden and Denmark, claim the right to control entry of warships into their territorial seas by means of prior notification and by limitations on the number of warships present at any one time.

This is not accepted by naval powers and in his materials, Harris (2010), has included the US and USSR joint statement on a uniform interpretation on rules of international law governing innocent passage which reflect agreement with the convention but included safe passage for warships without notification. **Arts 25** and **30 UNCLOS** provide that coastal states can demand that foreign warships comply with their regulations and the rules of passage set out in **Art. 19** and if a state fails to do so then the coastal state can order the warship to leave the territorial sea immediately and use according to **Art. 25** 'a degree of force proportionate to the threat which the continuing presence of the ship represents'.

Bardin (2002) gives examples of state practice. On 27 October 1981 a Soviet submarine grounded on the coast of Sweden. Sweden launched a formal investigation and claimed the right to require of any foreign warship, prior to entry into its territorial sea, official notification of the flag state. Another important incident discussed by Bardin was the *USS Pueblo* incident. In 1968, a US warship, *USS Pueblo* was seized by North Korea. Although the United States claimed that the vessel was on the high seas, North Korea argued that it was in territorial waters. The United States issued a statement that even if the ship had been in territorial waters the seizure was improper in the absence of an immediate threat of an armed attack. However, the ship was equipped with electronic devices and it could be argued that it was a violation of **Art. 19(2)(c)** '*collecting information to the prejudice of the defence or security of the coastal state*' and so this fact coupled with its refusal to leave the area justified the North Korean seizure.

The case law and state practice do not yet provide answers to these critical questions and the controversy between coastal states and naval powers continues. The fact that 40 states attempt to control entry into their waters by warships is an important element of state practice and might well result in a rule of customary law even though this is not a specific provision in **UNCLOS**. Given the United Kingdom's clear position, as commanding officer you will decide to continue with your voyage through the passage between Sweden and Denmark and hope that your ship is not stopped in its peaceful passage.

 Examiner's tip

This is not a question that has a definitive answer. The examiner will want to ensure that you have considered both sides of this issue. It is particularly important to mention the position of major naval powers such as the UK and USA.

 Question 4

The 1994 Implementation Agreement of Part XI UNCLOS has established a detailed and specific regime over the deep seabed.

Discuss the background to this agreement and why Western states were so intent on establishing this regime.

 Commentary

Regulation over the deep seabed of the high seas has been another area of controversy. Developed nations are those that have the technology and resources to exploit the natural resources of the seabed. Yet developing nations claim a share of those resources as they argue they are part of the common heritage of humankind. This controversy delayed the implementation of **Part XI UNCLOS** and this answer should discuss the divergent views and the regime that was specified within **Part XI UNCLOS** and its modification by the 1994 agreement.

The following would assist in the preparation of this answer: Nelson, 'The contemporary seabed mining regime: a critical analysis of the mining regulations promulgated by the International

Seabed Authority' (2005); and Guntrip, 'The common heritage of mankind: an adequate regime for managing the deep seabed?' (2003); and Churchill and Lowe (1999) has chapters on both the high seas and the international seabed area.

Answer plan

- Discuss the customary and treaty regime concerning freedom of the high seas.
- Discuss the divergent views concerning deep seabed exploration.
- Describe **Part XI UNCLOS**.
- Analyse the 1994 implementation agreement and how it modifies **Part XI UNCLOS**.

Suggested answer

Beyond the continental shelf and EEZ are the high seas containing the deep seabed which is rich in natural resources. Nelson (2005) argues that the oceans were long subject to the doctrine of the freedom of the high seas—a doctrine originating from Grotius in the seventeenth century. However, Nelson argues that in the twentieth century there was an increasing presence of maritime powers on the high seas intent on exploitation of the natural resources contained in the deep seabed.

The high seas were defined in the **1958 High Seas Convention** as '*all parts of the sea not included in the territorial sea or in the internal waters of a state*'. **Article 86 UNCLOS**, while not defining the concept, stated that it was '*all parts of the sea that are not included in the exclusive economic zone, in the territorial sea or in the internal waters of a state, or in the archipelagic waters of an archipelagic state*'. Churchill and Lowe (1999) argue that the **1958 Convention** codifies four customary examples of freedom of the high seas: freedom of navigation, fishing, laying of submarine cables and pipelines, and overflight. In **UNCLOS** these were extended in **Art. 87** to include the freedom to construct artificial islands and other installations, and the freedom to conduct scientific research. As Churchill and Lowe conclude, no state has the right to prevent ships of other states from using the high seas for any lawful purpose. All exercise of the freedom of the high seas is subject to the 'due regard' obligation. This means that where there is a conflict between two uses of the high seas it is necessary to determine which use is more reasonable. A good example discussed by Churchill and Lowe is the laying of fishing nets that could obstruct passage of other sea-going vessels. Obviously, that would not be due regard for the other states. Another example is weapons-testing. It is accepted that naval manoeuvres and conventional weapons-testing may be conducted on the high seas, but mariners must be notified of the areas and times these will take place. Nuclear testing may well be another matter. In the ICJ case, *Nuclear Tests* **(1974)**, Australia and New Zealand argued that atmospheric nuclear tests conducted by the French in the Pacific Ocean constituted infringement of the freedom of the high seas on account of the interference with ships and aircraft and by pollution caused by radioactive fallout. The case did not come to judgment, as France announced the termination of atmospheric nuclear testing.

In 1873 scientists aboard the *HMS Challenger* discovered polymetallic nodules on the deep seabed. These mineral deposits were large enough to enable commercial mining and developments in technology in the late twentieth century meant that mining became a real possibility. There was an important argument to be made with respect to the contents of the deep seabed. This was that these areas were part of the common heritage of mankind and, thus, not subject to any sovereign jurisdiction. The term 'common heritage of mankind' was first introduced in a speech by Maltese Ambassador Pardo in 1967. According to Guntrip (2003), there are four elements in the common heritage of humankind: states are prohibited from proclaiming sovereignty over any part of the seabed; states are required to use it for peaceful purposes; they must share in the management of the deep seabed; and they must share the benefits of its exploitation. In contrast to this, in 1974 a US company, Deep Sea Ventures Inc., filed a notice of discovery and claim of exclusive mining rights with the US State Department over a nodule discovered in the Pacific. The governments of Canada, the United Kingdom, and Australia stated that they did not recognize the claim, although they regarded the mining of the seabed as an exercise of the freedom of the seas. The developing states who favoured the common heritage principle were victorious first in the **General Assembly Declaration of Principles Governing the Seabed and Ocean Floor and the Subsoil Thereof** which confirmed the deep seabed as the common heritage of humankind and **Part XI UNCLOS** which also in very complex provisions provided for an authority, the International Seabed Authority, to control access to seabed mine sites and recovery of minerals from them.

Churchill and Lowe describe **Part XI** as an extraordinarily complicated legal regime. The rate of recovery was to be limited, to ensure that seabed minerals did no more than supply a certain proportion of the growth in world demand for nickel. Levies on miners were to be distributed among states as the '*common heritage of mankind*'. The Seabed Authority was to engage in the seabed exploitation itself through its mining arm, called the Enterprise. There was a complex parallel system of Enterprise and individual states mining ventures operating side by side.

In spite of the fact that this regime over the deep seabed was negotiated in 1982, because of the controversy between developed and developing states, it was not implemented until 1994. The developed states demanded alterations of the international regime to allow for economic profit from these enterprises and for a greater voice commensurate with their economic investment. According to Churchill and Lowe, the basic disagreement by the United States and other industrialized states was the lack of protection said to exist for the very substantial investments which had already taken place in seabed mining. Therefore, there were several more years of negotiation which culminated in the **Agreement Relating to the Implementation of Part XI UNCLOS**. According to Nelson (2005), the agreement, together with **Part XI UNCLOS**, constitutes the seabed-mining regime, which successfully manages the diverse interests of the international community.

The relevant authority established under **Part XI** is the International Seabed Authority which decides on the regulations for deep-sea mining and on approval of proposals for projects. There is not space enough in this answer to discuss the various organs of the International Seabed Authority, but it has three principles organs: the plenary Assembly, the 36-State Council; and the Secretariat. In 2000, it adopted regulations for the prospecting and exploration of the polymetallic nodules. As Nelson argues, these regulations are balancing economic benefit with protection of the marine environment which is in accordance with the aims of this part of **UNCLOS**. Churchill and Lowe also describe the **1994 Implementation Agreement** as a demonstration of the flexibility of international law at its best and has encouraged numerous states to become parties to the agreement and **UNCLOS** at the same time.

In summary, according to Churchill and Lowe, mining activities through the Enterprise and by commercial operators in the deep seabed area are to be carried out for the benefit of humankind as a whole, taking into particular consideration the interests of developing states. Therefore, although there may be commercial interests from developed states involved in the exploitation of deep seabed resources, this unique area of international law ensures the benefit of mining for all humankind.

 Examiner's tip

The successful student will have knowledge of the controversy concerning deep seabed development. Secondly, precise recounting of the new legal regime in **Part XI** and the establishment of the International Seabed Authority is essential.

Further reading

Bardin, A., 'Coastal state's jurisdiction over foreign vessels' (2002) 14 *Pace Int'l L. Rev.* 27.

Churchill, R. R. and Lowe, A. V., *The Law of the Sea*, 3rd edn (Manchester: Manchester University Press, 1999).

Freestone, D., Barnes, R., and Ong, D. (eds), *The Law of the Sea: Progress and Prospects* (Oxford: Oxford University Press, 2007).

Froman, F. D., 'Uncharted waters: non-innocent passage of warships in the territorial sea' (1984) 21 *San Diego L. Rev.* 625.

Galdorisi, G. and Kaufman, A., 'Military activities in the exclusive economic zone: preventing uncertainty and defusing conflict' (2001–2) 32 *California Western Int'l L. Jour.* 251.

Guntrip, E., 'The common heritage of mankind: an adequate regime for managing the deep seabed?' (2003) 4 *Melbourne Jour. of Int'l L.* 378.

Nelson, J., 'The contemporary seabed mining regime: a critical analysis of the mining regulations promulgated by the International Seabed Authority' (2005) 16 *Colorado Jour. of Int'l Environmental L. and Pol.* 27.

9

Jurisdiction

Introduction

Jurisdiction over people and property is a vital part of state sovereignty. Although it is also a subject canvassed in domestic law, it remains an important topic in public international law. The main focus of the questions in an examination usually involve enforcement jurisdiction. Prescriptive jurisdiction is the capacity to make laws but problem and essay questions generally concern the thorny issues of enforcement of crimes of international concern within domestic jurisdictions. A major debate within international law is whether a state by universal jurisdiction can try persons who have committed international crimes elsewhere. This topic is case-law intensive, with both domestic and international cases, and the student should be aware of the developing jurisprudence in this area. There is a key International Court of Justice (ICJ) decision on this topic—*Arrest Warrant of 11 April 2000 (Democratic Republic of the Congo v Belgium)* decided in 2002. As with all of the other topics, students will be rewarded by keeping up to date with the developing case law.

The first question in this chapter enables students to discuss the various heads of criminal enforcement jurisdiction and to demonstrate their knowledge of this important topic. The second question is one of the most likely to be asked in this area and it concerns universal jurisdiction. The third question is a problem question asking the student to apply the various heads of jurisdiction to a fact situation and relates to existing jurisprudence in the area. Finally, there is a question, particularly pertinent in the United States about the **Alien Torts Claims Act (ATCA)**, which has a growing body of jurisprudence on international jurisdiction for civil compensation for international delicts and a major pending case before the Supreme Court on the issue of universal civil jurisdiction, *Esther Kiobel et al. v Royal Dutch Petroleum Co. et al.*

Sources which may be of assistance include: Cassese (2008), which contains an excellent chapter on jurisdiction; Lowe has a comprehensive chapter on jurisdiction in Evans (2010); Ryngaert has written an excellent monograph on the jurisdiction in international law

(2008). A pertinent monograph on universal jurisdiction is Reydams (2005). An international instrument which provides important guidance on the various heads of jurisdiction is the *Harvard Research Draft Convention on Jurisdiction with Respect to Crime* (1935) **29 AJIL Supp. 443** (referred to in this chapter as **HRDCJ**) which, even though dating from 1935, still provides authoritative definitions of the various types of criminal jurisdiction. It was never incorporated into a binding treaty, and therefore this topic depends on doctrines of customary international law as reflected in international and domestic jurisprudence.

It should also be pointed out that various treaties might contain different rules of jurisdiction and of particular interest are the jurisdictional clauses in the **Geneva Conventions of 1949**, the **Genocide Convention of 1948**, the **Torture Convention of 1984**, and various conventions on airline hijacking, all with specific bases of jurisdiction. Treaties should also be referred to in the answers to these questions.

 Question 1

Define with reference to case law the various types of jurisdiction that arise in international criminal jurisdiction.

 Commentary

This question calls for a definition and description of the various types of enforcement jurisdiction. It is not enough, however, to define simply these heads of jurisdiction—reference to applicable case law is essential. The first place to start is with the **HRDCJ**, to begin this process of definition. Thorough knowledge is also required of ***Lotus (France v Turkey)***—the pivotal case on jurisdiction, as decided by the Permanent Court of International Justice (PCIJ) in 1927.

A danger in this question is to provide too much detail on each head of jurisdiction. Managing the time in answering this question will be critical. Although there are several types of jurisdiction, it is also important to emphasize whether or not this head of jurisdiction is generally accepted or controversial.

 Answer plan

- Discuss the **HRDCJ**: it is not a binding treaty but reflects customary international law.
- Describe the territorial principle.
- Describe the nationality principle.
- Describe the protective principle.
- Describe the universality principle.
- Discuss the doubtful status of the passive-personality principle.

Suggested answer

Jennings and Watts (1992) define state jurisdiction as the extent of each state's right to regulate conduct or the consequences of events. In this question the topic is particularly the state's right to take enforcement measures against criminal wrongs. The **HRDCJ** is the best source for the five main principles of jurisdiction that arise in international criminal jurisdiction. This was an effort to codify the following principles and though this is not a binding treaty, it is intended to reflect customary international law. The five main types of jurisdiction that arise in international criminal jurisdiction are the.

1   territorial principle;

2   nationality principle;

3   protective principle;

4   universal principle; and

5   passive-personality principle.

A draft convention was prepared reflecting these types of jurisdiction, but passive personality was omitted, as the permissibility of this basis of jurisdiction was thought to be doubtful. This convention was never implemented.

The first head of jurisdiction is the territorial principle—Ryngaert (2008) states that jurisdiction obtains over acts that have been committed within the territory. The territorial principle is the primary ground for exercise of jurisdiction the world over and perhaps the most intuitive as jurisdiction within one's borders is at the root of the creation of states. It is a fundamental aspect in a world order that is based on territorial integrity and independence of states.

Of primary concern under the territorial principle is the place where the offence is committed. Under this principle a country may prosecute for crimes which are committed upon its own soil. It is also the most convenient basis for exercise of jurisdiction, as witnesses will be located within the country, and with luck, so too will the offender. The **HRDCJ** does not limit the exercise of jurisdiction to offences committed completely within the territory; a state is allowed territorial jurisdiction when a crime is committed '*in whole or in part*' within its own territory, as in such cases where a weapon is fired over a frontier. As Ryngaert argues, in international criminal law it is commonly accepted that one constituent element of the act or situation has been consummated in the territory of the state that claims jurisdiction.

Perhaps the main case where the nature of territorial sovereignty in relation to criminal acts was examined was *Lotus*. The case involved a French steamer which collided in the high seas with the *Boz-Kourt*, a Turkish collier. Eight sailors and passengers died on the Turkish ship when it sank. The Turkish authorities arrested the French officer of the watch when the *Lotus* reached a Turkish port resulting in France claiming against Turkey in the PCIJ. The court rejected the claim and ruled that a state cannot exercise its powers outside its frontiers in the absence of a permissive rule of international law and, in this case, there was none. The court held that this did not mean that '*interna-*

tional law prohibits a state from exercising jurisdiction in its own territory, in respect to any case which relates to acts which have taken place abroad, and in which it cannot rely on some permissive rule of international law'. While the French attempted to claim that the flag state had exclusive jurisdiction over the ship at high seas, the damage done to the Turkish ship was equivalent to damage done to Turkish territory and allowed that country to exercise jurisdiction. This case established a means by which to define territory and how this is a far more malleable term than may be thought. It also holds that the principle of territory does not limit the power of a state to try crimes.

The nationality principle creates a basis for jurisdiction by reference to the nationality or national character of the person committing the offence. Ryngaert labels this basis of jurisdiction as the active personality principle. Every state must have a population or a collective of individual human beings to constitute a 'state'. The link connecting state powers of sovereignty and jurisdiction with the people is the concept of nationality. The commentary to the **HRDCJ** states that a person committing a crime owes allegiance to the state of which that person is a national, thereby emboldening the state with the competence to try and punish that national's crimes.

Many states claim jurisdiction under the nationality principle, regardless of where the offence was committed; meaning a state will claim jurisdiction even if the crime occurred within the territory of another state. This is much more the case in civil law countries, as common law countries tend to restrict these crimes to very serious offences when committed abroad.

Ryngaert (2008) defines the protective principle as protecting the state from acts perpetrated abroad which jeopardize its sovereignty or its right to political independence. This principle allows states to exercise jurisdiction over non-citizens who have committed an act abroad, which is deemed prejudicial to the vital security of the particular state concerned. This exercise of jurisdiction is justified on the basis of protecting the state's national interest. Since the non-citizen may not have committed a crime under the law of the country in which the non-citizen is residing, and if the crime encompassed political offences, an extradition order may be refused; this principle allows a state to gain jurisdiction by other means.

The protective principle exists, in part, because of the insufficiency of most municipal laws concerning offences against the security and integrity of foreign states. Most states utilize this principle and it is often used in treaties providing for multiple jurisdictional grounds. An important case law example provided by Shaw (2008) is the British case *Joyce v Director of Public Prosecutions*. This case involved the infamous pro-Nazi broadcaster 'Lord Haw-Haw'. Joyce, the accused, was born in the United States but in 1933 fraudulently acquired a British passport. In 1939 he left Britain and went to Nazi Germany. The case turned on whether the British court had jurisdiction to try him after the war on a charge of treason. The court took jurisdiction based on the protective principle, as, according to Shaw, the fact that treason occurred outside UK territory was immaterial, since states were not obliged to ignore the crime of treason committed against them outside their territory. Joyce was convicted and executed for this crime.

The universality principle is perhaps the most widely discussed form of jurisdiction to be used in modern times. This jurisdiction is claimed over persons for their committing a crime offensive to the international community as a whole, regardless of where the crime occurred. Under the universality principle, every state has the jurisdiction to try certain offences. These usually include heinous crimes, such as war crimes, crimes against humanity, crimes against peace, torture, piracy, and so on. **Article 10(a) of the HRDCJ** recognizes universal jurisdiction over all crimes, save those listed under **Arts 6–9** (crimes subject to nationality jurisdiction, security offences subject to protective jurisdiction, and piracy subject to universal jurisdiction).

The basis for this principle is that the crimes committed are offensive to the international community as a whole. Along with those crimes mentioned, there are a growing number of other offences that, through the creation of treaties, may subject states to the jurisdiction of other contracting parties. The **1949 Geneva Conventions** suggest a duty of the international community to make 'a common endeavour in the face of atrocities' and emboldens nations of the world with the right to claim jurisdiction over perpetrators of crimes which offend the international community as a whole. So too does the **Hague Convention** use language which imposes—rather than suggests a duty to seek—jurisdiction over international law violators: '*A state party in whose jurisdiction the alleged perpetrator of such offences is found **shall** prosecute him or extradite him*'.

Noteworthy cases in the further definition and expansion of universal jurisdiction, include *Eichmann*'s trial in Israel and the House of Lords' decision *Pinochet No. 3*—particularly Lord Millett's opinion. In *Eichmann* the Nazi head of the Jewish Office of the German Gestapo was found in Argentina, after years of no prosecution for his violations of human rights and international laws, and he was abducted to Israel and prosecuted under the jurisdictional basis of universal jurisdiction. The arrest of General Pinochet in London was a groundbreaking case for the international community and the expansion of the universal principle. It was one of the first instances where European judges applied universal jurisdiction to try the crimes committed by former heads of states. However, it was only Lord Millett in the judgment who actually confirmed the universality principles and jurisdiction over Pinochet by the majority was based on the **Torture Convention**.

The passive-personality principle is the last of the main types of international criminal jurisdiction and the one least utilized, because its permissibility is somewhat questionable. Passive personality is defined as jurisdiction by reference to the nationality or national character of the person injured by the offence.

A state may claim jurisdiction to try an individual for offences committed abroad which have affected, or will affect, the nationals of the state. Over 20 states utilize this principle but it has been opposed in Anglo-American countries. Though there are a number of treaties which include passive personality, the overall opinion is that the principle is uncertain grounds on which to base claims of jurisdiction under international law.

Judge Moore made an attack on the principle, in his dissent in the *Lotus* (discussed previously). Since the Turkish criminal code provided for jurisdiction where harm resulted to a Turkish national this appears to fit within the definitions of passive-personality jurisdiction and would thus allow Turkey to claim jurisdiction over the *Lotus* matter. The *Cutting* case of 1886 is similarly critical of the concept. An American published a defamatory statement about a Mexican citizen and, while in Mexico, the American was arrested and charged on the basis of damage to the Mexican in the United States. In the wake of strong protest from the US government, the charge was withdrawn. Because of its dubious and infrequent usage, the definition and utilization of passive personality has not developed into custom and is not widely used as a means of gaining international criminal jurisdiction.

 Examiner's tip

It is vital to define all of the areas of jurisdiction with reference to the Harvard Principles. The examiner will want to establish that the student has referred to the key cases under each head of jurisdiction.

 Question 2

It has been argued that universal jurisdiction is an established basis of jurisdiction for the criminal authorities of a state to try someone present in its territory with crimes against humanity even if the crimes did not take place in that territory.

Discuss with reference to case law and international treaties.

 Commentary

Universal jurisdiction is still a very controversial head of jurisdiction and perhaps even more so after the 2002 ruling in ***Arrest Warrant of 11 April 2000 (Democratic Republic of the Congo v Belgium)*** in which the influential separate opinion of Judges Higgins, Koojimans, and Buergenthal considered the concept of universal jurisdiction. This answer requires reference to the case law and international instruments. However, the answer also allows students to give their own opinion on the premise of the question—whether indeed this is an established head of jurisdiction.

The question, however, is based on universal criminal jurisdiction and the student should not stray into areas covered in a later question of universal civil jurisdiction. The student will be rewarded for reading this question carefully.

Answer plan

- Define the concept according to the **HRDCJ**.
- Discuss modified universal jurisdiction in treaties: **Geneva Convention**, **Hague Convention**, **1984 Torture Convention**.
- Discuss the jurisprudence on the issue: *Eichmann*, *Pinochet*, *Alvarez-Machain*, *Congo v Belgium*.

Suggested answer

The concept of universal jurisdiction may be looked to when crimes are committed which offend the international community as a whole. Ryngaert (2008) argues that genuine universal jurisdiction may be exercised by any state over a specific offence, without the offence having any link with that state except for the presence of the offender. It contends that certain crimes are so egregious they may be prosecuted in any court in the world. These usually include heinous crimes, including crimes against humanity, crimes against peace, torture, piracy, and slavery. War crimes are now accepted by most authorities as subject to universal jurisdiction, though the issues involved are extremely sensitive and highly political.

As the basis for this principle is that the crimes committed are offensive to the international community as a whole, it follows that as the international community and its laws develop, so too does the application of universal jurisdiction. Along with those crimes mentioned, there are a growing number of other offences, which through the creation of treaties may subject states to the jurisdiction of other contracting parties and transcend territorial boundaries. The **1949 Geneva Conventions** suggest a duty of the international community to make '*a common endeavour in the face of atrocities*' and emboldens nations of the world with the right to claim jurisdiction over perpetrators of crimes that offend humanity. It contains provisions for universal jurisdiction over grave breaches which include wilful killing, torture, or inhuman treatment, unlawful deportation of protected persons or taking of hostages and **Additional Protocol 1 of 1977** expands this list to attacks against civilian populations. The **1984 Torture Convention** seemed to concur with the sentiments of the **Geneva Conventions** claiming if a state cannot or will not prosecute a violation of international law, other states have the responsibility to do so. The **Hague Convention** continues the **Geneva Conventions** and the **Torture Convention**'s suggestion of a *right* to try cases despite a territorial basis for jurisdiction. It uses language which imposes—rather than suggests—a duty to seek jurisdiction over international law violators: '*A state party in whose jurisdiction the alleged perpetrator of such offences is found* **shall** *prosecute him or extradite him*'.

Such a situation arose both in the case of *Eichmann*'s trial in Israel and General Pinochet's arrest in London. In *Eichmann*, the Nazi head of the Jewish Office of the German

Gestapo was prosecuted and convicted under an Israeli law of 1951 for war crimes, crimes against Jewish people, and crimes against humanity. He was found in Argentina, after years of no prosecution for his violations of human rights and international laws, and he was abducted to Israel and prosecuted under the jurisdictional basis of universal jurisdiction. The District Court declared that far from limiting states' jurisdiction with regard to such crimes, international law was actually *in need* of the legislative and judicial organs of every state giving effect to its criminal interdictions and bringing criminals to trial. Thus the courts reflect the stance of the conventions and treaties relative to the overarching importance of universal jurisdiction to transcend any traditional and limiting territorial jurisdictional arguments.

There is an issue to be discussed here which regards the nature in which those to be brought under the jurisdiction of a foreign state for international law violations are obtained for trial and whether illegally obtaining a defendant may be grounds to refuse jurisdiction. While the United Kingdom will not try defendants if they are brought in illegally, *United States v Alvarez-Machain* suggests that this determination may be on a state-by-state basis. In 1990 Alvarez was abducted from Mexico by bounty hunters hired by the DEA to face charges for his involvement in the kidnap, torture, and murder of a DEA agent. The abduction was made because of the Mexican state's refusal to release the subject. The US Supreme Court ruled that the respondent's forcible abduction did not prohibit his trial; because of the nature of the crimes involved, and the unwillingness of the defendant's state to release him, the United States found no issue with bringing a violator of this kind to trial, despite the questionable means of getting him to court.

The arrest of General Pinochet in London was a groundbreaking case for the international community and expanded the usage of the universal principle into the realm of governmental figures and heads of state. Non-governmental organizations (NGOs) and their community had been pushing for Pinochet's arrest for years on account of his violations of human rights in Chile and the failure of any state prosecution to bring him to justice. On a visit to the United Kingdom for health-related reasons, Pinochet was brought under the jurisdiction of the United Kingdom and the House of Lords held that a leader must be responsible for his violations of human rights, regardless of what diplomatic immunity he may be awarded. It was one of the first instances where European judges applied universal jurisdiction to try the crimes committed by a former head of state. However, it was only Lord Millett who argued for pure universal jurisdiction with the other Lords finding their basis of jurisdiction under the United Kingdom's adoption of the **Torture Convention**.

The *Arrest Warrant of 11 April 2000 (Democratic Republic of the Congo v Belgium)* and the influential separate opinion of Judges Higgins, Koojimans, and Buergenthal is perhaps one of the best examples of universal jurisdiction's necessity and place to be utilized as a bridge over territorial jurisdictional lines. In 2000, Belgium issued an arrest warrant for Ndombasi with charges amounting to war crimes and crimes against humanity, which were allegedly committed by speeches that incited racial hatred and led to murders and lynchings. As Ndombasi was not in Belgium at the time of the issuance, the Democratic Republic claimed that Belgium lacked jurisdiction and argued that Ndombasi had diplomatic immunity. As discussed in the *Pinochet* case, Ndombasi's claim of diplomatic immunity would not shield him from universal jurisdiction, when charged with war crimes or crimes against humanity. While the court did not rule in Belgium's favour, the separate opinion suggests, as do the treaties enumerated here, that there is a principle of obligation when international laws are violated and that there is always some connection or some way to bring perpetrators under jurisdiction, save pure universal jurisdiction. In the separate opinion, the judges state '*virtually all national legislation envisages links of some sort to the forum state; and no case law exists in which pure universal jurisdiction has formed the basis of jurisdiction*'.

Universal jurisdiction has, in part, established itself as a basis of jurisdiction for the criminal authorities of a state to try someone present in its territory, because of a trend in the international community. As in the *Congo* case, cases will be dismissed because of the lack of presence of the individual to be tried in the territory of the state attempting to assert jurisdiction, but the separate opinion suggests that there is a trend moving away from territoriality and towards other bases of jurisdiction. In the opinion, there is discussion of the 'effects' or 'impact' jurisdiction, embraced by both the United States and, with certain qualifications, the European Union.

The international community has been wrestling with this issue and in October 2011 the 6th Committee (Legal) of the General Assembly debated the issue without any resolution, with some states arguing for universal jurisdiction for genocide, war crimes, and crimes against humanity and others arguing for state sovereignty. This is a continuing agenda item for the Legal Committee and the Secretary-General has prepared reports on this issue, two being prepared in 2010 and 2011.

Nevertheless there has been a trend and an evolution to depart from territoriality as the main basis by which to adjudicate jurisdiction and, as the separate opinion points out, the international community is instead looking, or perhaps *should* be looking, at where the 'effects' and 'impacts' of the violations are felt. If the court in the *Congo* case had used this as a basis of its jurisdiction, rather than Ndombasi's lack of physical presence in Belgium, the ruling would arguably have gone the other way. As universal jurisdiction has now been used widely within the international community and has made its way into custom, it is possible that its determination by means other than territoriality will evolve as well.

 Examiner's tip

The examiner would be impressed with the up-to-date information on the action in the United Nations on universal jurisdiction.

Question 3

Danie, a citizen of state A, is opposed to the current government of state B. He sets up an Internet site critical of state B's policies in a number of areas and revealing personal information about senior state B government officials. While on a visit to state B, he is arrested and charged with two crimes:

1   the promotion of dissatisfaction against the government of state B; and

2   encouraging attacks on officials of the government of state B (by revealing details about officials which could assist attackers).

To what extent could state B claim jurisdiction to try Danie of such crimes? To what extent did the criminalization of such content violate the principles of jurisdiction in international law?

Commentary

The problem in this case relates directly to a famous US case—the **Cutting** case which was discussed in the **Lotus** decision. It relates to other controversial type of jurisdiction—the accepted protective principle and the controversial passive-personality principle. However, the student must dismiss the other heads of jurisdiction on the way to the discussion of this important controversy. Although this is an area not as popular as universal jurisdiction, in the war on terror, claims of jurisdiction on vital interests have been advanced by states.

It is important to discuss the case law in this area and reprise the definitions of the various types of jurisdiction. The two leading cases are discussed in Shaw, who also gives an excellent summary of these two controversial heads of jurisdiction.

Answer plan

- Dismiss principles as justifications: nationality (not a national); universal (not a violation of international law); territorial (discuss the possibility that the website could be argued to be on *state B's* soil).

- Discuss the two possible bases of jurisdiction: first, the passive-personality principle and second, the **Cutting** case.

- Protection principle: protection of national interest, citizens, leaders, security, and **Joyce v DPP**.

Suggested answer

Under the five principles numerated in the **HRDCJ**, state B would be best to claim jurisdiction under the protective principle. It could not rely on the nationality principle, because Danie is not one of its citizens and therefore owes no allegiance to state B. The offences alleged against Danie do not fall under the umbrella of universal jurisdiction, which are violations against the international community, including crimes against humanity and human rights violations. It is not a persuasive argument for state B to claim the establishment of an Internet site opposed to the current government would fall under any of these classifications. State B may try to claim jurisdiction by means of the territorial principle, but, like its possible claim for universal jurisdiction, its argument would not have much weight. Because the Internet is a worldwide conception and may be accessed from almost all points on the globe, there could potentially be a claim that Danie's offences were committed within the boundaries of state B's territory. However, Danie's actual physical location was still confined to state A and this physical positioning will likely have greater weight when tried in court. It still remains to be determined by courts the nature of violations that occur through means of the Internet and no doubt legislation and judicial rulings will continue to redefine what is meant by territorial boundaries.

The first likely means by which state B may gain jurisdiction over Danie is by the passive-personality principle, which allows individuals to be tried for offences committed abroad which have affected or will affect nationals of a state. State B may claim that state A has continually failed to prosecute Danie for the offences committed and that the broadcasts are actually endangering the government officials. The relevant case and closely related to the facts in this problem is the *Cutting* case in 1886 which involved the publication in Texas of a statement made by a US citizen which was defamatory of a Mexican. Mr Cutting was arrested in Mexico but after vigorous protests the charges were withdrawn. However, this head of jurisdiction according to Shaw (2008) would be controversial as Judge Moore in a dissenting opinion in the *Lotus* case attacked this basis of jurisdiction, which was also claimed by the Turkish government. As Shaw argues, overall opinion is that it is a dubious ground.

State B is left with its most persuasive option—the protective principle. Jurisdiction is claimed under this principle by reference to the national interest injured by the offence. It allows states to exercise jurisdiction over non-citizens who have committed an act abroad, which is deemed prejudicial to the vital security of the particular state concerned. State B will argue that Danie's critique of the current government could have had palpable ramifications within its nation and that this created a real threat to the security of its people and territory. Whether this argument will prove persuasive, rests on the nature and the extent of Danie's discussion of the opposed policies and whether the court finds that there is a cause of action. This determination will likely be similar for any information revealed about senior staff, although arguments made may be more persuasive on this matter because of the personal nature of the information involved, rather than the simple commentary on public policies, arguably known to those within state B and to those who can access **ATCA**.

As this exercise of jurisdiction is justified on the basis of protecting the state's national interest, state B will have to establish a justifiable and persuasive case for Danie's site to have affected their national security or interest. Since the non-citizen—Danie—may not have committed a crime under the law of the country in which he is residing (depending on territorial arguments), this principle allows a state to gain jurisdiction by other means, save the few dubious options listed here. Again there is relevant jurisprudence of the House of Lords in *Joyce v Director of Public Prosecutions*. In that case a broadcaster, 'Lord Haw Haw', broadcast vitriolic anti-British propaganda from Nazi Germany and was tried, convicted, and hanged for treason based on this head of jurisdiction.

This is a principle which is easily abused and especially, as in this case, if the crime encompasses political offences, such as criticizing a current government or governmental policies, an extradition order may be refused. The protective principle exists, in part, because of the insufficiency of most municipal laws concerning offences against the security and integrity of foreign states.

Criminalization of content of the kind published over the Internet by Danie would have serious ramifications in the international community. The five principles outlined in the **HRDCJ** are to be used only in criminal jurisdictions and only for violations of international law. Violations of this nature usually include crimes, such as torture, genocide, rape, and serious human rights violations, not the freedom for one person to speak out about their views on government policies. Were a court to gain jurisdiction and thus criminalize Danie's acts, this opens the door for international law to adopt crimes of this kind into the international law vernacular and possibly stunting human rights to freedom of speech and expression.

This would also be a serious encroachment on state A's right and ability as a law-making nation. A state has a right to prescribe and make laws for their citizens to follow and to enforce these laws as it sees fit. Were state B to be able to try a citizen of state A for crimes that state A has neither prescribed nor enforced, this would be a violation of state A's right as a nation and law-making entity. This would also strip Danie of his rights as a citizen of a foreign state to be secure in the establishment in place in his nation. A criminalization of crimes such as the ones alleged against Danie would have a very negative impact on the international community as a whole and, as such, would not likely be allowed.

 Examiner's tip

The key to success in this question is to name the relevant heads of jurisdiction and to quickly dismiss the others. The importance of *Cutting* and *Joyce v DPP* cannot be over-emphasized. It is important to stick to the facts in this situation and to apply the law to those facts.

Question 4

The **Alien Torts Claims Act 1789 (ATCA)** is a unique method of establishing international civil jurisdiction.
With reference to case law, discuss the impact of **ATCA**.

 Commentary

This is a question directed primarily to students in the United States but it has become a topic of great interest in other jurisdictions. Although **ATCA** is a particular piece of legislation, many NGOs (including one devoted almost exclusively to this topic—Redress—based in London) seek to introduce the notion of universal civil jurisdiction. This would allow victims of torture, crimes against humanity, and genocide to seek compensation for their injuries and property losses. It might also allow punitive damages to be assessed against perpetrators. However, in this answer, the student must be aware that it is only in the United States that this type of claim has been successfully pursued.

 Answer plan

- Definition of **ATCA** and discussion of its evolution.
- *Filàrtiga* case and the court's positive application of **ATCA** to allow jurisdiction.
- Universal jurisdiction analogy.
- *Kadic v Karadžić* and the private versus public figure.
- *Tel-Oren* and the court's dismissal: was it the statute's fault or the drafters of the complaint?
- The Current United States Supreme Court case on universal civil jurisdiction is *Ether Kiobel et al. v Royal Dutch Petroleum*, once it is decided it will impact on this whole area and should be considered.

 Suggested answer

Under **ATCA,** the First Congress established original district court jurisdiction over all causes where an alien sues for a tort committed in violation of the laws of nations or a treaty of the United States. This act is codified in **s. 28 USC §1350** of the **US Code.** It essentially allows for any non-US citizen to utilize the US court system in situations where there may have been violations of international law. It is a unique method of establishing international civil jurisdiction in that it immediately brings what would otherwise be an international issue into the federal court system. Although **ATCA** was established over 200 years ago, it is still utilized today, though the scope of its use is in debate, as international law has developed and treaties are recognized. It is an important mechanism for establishing financial accountability for heinous crimes as universal civil jurisdiction has not been recognized in other nations.

In *Filàrtiga v Pena Irala* a Paraguayan national was allegedly kidnapped, tortured, and ultimately killed by Pena Irala, then the inspector general of police in Asuncion. After a fruitless attempt by the Filàrtiga family to bring suit for murder in their native Paraguay and the imprisonment and threats of death to their attorney the Filàrtigas sought asylum in the United States. In a separate move, Pena Irala also removed to the United States and, while there, the Filàrtigas lodged a complaint under **ATCA** in the US court system. Although their suit was initially dismissed in the District Court, the US Court of Appeals interpreted the statute to permit a private tort action for the acts of torture committed by Pena against Filàrtiga in Paraguay. It was held that torture was a violation of international law. This amounted to a rights violations, although clearly based on domestic laws.

It might be suggested that the nature of the crime involved be part of the determination when allowing jurisdiction under **ATCA**. Much like universal jurisdiction, perhaps crimes particularly heinous and egregious to the international community as a whole should be considered. As was suggested in the *Filàrtiga* ruling, the exercise of jurisdiction was based mainly on domestic laws. In addition, because of the inaction of the Paraguayan government to try the case, the Filàrtiga family could have used other justifications, such as passive personality and nationality (if, as asylum seekers, the United States government considered them to have become US citizens) to bring their claim.

Kadic v Karadžić raises the issue of public versus private citizens committing violations of international law and whether this has an effect on the utilization of **ATCA**. The statute cannot be used against a nation as an entity, as it states that an alien must bring the suit as an individual. In *Karadžić*, the court had to consider not only the applicability of the statute, but whether Karadžić's violations were acts of state or the acts of an individual. Radovan Karadžić was charged with genocide, murder, rape, and torture, among other violations of human rights, and the laws of war, against Bosnian Muslims and Bosnian Croats. His actions were a clear violation of international law and the court found that it could exercise jurisdiction and bring him to trial.

When considering the issue of state action versus private action, the court found that Karadžić was acting as an individual and questions whether such a violation would ever be seen as an act of state, even if the state in question were an established nation, unlike Karadžić's Republika Srpska. The defendant was awarded *no* immunity as a head of state and especially not as the head of an unrecognized entity. The court stated that '*the customary international law of human rights, such as the proscription of torture, applies to states without distinction between recognized and unrecognized states*'.

In *Tel-Oren v Libyan Arab Republic*, the court dismissed an action under the same statute brought by survivors and representatives of persons murdered in an armed attack on an Israeli bus in 1978. In March of that year, 13 members of the Palestine Liberation Organization (PLO) seized a civilian bus and, after holding the victims hostage and subjecting a number to torture, blew up the bus with grenades. The suit was brought by those injured and the survivors of those killed by the actions of the PLO. The plaintiffs were citizens of the United States, the Netherlands, and Israel. The court's reason for the dismissal was a lack of subject-matter jurisdiction, in that, because the offence did not occur within the jurisdiction of the US courts, and, on the face of the suit, the jurisdiction was not clearly for the US courts, the court could not claim to have connection with the matter at hand. The crime did not occur on US soil, nor did it directly affect or infringe upon US security, although, since a number of the plaintiffs were US citizens, one can question why the court did not seek jurisdiction in order to protect US security and its nationals.

One may question whether legal remedies were first sought and exhausted in the victims' national courts, as was the case in *Filàrtiga*, and whether this played a role in the cases being dismissed. Other international courts, such as the European Court of Human Rights, first requires victims of a human rights violation to seek remedy in their national court system before applying to the court. However, as the court in *Filàrtiga* ruled, when a violation of international law occurs, every nation, including the United States, has an overarching right to prosecute offenders who violate laws of this kind.

The opinion by Bork suggests a rather more simplistic reason for why the court in *Tel-Oren* ruled as it did. In Bork's opinion '*an explicit grant of a cause of action had to exist before a private individual will be allowed to enforce principles of international law in a federal tribunal*'. He goes on to say that the cause of action filed was '*vague, devoid of factual detail*' and that it is not within the rights of a court to *infer* a cause of action, regardless of the fact that the crimes committed *could* be inferred as violations of human rights treaties and the law of nations.

With this perspective, one must consider **ATCA** within the context of those who seek to use it and the position of the courts within the confines of the US court system, which must restrict itself to issues of established jurisdictional proof. If allowed to exercise jurisdiction in dubious situations, **ATCA** may lose its validity and use if people are seen to be abusing the situation. Because it is used so infrequently and with discretion, it has continued to be a tool by which victims may bring their violators to justice in the US court system. The court in *Karadžić* stated there are '*special questions regarding the judiciary's proper role when adjudication might have implications in the conduct of this nation's foreign relations*'. With increased globalization and the growing international body of laws and treaties, the US courts must consider—as must those seeking to avail themselves of the courts for international justice—the nature and validity of the claims they bring. Though the ruling in *Tel-Oren* may seem harsh to most, it is proper for the court to admit only those cases that clearly fit within the statute so that it continues to have an impact in the international community.

Examiner's tip

This question would be likely to be asked in a university in the United States. It is very important to be up to date on the litigation under the **Alien Torts Claims Act**. A new case concerning international civil jurisdiction has worked its way up to the Supreme Court. Students should be on guard for a decision in ***Esther Kiobel et al. v Royal Dutch Petroleum et al.*** where once again the issue of jurisdiction over torts committed outside of the United States is being considered.

Further reading

Cassese, A., *International Law*, 2nd edn (Oxford: Oxford University Press, 2004).

Evans, M., *International Law*, 2nd edn (Oxford: Oxford University Press, 2006).

Jennings, R. and Watts, A., (eds), *Oppenheim's International Law*, 9th edn (London: Longman, 1992).

Lowe, V., 'Jurisdiction' in M. Evans (ed.), *International Law*, 2nd edn (Oxford: Oxford University Press, 2006).

Reydams, L., *Universal Jurisdiction: International and Municipal Legal Perspectives* (Oxford: Oxford University Press, 2005).

Ryngaert, C., *Jurisdiction in International Law* (Oxford: Oxford University Press, 2008).

Shaw, M., *International Law*, 6th edn (Cambridge: Cambridge University Press, 2008).

10

State and diplomatic immunity

Introduction

Although state immunity is often combined with jurisdiction, in this book it will be treated separately on account of the importance and complexity of this issue and the recent case law in the International Court of Justice. In addition there is an important legal instrument on this topic entitled the **United Nations Convention on Jurisdictional Immunities of States and their Property 2004** which joins the **European Convention on State Immunity 1972** and various domestic state immunity acts. Although the **UN Convention** is not yet in force, some of its provisions represent customary international law in this area. State immunity is the reverse situation from the previous chapter of a state assuming jurisdiction over legal matters. In this case we are examining those situations where a state cannot exercise its jurisdiction over another state or its representatives because of this important doctrine.

The first two questions in this chapter will focus on the major area of examination in this topic, the two competing theories of immunity—absolute and restrictive—requiring analysis of the leading domestic cases on this issue. Included in this chapter is a problem question dealing with an employment situation. Although it is very common that employment matters can be brought before domestic courts even if another state is involved on the basis of restrictive immunity, there are important exceptions within the existing case law which might still lead to immunity being granted to the state involved. In addition there is problem canvassing the critical topic of immunity for representatives of the state. Finally, there will also be a question on the specific and interesting topic of diplomatic immunity and the two **Vienna Conventions on Diplomatic and Consular Relations**. Issues of diplomatic immunity are discussed by Wickremasinghe 'Immunity of state officials and international organizations', in Evans (2010).

There is an authoritative text on the issue of state immunity—Fox (2008), which would be an excellent source for revision. This book provides commentary on the **United**

Nations Convention on Jurisdictional Immunities of States and their Property which is the result of the work of the General Assembly's ad hoc committee established on this subject in 2000. The website of this important committee is located at http://untreaty%20.un.org/cod/jurisdictionalimmunities/index.html and it contains all of the reports of the drafting committee. It is also a topic that is very dense with case law from a number of jurisdictions. A source which summarizes European case law as a result of a project for the Council of Europe is Hafner *et al.* (2006). However, case law in this area is constantly developing and the student will be well rewarded for keeping up to date on cases of state immunity brought in their particular jurisdiction. Since the last edition of this book the International Court of Justice released its important judgment entitled *Jurisdictional Immunities of States (Germany v Italy: Greece Intervening)* which reviews many of the issues discussed in this topic.

Question 1

The United Nations Convention on Jurisdictional Immunities of States and their Property has finally resolved the issue of whether state immunity is restricted or absolute.

With reference to the convention and jurisprudence discuss the historical development of the current restricted doctrine of state immunity.

Commentary

This essay question invites a historical discussion of the development of the doctrine of restricted immunity. The first task is to define immunity and then to discuss the development of absolute and restricted state immunity. The **United Nations Convention on Jurisdictional Immunities of States and their Property** is not yet in force and the student must be careful to argue that the restricted doctrine contained within the convention also constitutes customary international law.

The chapters on state immunity in the recent textbooks discuss the development of this convention together with the evolution of the case law on this topic. There is no substitute for studying in careful detail the leading decisions and incorporating them in this question. Mentioning the names of the cases will not be sufficient: an analysis of the rulings on this question is vital. Furthermore, the types of commercial cases that might be heard in the domestic courts must be enumerated.

Answer plan

- Definition of state or sovereign immunity.
- Development of the doctrines of absolute and restricted immunity.

- Development of case law on restrictive immunity.
- Discuss the provisions of the **UN Convention** and list the categories of commercial cases that are not immune.

 Suggested answer

State immunity historically involved the right of the sovereign to be immune from prosecution in either the criminal or civil courts of another state. This evolved into the right not only of the sovereign but also any representative of a state present in another country or the entity of the state itself. Sovereign immunity is closely related to two other legal doctrines—non-justiciability and act of state. These two concepts mean that the domestic court cannot adjudicate upon the transactions of a foreign state. On the other hand, the principle of jurisdictional immunity asserts that in particular situations a court is prevented from exercising the jurisdiction it already possesses. The question of sovereign immunity is a procedural one and is a preliminary issue to be decided in any court case brought against a state. This becomes confusing in practice as act of state and immunity are similar, but one way to distinguish is that the act of a state takes place within the territory of that state and immunity deals with acts within the state where the court is located.

Shaw (2008) argues that the relatively uncomplicated role of the sovereign and of government in the eighteenth and nineteenth centuries gave rise to the concept of absolute immunity, whereby the sovereign was completely immune from foreign jurisdiction in all cases, regardless of circumstances. *The Schooner Exchange v McFaddon* was the first leading case in the US Supreme Court on state immunity decided in 1812. In this case a French naval vessel put into Philadelphia for repairs. The plaintiffs sought possession of the ship, as it was actually a US vessel seized on high seas during the Napoleonic wars. Chief Justice Marshall declared that the jurisdiction of a state within its own territory was exclusive and absolute but it did not encompass foreign sovereigns. He argued that perfect equality and independence of sovereigns meant that every sovereign waived the right of complete and exclusive territorial jurisdiction over the sovereign which meant the state. Therefore, the court found that the vessel in question was exempt from US jurisdiction. This was the ultimate statement of absolute immunity.

However, the rise in the commercial activities of states led to a modification of this rule of absolute immunity. In the twentieth century, states began to follow a doctrine of restrictive immunity, under which immunity was available with respect to government activity, but not where the state was engaged in commercial activity. In 1952, in the Tate letter, the US Department of State declared that the increasing involvement of governments in commercial activities coupled with the changing views of foreign states to absolute immunity rendered a change necessary and that thereafter '*the Department will follow the restrictive theory of sovereign immunity*'. This approach was followed by the courts in the United States in such cases as the *Victory Transport Inc. v Comisaria General de Abastecimientos y Transportes* and *Alfred Dunhill of London Inc. v Republic of Cuba* (66 ILR 212).

The first major case in the United Kingdom on restrictive immunity was heard by Lord Denning in 1977—*Trendtex Trading v Central Bank of Nigeria*. The Central Bank of Nigeria had issued a letter of credit in favour of the plaintiffs, a Swiss company, for the price of cement to be sold by the plaintiffs to an English company which had secured a contract with the Nigerian government to supply it with cement. The bank refused to honour the letter of credit. The plaintiffs brought an action *in personam* against the bank in the English High Court. The Nigerian bank claimed sovereign immunity. Lord Denning held that the bank was liable for the loan under the doctrine of restrictive immunity, as this case concerned a commercial contract. The relevant act was simply a breach of a commercial contract. In this case the bank was not an agent of the Nigerian government, and therefore there was no immunity at all but, even if it had been an agent, there would be no immunity on account of the commercial nature of the contract.

The second major case on restrictive immunity was *I Congreso del Partido* in the House of Lords. In this complex case there was consideration of the activities of two ships. The issue was whether the action was commercial and therefore an area of non-immune activity, or whether the ships were involved in sovereign activity. This case followed the nature and purpose of the act test to determine this important question. Lord Wilberforce emphasized that in considering whether immunity should be recognized one had to consider the whole context in which the claim was made in order to identify the relevant act which formed the basis of that claim. The court was to look at the nature of the contract and also the nature of the breach. If the contract is an act *jure imperii*, there is sovereign immunity. If it is an act *jure gestionis*, in other words, an act of a private law character, such as a private citizen might have entered into, there is no immunity. The particular issue raised in this case was whether immunity could be granted where, while the initial transaction was clearly commercial, the cause of the breach of the contract in question appeared to be an exercise of sovereign authority. In this case, two vessels operated by a Cuban state-owned shipping enterprise were supposed to deliver sugar to a Chilean company. However, the ships were ordered by the Cuban government to stay away from Chile after the Allende government was overthrown. The Cuban government pleaded sovereign immunity on the grounds that the breach of contract was a foreign policy decision. The House of Lords did not accept this and argued that once a state entered into the trading field it would require a high standard of proof of a sovereign act for immunity to be introduced.

As a result of the development in the case law, the majority of states have now accepted the restrictive immunity doctrine and this has been reflected in domestic legislation, as in the **US Foreign Sovereign Immunities Act of 1976** and the **UK State Immunity Act of 1978**. It is critical to note that they still provide a general rule of immunity with exceptions for commercial activities. This was also the approach adopted in the **European Convention on State Immunity of 1972**. The last countries that clung on to the theory of absolute immunity were the states of the former Soviet Union.

The UN in 2004 adopted the **United Nations Convention on Jurisdictional Immunities of States and their Property** which is now open for signature and will be in operation after the deposit of the thirtieth instrument of ratification. The approach in the convention is very similar to the US and UK statutes. The state is broadly defined and includes the political subdivisions and agencies and instrumentalities of the state. The test for whether an act is *jure imperii* or *jure gestionis* is a modified nature approach, which also allows courts to take into account the nature and the purpose of the transaction. This is to help developing countries promote national economic development.

First, reference should be made primarily to the nature of the contract or transaction and, if it is established that it is non-commercial or governmental in nature, no further enquiry is needed. However, if the contract or transaction appears to be commercial, then reference to its purpose should be made to determine whether the contract or transaction is truly sovereign or not. Examples of a sovereign act could be the procurement of medicine to fight an epidemic, or the procurement of food supplies.

In the convention there is an enumeration of the activities that are not subject to state immunity. These are:

1 commercial activities;

2 contracts of employment;

3 personal injury or damage to property;

4 title to or possession of property;

5 patents and trademarks; and

6 commercial shipping.

States can also waive their immunity and they often do so in arbitration agreements. There is also a regime of immunity from execution which is broader, as it often involves government assets such as embassies.

In summary, it is clear that the **UN Convention** has accepted the customary law of the restricted doctrine of state immunity but adopted the same approach of exceptions to the doctrine of absolute immunity. However, the convention only has 13 parties and will not come into effect until there are 30 states depositing instruments of ratification. Customary law in this area remains extremely important.

 Examiner's tip

The student must show knowledge of the case law that led the drafters of the **UN Convention** to the conclusion of the restricted doctrine of state immunity. The key is to develop the case law prior to consideration of the treaty as a big risk is to simply discuss the convention without the development of the case law. Knowledge of your domestic legislation in state immunity is also critical as is the development of the domestic cases.

Question 2

Until recently, Jane, a citizen of Ruritania, has been employed in Appolonia as a teacher on the Ruritanian air force base located in Appolonia. She was fired because her immediate superior did not like the fact that she wore short skirts to work. She wishes to bring an action in Appolonia against her employer for unjust dismissal. Ruritania appears before the employment tribunal at the first instance and claims state immunity. Neither party is yet a party to the **United Nations Convention on Jurisdictional Immunities of States and their Property** and there is an understanding that military activities will not be covered by that convention.

You are counsel for Jane. Advise her on the prospects of the matter proceeding in an Appolonian court.

Commentary

This case concerns a contract of employment between Jane and the State of Ruritania and she seeks to bring a claim in Appolonia. Be careful, as this problem is not as straightforward as it may seem. At first blush, the state of Ruritania is not entitled to immunity on the basis of employment contracts. However, there are two complicating factors: Jane is a citizen of Ruritania; and she is working for a government body which might just be involved in activities which still attract absolute immunity.

This problem is very similar to **Holland v Lampen Wolfe** decided in the House of Lords. You need to read this case carefully and also examine the issue of employment contracts discussed in Fox (2008). A shorter version is available: 'International law and restraints on the exercise of jurisdiction by national courts of states', in Evans (2010).

Answer plan

- Discuss the restricted doctrine of state immunity and the exception for employment contracts in both customary law and in the treaty.
- Discuss the exceptions to the doctrine of restricted immunity in the treaty and in customary law.
- Discuss relevant case law concerning the distinction between public and private activity, particularly the House of Lords' decision in **Holland v Lampen Wolfe**.
- Provide an opinion as to the outcome of this action.

Suggested answer

Jane seeks to sue in Appolonia a representative of the State of Ruritania for unjust dismissal. The critical facts are that she has been employed as a teacher on a Ruritanian air force base. This triggers an examination of the customary law of state immunity. Recently, the international community concluded a treaty on this issue. According to **Art. 5 United Nations Convention on Jurisdictional Immunities of States and their Property** a state enjoys immunity in respect of itself and its property from the jurisdiction of the courts of another state. However, there are exceptions to that absolute immunity and the convention adopts the restrictive immunity doctrine which provides for exceptions to immunity for commercial activities. However, there is a general understanding that this convention is not to cover military activities, so customary international law on state immunity is relevant. This is reasonable, as the restrictive doctrine has been accepted as part of customary law based on a long line of domestic cases.

The first item that Jane will argue is that employment is a commercial activity, and so at first glance Jane's claim seems entirely possible. Although not binding, **Art. 11(1) United Nations Convention on Jurisdictional Immunities of States and their Property** specifies that a state cannot invoke immunity before a court of another state in a proceeding which relates to contracts of employment between an individual and the state for work performed on the territory of that other state. Regrettably for Jane, even if the treaty had applied, this would not end the issue, as there are important caveats contained within the provision which apply in Jane's situation. Crucially **Art. 11(2)(a)** indicates that **para. 1** does not apply if the employee has been recruited to perform particular functions in the exercise of government authority.

As this treaty is not yet in force, and, even if it were, it will not cover military situations, it is necessary to examine the customary law doctrine of restricted immunity. According to Fox, in conducting a survey of various common law and civilian law jurisdictions, there is a clear trend towards the restricted doctrine of state immunity, which is now reflected in the convention. Therefore, it can be argued that the provisions regarding employment law might reflect customary international law. Fox argues that exceptions from state immunity which are widely recognized, include contracts of employment other that those with nationals of the sending state engaged in public service. Once again the exception seems to be the notion of public service which would be similar to the idea of functions in the exercise of government authority.

However, in this case, Jane has been a teacher on a military base and it is necessary to examine carefully the relevant case law on the distinction between regular employment and employment in the public service. This main legal issue is discussed by Fox and by Shaw who review the case law distinguishing between acts conducted either in a private or public function. Fox cites the test employed by Lord Wilberforce in *I Congreso del Partido* where he stated that the court must consider the whole context in which the claim against the state is made, with a view to deciding whether the relevant acts on which the claim is based should, in that context, be considered as fairly within an area of activity, trading or commercial or otherwise of a private law character. Or whether the relevant activity should be considered as having been done outside the area and within the sphere of governmental or sovereign activity.

Shaw indicates that there have been a number of cases on this issue particularly with regard to employment in foreign embassies. In *Sengupta v Republic of India* 65 ILR 325 the Employment Appeal Tribunal held on the basis of customary law that immunity existed for a contract of employment involving the workings of a mission since that constituted a form of sovereign activity. The Supreme Court of Canada decided *United States of America v Public Service Alliance of Canada and others* and held that the conduct of labour relations at a foreign military base was not a commercial activity. At first glance, the fact that Jane is a teacher on an air force base would not seem to be a sovereign activity, yet her situation is very similar to the House of Lords' decision in *Holland v Lampen Wolfe* (2000).

In this case the House of Lords considered the case of a US citizen who was a teacher on a US air force base in the United Kingdom. The plaintiff was arguing that a memorandum written by her superior was libel. The House of Lords granted immunity to the United States, arguing that the act concerned took place in the context of the provision of education on a military base, which was an activity serving the needs of the US military and therefore a sovereign activity. This case also cited with approval the *Littrell v United States of America (No. 2)* case which held that military treatment for US personnel on a US base in the United Kingdom was a sovereign activity.

Therefore, although Jane may have been an employed teacher, the whole context of her activity must be considered. In examining the similar cases of *Holland v Lampen Wolfe* and *Littrell*, Fox argues that, although the acts by their nature were ones which a private person might commit, they were immune because they were performed in the exercise of sovereign authority by reason of the service personnel involved and the commission of the acts in pursuance of the purpose of maintaining an efficient fighting force. It is likely, then, that Jane, who performed these same acts, will not be able to sue her employer Ruritania in Appolonian courts and that the doctrine of absolute immunity will apply.

 Examiner's tip

As the provision in the new **United Nations Convention** is not as of yet binding on many states, it is vital to develop the case law in this problem question. Furthermore, the case of *Holland and Lampen Wolfe* is a relatively recent consideration of the employment provisions and the issue of customary international law and state immunity. Knowledge of the convention and this case would be essential elements of a good answer.

Question 3

You are a lawyer for the Australian Attorney-General's department. It has come to your attention through the media that a group of Australian ex-service members and relatives of service members, who were prisoners of war of Germany during the Second World War, intend to bring civil claims of torts on claims of torture and murder.

You are a lawyer for the Australian Attorney-General's department and have been asked to prepare a memorandum on whether Australian courts could take jurisdiction in the wake of the judgment of the International Court of Justice in *Jurisdictional Immunities of States (Germany v Italy: Greece Intervening)*

Commentary

A major political issue in state immunity is whether public officials should be permitted to escape tort liability for violations of *jus cogens* rules of international law—such as the prohibition on violation of fundamental rules of humanitarian law on grounds of sovereign immunity. This is particularly so for cases arising from the Second World War. Although heinous crimes were committed by the Nazi and Japanese regimes of the day, state immunity for sovereign acts was also a well settled doctrine of customary international law. The case of *Jurisdictional Immunities of States (Germany v Italy: Greece Intervening)* is an excellent opportunity to revisit this important issue which has also occupied the European Court of Human Rights, although they dismissed the cases against Germany in that court.

Answer plan

- Discuss the importance of the new case of *Jurisdictional Immunities of States (Germany v Italy: Greece Intervening)* to the law of state immunity.
- Discuss the issue of customary international law and the definition of state immunity.
- Discuss the impact of the decision of the International Court of Justice on the issues of tort liability and violations of peremptory norms of international law. Refer to the academic literature on the issue of violations of international law and state immunity.

Suggested answer

Dear Attorney:

It is my respectful opinion that, in light of a major case in the International Court of Justice, the judgments in the Australian Courts against Japan for its treatment of prisoners of war during World War II cannot stand. Although the issue of liability in tort for crimes committed during that war has been canvassed in detail in the European Court of Human Rights and in Italian and Greek courts, these rulings were not binding on Australia. However, case law from the International Court of Justice, while not binding, is highly persuasive, particularly with respect to the interpretation of customary international law which is binding on Australia. The position of Greece is instructive in this regard. In its pleadings Greece argued that any ICJ decision on the effects of the principles of jurisdictional immunity of states would have a significant effect on pending and potential lawsuits brought by individuals before those courts—this is precisely the situation we are faced with in Australia.

The relevant case is *Jurisdictional Immunities of States (Germany v Italy: Greece Intervening)*. Germany issued a claim in the International Court of Justice against Italy alleging that by allowing civil claims based on violations of international humanitarian law by the German Reich during World War II, it had violated its obligations under international law by failing to respect the jurisdiction immunity which the Federal Republic of Germany enjoyed under international law.

State immunity is a very important doctrine of international law as it reflects according to Fox (2010) respect for state independence and equality. **Article 2(1)** of the **United Nations Charter** confirms that the principle of sovereign equality is a fundamental principle of the international legal order. Included in sovereignty is the jurisdiction of states over their own people. State immunity according to Fox (2010) is the protection of the legal entity of the state itself from another state's courts. Balanced against this are the responsibilities of states to the international community '*erga omnes*' not to violate fundamental norms of international law, norms of *jus cogens*.

Importantly, in this recent case before the ICJ, the court canvasses customary international law on state immunity, as, although Germany is one of the eight states parties to the **European Convention on State Immunity of 16 May 1972**, Italy is not a party and the convention is accordingly not binding upon it. Neither state is party to the **United Nations Convention on the Jurisdictional Immunities of States and their Property**, adopted on 2 December 2004 (hereinafter the 'United Nations Convention'), which is not yet in force in any event as it requires 30 ratifications. In its discussion of customary international law the court declared that state practice of particular significance was to be found in the judgments of national courts faced with the question of whether a foreign state is immune. Also important practice are domestic legislation on state immunity, the claims to immunity advanced by states before foreign courts, and the statements made by states in the extensive study of the subject by the International Law Commission and with respect to the adoption of the **United Nations Convention**. *Opinio juris*, according to the ICJ, was reflected in the assertion by states claiming immunity that international law accords them a right to such immunity from the jurisdiction of other states; in the acknowledgement, by states granting immunity, that international law imposes upon them an obligation to do so; and, conversely, in the assertion by states in other cases of a right to exercise jurisdiction over foreign states.

The court begins by classifying the acts alleged to have been committed by German soldiers (in this case murders and forced labour) as *acta jure imperii*. These are acts of a state's sovereign power and whether they were lawful or not is not relevant to the consideration of state immunity. In this case the parties and the court agreed that states are generally entitled to immunity in respect of *acta jure imperii*. This is a rule of customary law also included in the **European** and **United Nations Conventions**. However, Italy argued that customary international law had developed to the point where a state was no longer entitled to immunity in respect of acts occasioning death, personal injury, or damage to property on the territory of the forum state (the state in which the court case is launched), even if the act in question was performed *jure imperii*. The court refused to rule on whether there was a tort exception to state immunity as reflected in **Art. 12** of the **UN Convention** (not in force). The court narrowed the issue to acts committed on the territory of the forum state by the armed forces (and other state organs working with the armed forces) of a foreign state, in the course of conducting an armed conflict.

Article 12 of the **United Nations Convention** is so important that it will be set out in full and would have a serious impact on this opinion were it to be in force for Australia. It states:

> Unless otherwise agreed between the States concerned, a State cannot invoke immunity from jurisdiction before a court of another State which is otherwise competent in a proceeding which relates to pecuniary compensation for death or injury to the person, or damage to or loss of tangible property, caused by an act or omission which is alleged to be attributable to the State, if the act or omission occurred in whole or in part in the territory of that other State and if the author of the act or omission was present in that territory at the time of the act or omission.

Unlike the **European Convention**, the **United Nations Convention** contains no express provision excluding the acts of armed forces from its scope. Therefore, if the convention was in force, suits in another country for tort against a state for compensation for acts of this type could be permissible.

However, like the court we are required to consider customary law as it stands now. In an extensive analysis of statements to convention bodies, national statutes, decisions in the **European Court of Human Rights**, and domestic case law, the court concluded that customary international law continued to require that a state be accorded immunity in proceedings for torts allegedly committed on the territory of another state by its armed forces and other organs of state in the course of conducting an armed conflict.

The court also considered a three-part Italian argument of why the courts should be entitled to deny state immunity for these acts *jure imperii*. Firstly Italy argued that the acts giving rise to the claims were serious violations of the principles of international law applicable to the conduct of armed conflict, amounting to war crimes and crimes against humanity. Secondly, Italy maintained that the rules of international law thus contravened were peremptory norms *(jus cogens)*. Thirdly, Italy argued that the claimants having been denied all other forms of redress, the exercise of jurisdiction by the Italian courts was necessary as a matter of last resort.

The court again canvassed customary law and indicated on the first point that other than the Italian decisions, there was almost no state practice which might be considered to support the proposition that a state is deprived of its entitlement to immunity in such a case. With respect to the second point the court held that in fact there is a substantial body of practice, as confirmed in the ICJ. In addition, there is a substantial body of state practice from other countries which demonstrates that customary international law does not treat a state's entitlement to immunity as dependent upon the gravity of the act of which it is accused or the peremptory nature of the rule which it is alleged to have violated. With respect to the third argument the court declared that national courts have to determine questions of immunity at the outset of the proceedings, before consideration of the merits. Immunity could not be made dependent upon the outcome of a balancing exercise of the specific circumstances of each case to be conducted by the national court before which immunity is claimed. Lack of reparation, then, could not be a factor in considering state immunity.

This important decision closes the door on state liability in other countries for acts of its officials, even though those officials may face international criminal prosecution. As Fox (quoting Justice Guillaume) states: 'to confer on all national courts jurisdiction against a foreign State for violation of fundamental human rights affecting the physical integrity of the person would…risk creating total judicial chaos'.

 Examiner's tip

Be sure and check whether or not the **United Nations Convention on the Jurisdictional Immunities of States and their Property** is in force by having received 30 ratifications (as of the date of writing it was not in force). It would fundamentally alter the opinion in this question.

Make sure you read this decision and understand the reasoning. A longer essay may also quote the jurisprudence of the European Court of Human Rights supporting this opinion.

Make sure you address the problem by providing a letter of opinion.

 Question 4

Diplomatic immunity is one of the oldest doctrines of public international law. Given the recent attack on the Consulate in Benghazi, Libya, it also might be one of the most important.

Discuss with reference to international instruments the scope of diplomatic immunity.

Commentary

Another issue frequently canvassed is the issue of diplomatic immunity, one of the oldest and accepted doctrines of public international law. There are two relevant conventions that must be discussed in this answer: the **Vienna Convention on Diplomatic Relations 1961** and the **Vienna Convention on Consular Relations 1963**. An excellent source to prepare this question is Wickremasinghe (2006).

Answer plan

- Define diplomatic law and diplomatic immunity.
- Discuss the customary international law in this area.
- Discuss the **Vienna Convention on Diplomatic Relations**.
- Discuss the **Vienna Convention on Consular Relations**.

Suggested answer

Wickremasinghe defines diplomatic law as the law by which international relations are conducted, and the processes of communications at the public international level are facilitated. Diplomatic immunity is the immunities that officials of states and international organizations enjoy from the jurisdiction of other states. This is a self-contained regime which includes rights for sending and receiving states of diplomatic and consular missions.

There are two major treaties governing this area. Wickremasinghe also argues that diplomatic law is not fully codified and certain categories of those working in international relations therefore enjoy immunity only by virtue of customary international law. He gives the example of the law governing the privileges and immunities of foreign heads of state and other senior government officials which remains largely uncodified at the international level. There are two types of customary law immunity—the first is immunity *ratione personae*. These immunities are enjoyed by certain categories of state officials by virtue of their offices. These immunities are often wide enough to cover both the official and private acts of such office holders and therefore such persons will enjoy personal inviolability (including freedom from arrest or detention) and absolute immunity from criminal jurisdiction. The second is immunity *rationae materiae*—these immunities attach to the official acts of state officials. According to Wickremasinghe, they are determined by reference to the nature of the acts in question rather than the person. These may apply to official acts of visiting state officials.

The first major treaty governing this area is the **Vienna Convention on Diplomatic Relations 1961**. This treaty is one of the most widely ratified of all international conventions. Some of the provisions reflecting long-term practice clearly also reflect customary international law. This treaty sets out in **Art. 2** that diplomatic relations take place by mutual consent. The various immunities of the diplomats and their missions begin with **Art. 22** which specifies that the premises of a foreign mission shall be inviolable. An example of practice in this area was the St James's Square incident of 1984 in which a police officer on patrol was killed in front of the Libyan Peoples Bureau in London from a shot fired from within the bureau. The UK Parliament and the UK government considered whether an amendment to this absolute bar should be sought, but rejected the idea. In **Art. 22(2)**, the receiving state has a special duty to take all appropriate steps to protect the mission. A famous case that dealt with this issue was *United States Diplomatic and Consular Staff in Tehran (US v Iran)* **ICJ Reports 1980**. In that case the court held that even though the demonstrators that took the embassy staff hostage were not acting on behalf of Iran, Iran was responsible for having failed to protect the premises. It is important to note, then, that it is not just diplomatic immunity which is preserved, but the obligation is on all nations to protect all diplomats stationed there. This might well be an issue again when one considers the situation in Benghazi when the Libyan officials failed or were unable to protect the consulate.

Articles 23–30 provide for immunities enjoyed by members of the mission. These include the inviolability of the private residence of a diplomat, immunity from taxes and customs, and, crucially, that the diplomatic bag containing correspondence may not be opened. **Article 31** is the first provision on jurisdictional immunities. Wickremasinghe summarizes the provisions that diplomatic agents and their families enjoy (provided they are not nationals of the receiving states), which include immunities such as freedom from arrest and detention and absolute immunity from criminal jurisdiction. A diplomatic agent is also immune from civil and administrative jurisdiction except in three types of cases:

1   a real action relating to immovable property situated in the receiving state, unless the diplomatic agent holds it on behalf of the mission;

2   an action in relation to succession in which the diplomatic agent is involved as an executor, administrator, heir, or legatee as a private person; and

3   an action relating to any professional or commercial activity exercised by the diplomatic agent in the receiving state outside the diplomatic agent's official function.

There are slightly lesser immunities afforded to administrative and technical staff, service staff, and diplomatic agents who are not nationals of the sending state. Their immunities only extend to immunity *ratione materiae* in respect of their official acts. An important limitation is that under **Art. 32** immunity could be waived and the local court enjoy jurisdiction. However, this is rare and ordinarily the sending state will simply recall the diplomat home for disciplinary action. The receiving state could also choose to expel the diplomat and that often happens when there is a suspicion of espionage.

The second relevant treaty is the **Vienna Convention on Consular Relations 1963**. Wickremasinghe argues that the role of counsels is to represent the sending state with an emphasis on technical and administrative matters, rather than political matters. The scheme of the treaty is very similar to the **Diplomatic Relations** treaty. The difference is that consular officers enjoy a more limited personal inviolability; they may not be arrested or detained except in the case of a grave crime—pursuant to a decision of a competent judicial authority (**Art. 41**). They also only enjoy immunity *ratione materiae* in respect of acts performed in the exercise of their consular function. Therefore, acts performed in their private capacity could result in enforcement by the country of their residence.

Wickremasinghe argues that despite the considerable constraints that these immunities place on the territorial jurisdiction of the receiving state, states generally observe them scrupulously. Although the Libyan and Iranian incidents are quite well known, there has been very little violation of the provisions of the two **Vienna Conventions**. A current controversy includes the payment of the congestion charge by the United States Embassy in London. The United States has taken the position that this charge is taxation and has refused to pay the amount owed. This area of the law will continue to cause controversy over the behaviour of some diplomats, but it illustrates the reciprocity of international law in that all countries seek to respect the provisions, so that their diplomats will be protected wherever they may serve.

 Examiner's tip

The examiner will be searching for detailed knowledge of the two relevant treaties. It would be worthwhile to discuss the situation in Tehran, Iran and the current attack on the consulate in Benghazi as examples of egregious violations of the immunity afforded to the persons, embassies, and consulates of states.

Further reading

Brownlie, I., *Principles of Public International Law*, 7th edn (Oxford: Oxford University Press, 2008).

Fox, H., *The Law of State Immunity*, 2nd edn (Oxford: Oxford University Press, 2008).

Fox, H., 'International law and restraints on the exercise of jurisdiction by national courts of states' in M. Evans, *International Law*, 3rd edn (Oxford: Oxford University Press, 2010).

Hafner, G., Kohen, M., and Breau, S., (eds), *State Practice Regarding State Immunities* (The Hague: Martinus Nijhoff, 2006).

Shaw, M., *International Law*, 5th edn (Cambridge: Cambridge University Press, 2003).

Wickremasinghe, C., 'Immunity of state officials and international organizations' in M. Evans, *International Law*, 3rd edn (Oxford: Oxford University Press, 2010).

11

State responsibility

Introduction

The law of state responsibility is one of the most challenging and interesting areas of international law. It is as a result of the breach of their international obligations by states that most international disputes arise. Jennings and Watts (1992) define the concept as a state, the main legal subject of public international law, bearing responsibility for its conduct in breach of international obligations. Therefore, responsibility attaches to a state by virtue of its position as an international person. To study the law of state responsibility is to study the legal consequences that might result from breaches of international agreements or custom. As Shaw (2008) indicates, the focus of analysis in this area is on principles concerned with second-order issues, in other words, the procedural and other consequences flowing from a breach of a substantial rule of international law. This area of study is now made much clearer with the adoption on 9 August 2001 of the **Articles of State Responsibility** by the International Law Commission (ILC). The General Assembly (GA) by **Resolution 56/83** of **12 December 2001** annexed the text of the articles and commended them to governments.

This chapter contains two types of questions, those which focus on the responsibility of states for protection of foreign residents and visitors (once known as aliens) and those which focus on economic disputes, particularly the expropriation of foreign property. Both types of questions must include discussion of the provisions of the **Articles of State Responsibility**. It is also very important in this complex area to be familiar with the large body of relevant case law. The sources for much of this case law are international arbitration commissions established between countries such as Mexico and the United States, and Iran. These commissions assessed claims for international responsibility.

There is a great deal of reading to be done in this area and the chapters on state responsibility are always voluminous in the textbooks. An important source which is of great assistance in this area is Crawford (2002). It not only contains authoritative statements (from the ILC's special rapporteur on state responsibility) on the meaning of the various articles and an excellent introduction to the subject with summaries of the pertinent case law, but it also contains a good bibliography on the subject useful for revision. Another useful and concise source is Crawford and Olleson, 'The nature and forms of international responsibility' in Evans (2010). The Lauterpacht Centre of International Law also has a project on state responsibility with voluminous materials from the International Law Commission on their website. A relevant International Court of Justice decision considering state responsibility for trans-boundary pollution is the ***Pulp Mills on the River Uruguay (Argentina v Uruguay)*** case Judgment 20 April 2010.

Once again, there can be a combination of essay topics and problem questions in this complex area and it is important to prepare a comprehensive outline including the relevant **Articles of State Responsibility** and the case law prior to answering any question.

? Question 1

1. What obligations does a state have in international law towards nationals of another state present within its territory?
2. If a state fails to meet its international law obligations owed to a non-national, what rights are acquired by:
    (a) the non-national individual; and
    (b) the state of nationality of that individual?

Commentary

The law of state responsibility historically began with a concern for the protection of what were termed aliens who were present in another state and fell victim to violations of international law. This question requires the student to be familiar with a number of cases from the late nineteenth to early twentieth century that were heard in various International Arbitration Commissions (IACs). Recent relevant case law is from the US–Iran Claims Tribunal located at The Hague. The reports of the many rulings in this tribunal provide a rich source of case law.

An important issue is to distinguish between the primary and secondary rules of state responsibility. The primary rules concern the standards which a state might have to meet in the treatment of aliens. The secondary rules concern how a state might be made legally responsible for the violations of these standards. This question concerns the primary rules of standards of treatment and the kinds of violations that might occur and the secondary rule issue of who might pursue the claim on behalf of the alien.

Answer plan

- Definition of the law of state responsibility and the secondary rules of state responsibility.
- Describe the jurisprudence relative to the primary rules of state responsibility towards aliens.
- Discuss the controversy over a national or international standard on treatment of aliens.
- Establish the jurisdiction of the state to pursue claims on behalf of its nationals.

Suggested answer

State responsibility is defined as liability of a state for failure to observe obligations imposed by rules of international law. This is known in international law as responsibility. Examples of breach of the rules of state responsibility are: a state failing to honour its treaty obligations; a state violating the territorial integrity of another state; a state damaging the territory or property of another state; where a state employs armed force against another state; where state officials injure the diplomatic representatives of another state; where officials of a state mistreat the nationals of another state. This mistreatment could include violations of the right to life, torture, expropriation of property, unlawful imprisonment, or violations of the right to fair trial, to name but a few.

The **Articles of State Responsibility** adopted by the ILC in 1996 and recommended to state by the GA by **Resolution 56/83 of 12 December 2001** lists the secondary rules of state responsibility. This means the provisions that set out the way that liability is determined and sets out the consequences to the state of the violation of the primary rules. **Article 1** specifies that every internationally wrongful act of a state entails the international responsibility of that state. In the *Chorzow Factory* case in the Permanent Court of International Justice (PCIJ) the ruling established that it is a principle of international law that any breach of an engagement involves an obligation to make reparation.

The primary rules of international law of state responsibility developed as a result of concern over treatment of aliens (not extra-terrestrials!), i.e. persons residing in a country other than their country of nationality. As one might expect these claims arose out of injury to persons or property and often led to arbitration commissions between two nations to resolve these issues of state responsibility.

However, within the jurisprudence of these commissions, a major international controversy was over a minimum international standard or national standard in treating aliens. In Latin American the *Calvo* doctrine was formulated which held that aliens are only to be accorded such rights as nationals and have to seek redress for grievances in the domestic arena. According to Shaw (2008), the developed states of the West argued historically that there exists an international minimum standard for the protection of foreign nationals. The case law seems to support that position. In the *Neer Claim* in the US–Mexico Claims Commission, a US superintendent of a mine in Mexico had been killed. The commission held that the propriety of governmental acts should be put to the test of international standards and that the treatment of an alien to constitute an international delinquency should amount to an outrage, to bad faith, to wilful neglect of duty or to an insufficiency of governmental action so far short of international standards that every reasonable and impartial individual would readily recognize its insufficiency.

In the *Garcia* case, the same commission emphasized that there existed an international standard concerning the taking of human life and in the *Roberts* claim reference was made to the test whether aliens were treated in accordance with ordinary standards of civilization. The test involved improper administration of civil and criminal justice as regards an alien. See also the *Janes* claim, where a US citizen was killed in Mexico. The identity of the murderer was known, but no action was taken for eight years. The widow was awarded £12,000 in compensation for the non-apprehension and non-punishment of the murderer.

The PCIJ in *Certain Interests in the Polish Upper Silesia* supported this position by recognizing that there was a common or generally accepted international law respecting the treatment of aliens which was applicable in spite of municipal legislation. However, Shaw (2008) argues, in examining all of these cases, that the standard of treatment was not clear. However, one could take issue with that opinion, as the case law certainly seems to conform to the basic human rights that were later developed by the UN. These arbitration cases concerned right to life, detention, criminal justice, and torture, all of which have standards later specified in international human rights law.

In 1958 Garcia-Amador, in a report on international responsibility to the ILC, argued that the two approaches were now synthesized in the concept of international recognition of the essential rights of humankind. The two principles are that aliens have the same rights as nationals which should in any case not be any less than the fundamental human rights recognized and defined by international agreements. At the time, the ILC was deadlocked over international versus local standards and did not adopt this approach, but, as Shaw points out, international human rights law has developed since 1957 and the **United Nations Declaration on the Human Rights of Individuals who are not Nationals of the Countries in which They Live (GA resolution 40/144)** and concern with migrant workers have led to a final resolution that a minimum international standard applies with regards to civil and political rights.

Another key issue in the law of state responsibility is the right to make a claim. In the PCIJ's *Mavrommatis Palestine Concessions Case (Greece v UK)*, the court stated that it is an elementary principle of international law that a state is entitled to protect its subject, when injured by acts contrary to international law committed by another state, from whom they have been unable to obtain satisfaction through the ordinary channels. A state is asserting its own rights but it is totally discretionary on the state. The injured non-national has a responsibility to pursue domestic remedies but, if they are exhausted or not available, then it is up to the injured non-national's state of nationality in its own discretion to pursue the claim. There is no provision for the national of the state with the right to make the claim to force the state to claim and often diplomatic or policy considerations intervene. The individual has every right to his or her domestic remedies in the state where he or she has suffered the financial and/or personal injury but if those remedies are not successful or inadequate and his or her home state refuses to pursue the claim, the matter ends there. This may seem unduly harsh but the whole basis of state responsibility is the right of the state to pursue international claims against another state.

 Examiner's tip

In this question the student is required to discuss the arbitration cases that laid the foundation for responsibility of states towards aliens. It is also critical to discuss the development of human rights standards that now establishes the minimum standard necessary.

 Question 2

You are the Attorney-General of Pakistan. It has been brought to your attention that groups of al-Qaeda terrorists are training in your North-West Frontier provinces and that some of your security forces are conducting the training and that some of your defence officials are providing the group with arms.

You must advise the Prime Minister of Pakistan whether other countries could argue, based on the international law of state responsibility, that any conduct of al-Qaeda in any other countries could be attributed to your state.

 Commentary

As there are numerous persons who act or purport to act on behalf of a state it is vital that you demonstrate an understanding of how the conduct of those officials can be attributed to the state. This is a threshold consideration; before any court or tribunal can consider defences or matters of compensation the conduct has to be attributed to a state.

This answer must contain reference to a number of key cases on the law of state responsibility and complete discussion of the **Articles of State Responsibility**. It is fortunate that the leading textbooks discuss the doctrine of attribution and the relevant cases as does the commentaries to the **Articles of State Responsibility** in Crawford (2002).

Answer plan

- Discuss in detail the relevant **Articles of State Responsibility** on attribution.
- Describe how conduct might be imputed to a state with reference to relevant case law.
- Discuss the particular issue of acts of insurrectionaries.

Suggested answer

A preliminary issue in the law of state responsibility is how a state might become responsible for the actions of its officials. As Crawford (2002) argues, one of the essential conditions for the international responsibility of a state is that the conduct in question is attributable to the state under international law. **Chapter II Articles of State Responsibility** entitled 'Attribution of conduct to a state' defines the circumstances when an act or omission is to be considered as the conduct of the state. The general rule according to Crawford is that the only conduct to be attributed to the state at the international level is that of its organs of government, of others who have acted under the direction, instigation, or control of these organs; these are called agents of the state. A case that considers these rules of attribution in the Articles as reflecting customary international law is the *Application of the Convention on the Prevention and Punishment of the Crime of Genocide (Bosnia and Herzegovina v Serbia and Montenegro)*, the 2007 Judgment of the ICJ. In determining what constitutes an organ of a state for the purposes of responsibility, the internal law and practice of each state are of prime importance. But while the state is free to determine its internal structure, international law has an important role. The example given by Crawford is that the conduct of certain institutions performing public functions and exercising public powers, such as the police, would be attributed to the state even if those institutions were regarded domestically as autonomous of the executive of the government.

Chapter II contains eight articles (**Arts 4–11**). First, **Art. 4** sets the basic rule in international law that the conduct of any state organ shall be considered an act of state, whether the organ exercises legislative, executive, judicial, or any other function. This rule was confirmed by the ICJ in the *Application of the Convention on the Prevention and Punishment of the Crime of Genocide* Judgment as being a rule of customary international law.

Article 5 specifies that the conduct of a person or entity which is not an entity of the state but which is empowered by the law of that state to exercise elements of governmental authority is an act of that state. This rule was used in a case before the Iran–US Claims Tribunal in the case of *Hyatt International Corporation v Government of the Islamic Republic of Iran*, where a foundation established by the state of Iran held property for charitable purposes and its powers included identification of property for seizure. The tribunal held that this foundation was a public entity. However, in *Schering*

Corp v Iran a US company was expropriated by the workers' council. The Iran–US Claims Tribunal held Iran was not responsible, as the workers' council, although brought into being by the state, was not intended to function as an organ of state.

Article 6 deals with a particular case and includes within state responsibility the contact of an organ placed at the disposal of a state by another state. Article 7 is perhaps the beginning of the departure from the straightforward situation and interestingly attributes state responsibility to persons or entities empowered to exercise elements of governmental authority *even if it exceeds* its authority or contravenes instructions. The *Caire* case helped to formulate this rule. This case involved two Mexican officers murdering a French national after he refused to pay them money. The commission stated that even though these officers acted outside of their authority, Mexico was responsible because the two officers acted under the cover of their status and used means (arms) at their disposal because of their status.

Article 8 widens the ambit to the conduct of a person or group if it acts under the instructions of, or under the direction or control of, that state. This was a key issue in *Military and Paramilitary Activities in Nicaragua*, where the ICJ held that although the United States was not responsible for all acts of the rebel group the *contras*, they were responsible if they had actually been in effective control of the military or paramilitary operations, that is giving directions to the *contras*. This rule is further discussed as customary in the *Application of the Convention on the Prevention and Punishment of the Crime of Genocide* case where the court was unable to attribute to Serbia the activities of those who caused the massacre at Srebrenica. The court held that the 'overall control' test proposed by the ICTY in the *Tadić* Judgment was 'unpersuasive' and maintained the *Nicaragua* test.

Article 9 is an interesting section which states that the conduct of a person or group of persons shall be considered an act of a state if the person or group of persons is in fact exercising elements of governmental authority. Crawford argues that the principle underlying Art. 9 owes something to the old idea of the *levée en masse*, the self-defence of the citizenry in the absence of regular forces. A modern example is *Yeager v Iran* in the Iran–US Claims Tribunal. A businessman was held by the Islamic Revolutionary Guard for several days then deported. The tribunal held that the revolutionary guards were acting on behalf of the new government or at least exercised elements of governmental authority. The burden was on Iran to show that the government could not control guards or that they were not exercising elements of governmental authority.

Another interesting aspect of attribution considered in the articles is liability for the acts of an insurrectional movement. Under Art. 10, an insurrectional movement which becomes the new government is then responsible for previous acts. The traditional rule as confirmed in the *Solis* case was that it was a well-established principle of international law that no government can be held responsible for a rebel group where the government itself is not guilty of breach of good faith, or of no negligence in suppressing insurrection. This rule changes, however, when an insurrectional movement becomes the new government. Crawford states that this is justified on the basis of continuity which exists between the new state and the insurrectional movement. Effectively, the same entity which had the characteristics of an insurrectional or rebel movement now became the established government and was, therefore, responsible for those acts.

The final rule of attribution is that conduct which is not attributable to a state under any of the preceding articles in **Art. 11** shall be considered an act of state under international law if and to the extent that the state acknowledges and adopts the conduct in question as its own. The ICJ in *United States Diplomatic and Consular Staff in Tehran* considered this doctrine. In that case it was held that Ayatollah Khomeini announced a policy of maintaining the hostage situation, thereby accepting the conduct of the students as Iranian conduct.

These rules of attribution confirm existing ICJ case law and provide an extensive list of rules to enable a state to be held responsible for a wide range of conduct, including conduct of terrorist groups within their borders.

 Examiner's tip

The student who understands the importance of the *Nicaragua* and *Genocide* opinions to the law of attribution will do well in this question.

 Question 3

Outline with case law examples the various defences available to a state accused of breaches of its international obligations.

 Commentary

The defences to allegations of breaches of state responsibility are a key part of the **Articles of State Responsibility**. Crawford (2002) has a complete and comprehensive discussion of the defences available together with the relevant case law.

This is an area that is well worth attempting, as the defences are clearly set out in the articles and there are interesting case law examples for each defence. However, there are complexities involved in advancing these defences and limitation clauses within most of the **Articles of State Responsibility** which should also be cited in this answer.

Answer plan

- Outline defences with reference to customary international law and the **Articles of State Responsibility**.
- Discuss the relevant case law on each defence.
- Summarize the nature of defences to state responsibility.

Suggested answer

There are defences to state responsibility that have been developed within customary international law and included in the **Articles of State Responsibility**. These defences include consent of the injured state, countermeasures, *force majeure*, distress, necessity, and self-defence. A general comment on these defences is that they are extremely difficult to advance in response to claims that a state violated its international obligations. These defences are set out in **Chapter V, Part I Articles of State Responsibility** and are entitled 'Circumstances precluding wrongfulness'.

The first and obvious defence is consent. **Article 20 Articles of State Responsibility** states that a valid consent by a state to the commission of a given act by another state precludes the wrongfulness of that act. Crawford (2002) gives examples of consent given by a state, which include commissions of inquiry sitting on the territory of another state, the exercise of jurisdiction over visiting forces, humanitarian relief and rescue operation, and the arrest or detention of persons on foreign territory.

The next defence in the articles is self-defence as set out in **Art. 21**. A state is precluded from wrongfulness if it is taking action in self-defence in conformity with the **UN Charter**. It has to be noted that the self-defence has to be in conformity with the Charter which includes obligations of reporting to the Security Council. There are also customary law limitations of necessity and proportionality.

The **Articles of State Responsibility** next list countermeasures in **Art. 22** as a defence even though these acts might not be in conformity with an international obligation; countermeasures is now the preferred term for reprisals not involving the use of force. A state whose demands for reparation have not been met is entitled not to comply with one or more of its obligations towards the state committing the wrongful act, but it may not include the threat or use of force or extreme economic or political coercion designed to endanger the territorial integrity or political independence of the state. Countermeasures must be proportional to the wrong incurred.

The next defence is if the internationally wrongful act is due to *force majeure* which is defined as an occurrence of an irresistible force or to an unforeseen external event beyond the control of the state which has made it materially impossible for the state concerned to conform with the international obligations in question. There are particular exclusions within **Art. 23 Articles of State Responsibility**. It does not apply if the situation of *force majeure* is due to the conduct of the state invoking it or if the state has assumed the risk of that situation occurring. There are a number of cases that consider this defence—see the *Gill* case, where a British national had his house destroyed in Mexico as a result of a sudden uprising. The Arbitration Commission held that the Mexican government could not be held responsible because it was not due to negligence but a genuine inability to act. However, as Shaw (2008) argues, the standard of proof is high. This is evident in the *Serbian Loans* case, in which the PCIJ declined to accept the claim that the First World War made it impossible for Serbia to repay loans. Finally, in the *Rainbow Warrior* case, *force majeure* was raised by France when it argued that French agents were repatriated to France without the consent of New Zealand due to medical emergency. The tribunal stressed that the test of the applicability of this doctrine was one of absolute and material impossibility and a circumstance rendering performance of an obligation more difficult or burdensome did not constitute a case of *force majeure*.

The next defence—distress—means that wrongfulness is precluded in the case of a state acting in conformity with an international obligation binding upon it if the author of the conduct concerned had not other means in a situation of extreme distress of saving his life or that of the person entrusted to his care. Once again there are clauses in the articles limiting this defence. It does not apply if the situation of distress is because of the conduct of the state invoking it or if the act in question is likely to create a comparable or greater peril. Usual examples of distress in practice are aircraft or naval vessels entering foreign airspace or ports without permission resulting from technical or bad weather conditions. The difference between distress and *force majeure* according to Shaw is that in the former there is an element of choice, but that choice is between observance of an obligation which would lead to inevitable loss since distress in this context is to be equated with extreme peril and breach of that obligation. The key case example again given by Shaw and Crawford is the *Rainbow Warrior* arbitration which reviewed the elements of this defence in relation to the French repatriating their two agents who were imprisoned on the Island of Hao according to an agreement between France and New Zealand. Although the arbitration tribunal considered the defence, it had to meet the following conditions to be successful:

1   The existence of very exceptional circumstances of extreme urgency involving medical or other considerations of an elementary nature, provided always that a prompt recognition of the existence of those exceptional circumstances is subsequently obtained from the other interested party or is clearly demonstrated.

2   The re-establishment of the original situation as soon as the reasons of emergency involved to justify the breach of obligation had disappeared.

3   The existence of good faith effort to try to obtain the consent of New Zealand in terms of the 1986 agreement.

The tribunal did not accept that these conditions had been met, as the illness of the agents was not life-threatening and held that France's action in removing its agents from the island where they were imprisoned was not justified.

Finally, **Art. 25** sets out the defence of necessity. Necessity is where the act concerned was the only means of safeguarding an essential interest of the state against grave and imminent peril provided that the essential interest of the second state or the international community is not seriously impaired by the act. Again there are exclusions: first, that the international obligation in question excludes the possibility of invoking necessity; and, second, it is excluded if the state has contributed to the situation of necessity. An example is the *Torrey Canyon* incident where a Libyan oil tanker ran aground off UK coastal waters and the UK bombed it to prevent a massive oil spill. It was held to be a necessary act to safeguard the essential interest of the state. It should be noted that the tribunal in the ***Rainbow Warrior*** case expressed the opinion that the defence of necessity was controversial. However, another important case that considered the exact wording of **Art. 25** is the ***Gabčíkovo-Nagymaros Project*** case in the ICJ which held that the state of necessity was a ground recognized in customary international law for precluding the wrongfulness of the act but that the conditions set out for necessity must be cumulatively satisfied. Therefore, it can be argued, based on that case that necessity is an established defence in international law and that the articles, as with all of the other defences, do express customary international law.

In conclusion, it is evident from the narrow scope of these defences and the case law decided on these issues that these defences will be very difficult to maintain.

 Examiner's tip

The student must have extensive knowledge of the ***Gabčíkovo-Nagymaros Project*** judgment. The student must also discuss all of the available defences before dismissing them. This will require reference to case law and the **Articles of State Responsibility**. Extra marks would also be given for discussion of Crawford's commentary on these defences.

 Question 4

Prima Oil, a company with headquarters in the UK, entered into an agreement in 1955 with the state of Liberationa to exploit its massive oil reserves for a period of 100 years. This agreement provided most favourable tax status to this company and most of the profits from the oil reserves are being realized in the UK. In 1999, a government of national unity took power in a military coup and declared in 2006 that it intended to nationalize all oil fields and pay only a break-up value to the companies located on these fields.

In the agreement there is an arbitration clause between the state of Liberationa and Prima Oil. You have been assigned to arbitrate the dispute.

Indicate what kinds of factors will influence your decision, what case law and legal instruments you will rely upon, and what kind of compensation Prima Oil might expect to receive.

Commentary

One of the most complex parts of the law of state responsibility is expropriation. The major legal issue is the amount of compensation that can be ordered for the loss of the business. Again there is disagreement on the standard of compensation between the post-colonial and developed countries. Students must be familiar with the range of case law available on this issue.

The student who attempts this question should be aware of the difficulty involved and should only be attempting this answer if the aim is to obtain a first class mark! The lecturer will be most impressed if this answer is attempted. The sources to review for this question would be: Brownlie (2008), which has a section on the expropriation of foreign property; Harris (2010) contains sections from the key expropriation cases, and provides an excellent place to start in researching this important area.

Answer plan

- Discuss the general law of reparations or damages arising out of breach of state responsibility as set out in **Chorzow Factory**.
- Discuss the GA resolutions dealing with expropriation, and the debate over compensation.
- Apply the relevant case law to this issue.

Suggested answer

As arbitrator in the case between Prima Oil and the state of Liberationa, I am aware that a primary rule in the law of state responsibility is the obligation of a state to make reparation for its international wrong. This is obviously the case when private assets are seized or expropriated by a state, which is the situation in this case. The first relevant case is the **Chorzow Factory (Germany v Poland)** case decided in 1928. There was a seizure by Poland of a factory at Chorzow contrary to the **Geneva Convention 1922** between Germany and Poland on Upper Silesia. There was a claim by Germany for damage caused by what was called an illegal expropriation. This case in the PCIJ held reparation '*must, as far as possible, wipe out all the consequences of the illegal act and re-establish the situation which would, in all probability have existed if that act had not been committed*'.

In the case at hand we first must determine whether we are dealing with a seizure of property such as the **Chorzow Factory** or an expropriation. In either case the principle of reparation must be borne in mind but it might affect the final award. For the purposes of this arbitration, 'expropriate' can be defined as the compulsory taking of private property by a state, which was the case in these circumstances. It has become a very important area of state responsibility according to Shaw (2008) because the expansion of Western economies since the nineteenth century resulted in investment in the developing areas of the world. However, with the granting of independence to former colonies, the influence of Western companies has come under pressure and there are cases all over the world of companies being nationalized. Nationalization is a perfectly legal tool of economic and social reform. However, at the same time, there is a requirement under international law to make reparation.

According to Shaw, there are circumstances, however, where it might be held (as the court did in *Chorzow*) that an expropriation is unlawful, either because of the discriminatory manner in which it was carried out or because of there being no offer of, or inadequate, compensation. Liberationa has only offered break-up value to Prima Oil and therefore might be offering inadequate compensation. It should be noted, however, that one of the most controversial areas in expropriation is to determine the appropriate level of compensation.

A first requirement of expropriation as established by the PCIJ in *Certain German Interests in Polish Upper Silesia* is that expropriation must be for reasons of public utility, judicial liquidation, and other measures. I am prepared to find in this case that the expropriation was for a public purpose. The next issue is that it should be done without discrimination. In the *BP v Libya* arbitration case the reason for expropriation of the BP property was the Libyan position that the UK had been a party in urging Iran to occupy the Persian Gulf Islands. The arbitrator in that case held that the expropriation violated international law, as it was discriminatory in character. I am not prepared to find such evidence in this case, as there was an intention by the government of Liberationa to nationalize *all oil fields* not just those belonging to the United Kingdom.

I am urged to consider different standards of compensation. Prima Oil has brought my attention to the formula proposed by US Secretary of State Hull developed during expropriations of US property in Mexico. This standard is for prompt, adequate, and effective compensation. Liberationa urges me to use the formula provided in the **1962 General Assembly Resolution on Permanent Sovereignty over Natural Resources** which uses the phrase '*appropriate compensation*'. They support their argument that this resolution should apply by stating that the arbitrator in the *Texaco v Libya* arbitration approved of this formula as part of customary international law. In the *Aminoil* arbitration case the tribunal held that the standard of appropriate compensation codifies positive principles. The tribunal in that case also provides assistance as to how compensation might be determined under this standard by taking into account all the relevant circumstances. However, Liberationa asks that I go even further by only using domestic considerations in my determination as per the **1974 Charter of Economic Rights and Duties of States**. It accepts that the 1962 resolution was linked to both international and domestic law. Liberationa also refers me to the **1973 General Assembly Resolution 3171 declaring a New International Economic Order** which argues that each state is entitled to determine the amount of possible compensation and the mode of payment.

Although I can accept that there were incidents of compensation being paid according to domestic guidelines, there have been more recent legal developments which support the Prima Oil position. **Section IV(1) World Bank Guidelines on the Treatment of**

Foreign Direct Investment mandates that a state may not expropriate foreign private investment except where it is done in accordance with applicable legal procedure, in pursuance of a public purpose, without discrimination, and upon payment of *appropriate compensation*. **Article 13 European Energy Treaty** goes even further and returns to the Hull formula of prompt, adequate, and effective compensation.

I am, therefore, satisfied that the appropriate formula for compensation in this case should be in accordance with the World Bank guidelines of appropriate compensation but in accordance with international and domestic considerations. I rely also upon the case of ***Amoco International Financo Corp. v Iran*** heard in the US–Iran Claims Tribunal, in which the claimant was a Swiss company, a wholly owned subsidiary of Standard Oil, which entered in 1966 a joint venture with an Iranian company but the agreement was declared by Iran to be null and void. The arbitrator held that expropriation for nationalization is legal for public purposes. In this case it was ordered that there was a lawful expropriation and therefore fair compensation was ordered. The business was valued as a going concern. This is precisely the formula then which should be applied to Prima Oil and it should be valued as a going concern.

 Examiner's tip

The cases in this question are difficult and the excellent answer will organize and discuss them in detail. It is particularly important to give a clear but supported opinion on compensation. You must support your answer with the admittedly divided jurisprudence on oil arbitrations.

Further reading

Brownlie, I., *Principles of Public International Law,* 7th edn (Oxford: Oxford University Press, 2008).

Crawford, J., *The International Law Commission's Articles on States' Responsibility* (Cambridge: Cambridge University Press, 2002).

Crawford, J. and Olleson, S., 'The nature and forms of international responsibility' in M. Evans, *International Law*, 3rd edn (Oxford: Oxford University Press, 2010).

Harris, D. J., *Cases and Materials on International Law*, 7th edn (London: Sweet & Maxwell, 2010).

Jennings, R. and Watts, A., (eds), *Oppenheim's International Law*, 9th edn (London: Longman, 1992).

Shaw, M., *International Law*, 6th edn (Cambridge: Cambridge University Press, 2008).

12

Arbitration and judicial settlement of disputes

Introduction

Although it is argued that international law does not have a developed system of enforcement, there is an active dispute resolution system dealing with more and more international cases. The questions in this chapter will concentrate on this legal system for peaceful settlement of disputes, including the international system of arbitration and the procedures of binding judicial decisions and advisory Opinions in the International Court of Justice (ICJ). As resort to settlement of international disputes is one of the primary aims of the UN and incorporated in **Chapter VI UN Charter,** this topic is often discussed just before the topics on the use of force. Students are expected to understand the various methods of dispute settlement short of the final option of resorting to armed conflict.

The main judicial institution in the international system for binding dispute settlement is the ICJ. The **Statute to the International Court of Justice** is appended to the **UN Charter** and students are expected to have an understanding of the unique structure and procedure of the ICJ. Questions on the ICJ will elucidate the two types of cases heard—contested cases between states and advisory Opinions. It is critical that the student is familiar with the evolving jurisprudence in international law, particularly those emanating from the ICJ and the Permanent Court of Arbitration (PCA).

The chapter will begin with a general question on dispute settlement and then follow with three specific questions about the practice and procedure of the ICJ, as it is the most important and the busiest institution of adjudication of disputes. There is a question concerning the unique international mechanism of international organizations requesting advisory Opinions. Further, there is a question on the complicated preliminary issue of the court's jurisdiction. Finally, there is a question on whether the ICJ can review the decisions of the Security Council—that is, whether the ICJ is a body capable of judicial review of the actions of the UN.

An excellent source of reference and materials for this topic is Merrills (2005). Furthermore, the websites of both the ICJ and the PCA contain reports of their cases as well as the rules and procedures that each institution follows. Shaw (2008) contains an excellent description of the various methods of dispute settlement used in the first question in this chapter.

Question 1

Since the first Hague Conference in 1899 there has been an evolution of various methods of dispute settlement.

With reference to international instruments and jurisprudence give examples of various methods of dispute settlement as contemplated by **Art. 33 UN Charter.**

Commentary

This general question gives the student the opportunity to display knowledge of the various methods of international dispute settlement. These methods are neatly set out in **Chapter VI UN Charter** and this article should be repeated in its entirety. A good structure would be then to define the various methods suggested in the Charter with actual examples of international practice. A recent example is former Secretary-General Kofi Annan's peace plan in Syria, which although a failure, gives a good example of international mediation.

Answer plan

- Discuss the **UN Charter** provisions on dispute settlement.
- Expand on the various methods of dispute settlement and particularly emphasize the PCA.
- Discuss some leading arbitration panels.

Suggested answer

Article 2(3) UN Charter states that: '*all members shall settle their international disputes by peaceful means in such a manner that international peace and security and justice are not endangered*'. **Article 33, Chapter VI UN Charter** mandates that any parties to a dispute, the continuance of which is likely to endanger the maintenance of peace and security, *shall* first seek a solution by negotiation, enquiry, mediation, conciliation, arbitration, judicial settlement, resort to regional agencies or arrangements, or other peaceful means. It is clear that the charter system contemplates a resort to peaceful mechanism prior to any use of force. In this answer we will review these means save the resort to regional agencies. In fact, most international disputes are settled through negotiation between parties, third-party assistance, or court or arbitration procedures.

A dispute was defined by the Permanent Court of International Justice (PCIJ) in the *Mavrommatis Palestine Concessions (Jurisdiction)* case as '*a disagreement over a point of law or fact, a conflict of legal view or of interests between two persons*'.

There is no hierarchy of methods and states have a free choice unless their choice is likely to endanger the maintenance of international peace and security, in which case, under **Art. 37(1)**, they shall refer the matter to the Security Council.

Dispute settlement

Negotiation

The most common form of dispute settlement is by negotiation. Sometimes the treaties themselves specify a duty to negotiate—see the *North Sea Continental Shelf* case. Shaw (2008) gives the example of **Art. 282(1) United Nations Convention on the Law of the Sea** which specifies that the first step in a dispute is to engage in negotiation. The negotiation must be genuine and must comply with rules of good faith and not be a mere formality.

Good offices and mediation

This method involves the use of a third party in the negotiation. This process is aimed at persuading the parties to a dispute to reach satisfactory terms for its termination by themselves. Good offices can also be employed when a third party attempts to persuade one of the parties to enter into negotiations—for example, France encouraging the US–Vietnam talks.

According to Shaw, a mediator has an active and vital function seeking to cajole the disputing parties into accepting the mediator's own proposals. This can be the UN Secretary-General but often US presidents and their envoys will act, for example President Clinton's pivotal role in the Israeli–Palestinian dispute. Recently former Secretary-General Kofi Annan acted in this role for Syria and proposed a peace plan. Sadly, the conflict in Syria continued to escalate and Annan resigned from this role.

Inquiry

A commission of inquiry can be conducted by reputable observers to ascertain facts in contention in an international dispute. The 1899 Hague Conference first proposed this as an alternative to arbitration. An example given by Shaw is the Dogger Bank incident of 1904. In that case Russian naval ships had fired on British fishing boats thinking they were Japanese. This resulted in the 1907 Hague Conference support for international inquiries for settlement of disputes. This method has not been used very often, although it could be useful in settlement of disputes.

Conciliation

This method involves a third-party investigation of the basis of dispute and the submission of a report containing suggestions for a settlement. This report does not constitute a binding decision, only a proposal for settlement. It was used most often between the two world wars. The rules of conciliation were set out in the **1928 General Act on the Pacific Settlement of International Disputes** (revised in 1949). A panel of conciliation was composed of five persons, one from each side, the other three being neutral. Their investigation was to be concluded in six months and not to be held in public. This method is now proposed in a number of treaties—for example, the **1982 Convention of the Law of the Sea** and the **1985 Vienna Convention the Protection of the Ozone Layer**. This method was used in the Iceland–Norway continental shelf dispute. The panel proposed a joint development zone.

Bryan treaties

These are named after the US Secretary of State who negotiated the treaties. During 1913 and 1914, agreements were concluded with 30 nations in which pledges were made to submit troublesome issues to adjudicating panels. Many of the treaties also provided for one-year cooling-off periods which prohibited any other action until the time expired; then nations could accept or reject the commission's findings and act in their own best interests.

Adjudication or binding methods of dispute settlement

Arbitration

The **1899 Hague Convention for the Pacific Settlement of Disputes** included a number of provisions on international arbitration. Most importantly, the PCA was established at The Hague. This is not a fixed body of judges. The PCA consists of a panel of persons nominated by the contracting states—each one nominating a maximum of four, comprising individuals of known competency in international law, and of the highest moral reputation.

In a dispute, the contracting states can choose members of the tribunal from the panel. Between the years 1900 to 1932 some 20 disputes were arbitrated. Numbers fell off dramatically during the cold war but the numbers are increasing. The whole process is based on the consent of states which can be expressed in arbitration treaties.

In the PCIJ advisory Opinion *on the Treaty of Lausanne* arbitration was defined thus: *'arbitration is taken is a wide sense, characterized simply by the binding force of the pronouncement made by a third party to whom the international parties have had recourse, it may well be said that the decision in question is an "arbitral award"'*. An arbitral tribunal is competent to determine its own jurisdiction. Once an arbitral award is given, it is final and binding and adjudicators are required to base their decision on international law.

In recent years there has been an exponential rise in the number of interstate arbitrations from boundary or law of the sea disputes to bilateral investment treaty disputes which also involve commercial interests. The Iran–US Claims Tribunal was established in 1981 as an international arbitral body to adjudicate claims of US nationals against Iran and Iranian nationals against the United States as a result of seizures of property and the detention of hostages.

Another important arbitration procedure was established in the **Algiers Agreement 2000** between Ethiopia and Eritrea which established two arbitration commissions: the Boundary Commission and the Claims Commission. Each commission was composed of five members and located in The Hague and administered by the PCA. Each country appointed two commissioners who were not nationals of the country. The president of each commission was selected by the other commissioners. Provision was made whereby, if parties failed to agree on a president within 30 days, the Secretary-General of the UN would appoint a president after consultation with the parties. Both of these commissions have begun to issue influential awards which not only settle disputes but constitute important clarifications of international law.

International Court of Justice

The final element of dispute settlement is the ability to have a matter adjudicated by the ICJ. Merrills (2005) states that judicial settlement involves the reference of a dispute to permanent tribunals for a legally binding decision. The court is based on the consent of a sovereign state having a matter in dispute determined by the court. The court operates both through the Charter and through its own statute—The **Statute of the International Court of Justice**—appended to the Charter. Another way in which disputes are canvassed by this court is by way of advisory Opinions in which the main organs of the UN may ask the court's opinion on key issues of international concern, but which may also assist in resolving international disputes which was certainly the case in the *Namibia* advisory Opinion. In that case the ICJ held that South Africa's continued mandate over Namibia was unlawful and the dispute was eventually settled with South Africa relinquishing control over the territory.

 Examiner's tip

Using recent examples of any of these methods of dispute settlement would impress the examiner. Reference to the provisions in the Charter is essential as knowledge of **Chapter VI** is often neglected in favour of **Chapter VII**. Knowledge of how the International Court of Justice receives cases is also important.

Question 2

Part of the jurisdiction of the ICJ is the ability to give advisory Opinions. However, these opinions have caused some controversy in that some states argue that they have nothing to do with legal opinions and are rather politically motivated to punish certain states.

With reference to the jurisprudence of the ICJ, discuss this statement.

Commentary

A unique procedure has been developed by the **Statute of the International Court of Justice** and that is advisory Opinions set out in **Chapter IV Arts 65–8**. This question requires knowledge on the part of the international law student of the procedures set out in the statute but also examination of a sample of advisory Opinions. One advisory Opinion which discusses the procedural aspects is the first ruling at the request of the World Health Organization (WHO) to obtain an opinion on the legality of nuclear weapons which set out that the WHO did not have jurisdiction to ask for such an opinion, as its competence for activity did not include the question asked.

It is important to answer the question asked and to focus on those opinions such as the *Legality of Nuclear Weapons* advisory Opinion and the *Legal Consequences of the Construction of a Wall in the Occupied Palestinian Territory* case. Another pivotal case is the current advisory Opinion considering the independence of Kosovo, which was decided in July 2010.

Answer plan

- Set out the statutory provisions in the **Statute of the International Court of Justice** governing advisory Opinions.
- Discuss the jurisdictional aspect of requesting an Opinion.
- Provide examples of the types of advisory Opinions given.
- Conclude with a discussion of the importance of these Opinions to international law.

Suggested answer

The Statute of the International Court of Justice contains a specific part, Chapter IV, which deals with a unique procedure in the court—advisory Opinions. Under Art. 65 of the statute, the ICJ may give an advisory Opinion on any legal question at the request of whatever body may be authorized by or in accordance with the UN Charter to make such a request. The purpose is not to settle interstate disputes but rather to offer advice to the organs and institutions requesting the opinion. **Article 65(2)** speci-fies that questions upon which the advisory Opinion of the court is asked shall be laid before the court by means of a written request containing the exact statement of the question upon which an Opinion is acquired accompanied by all the documents likely to throw light upon the question. The issue that this essay is focused on is whether these questions contain political or legal Opinions. It is the opinion of this writer that these questions can be both and that the court is well able to deal with the issues placed before it.

In **Art. 67** the court delivers its advisory Opinion in open court with notice given to the Secretary-General and to the representatives of Members of the United Nations, of other states, and of international organizations immediately concerned.

There had been a similar procedure laid down before the PCIJ and from the jurispru-dence of that court it is in accepting jurisdiction that controversies occur. There are three main jurisdictional issues. The first is whether the advisory Opinion is dealing with a dispute between parties where one party refuses to proceed to dispute settle-ment. In the *Eastern Carelia* case in 1923, the PCIJ ruled that the court would not exercise its advisory jurisdiction in respect of a central issue in a dispute between the parties where one of the parties (Russia) refused to take part in the proceedings. How-ever, recently this principle has not been followed by the ICJ in the *Legal Consequences of the Construction of a Wall in the Occupied Palestinian Territory* advisory Opinion where Israel refused to take part. In the *Western Sahara* case, the ICJ gave an advisory Opinion as regards the nature of the territory and the legal ties with Morocco and Mauritania even though Spain, the administering power, objected. The case can be distinguished from the *Eastern Carelia* which was refused jurisdiction when Russia objected, as Russia was never part of the PCIJ, whereas Spain was a UN member and therefore a party to the court. For this reason, the court leans towards exercising its jurisdiction despite the objection of a concerned party.

The second issue is whether the organization is authorized to seek such an advisory Opinion. This was discussed in the *Legality of Nuclear Weapons* advisory Opinion. The court first denied the request of the WHO, as three conditions must be met:

1   the specialized agency in question must be duly authorized by the General Assem-bly (GA) to request Opinions from the court;

2   the Opinion must be a legal question; and

3   the question must be one arising within the scope of activities of the requesting agency.

The WHO mandate was the promotion of health, not peace and security, and therefore it was not a proper agency to ask for an advisory Opinion on the issue. The final Opin-ion was given on behalf of the GA. The case debated whether there was a legal question, but the court did take jurisdiction.

The third issue is the aspect of a legal question and it is in two Opinions particularly that this issue has been canvassed. The first again is the main Opinion in the *Legality of Nuclear Weapons* advisory Opinion. The issue was whether the legality of the possession or use of nuclear weapons was a legal or political Opinion. The court held that the question before posed to the court was both legal and political and that the judges were well able to deal with the legal aspects of the problem.

The second and more recent case was the *Legal Consequences of the Construction of a Wall in the Occupied Palestinian Territory* advisory Opinion where the court again took jurisdiction. There were two aspects to this objection: one that the question was too vague and the other that the question was a political rather than legal one. The court held that a lack of clarity did not prevent the question from being answered, as necessary clarifications of interpretation have frequently been given by the court. The issue of whether the question was a political one engaged both jurisdiction and propriety. In terms of jurisdiction the court had no difficulty in relying on its previous jurisprudence, that it could answer a legal question which also had political aspects. Examples of other advisory Opinions given include the *Conditions of Admission of a State to Membership in the United Nations*; *Competence of the General Assembly for the Admission of a State to the United Nations*; *Certain Expenses of the United Nations*, and *Legality of the Threat or Use of Nuclear Weapons*.

Finally, in this essay discussion should take place about the importance of these Opinions. In fact the advisory Opinions such as the *Nuclear Weapons* Opinion, the *Wall Case*, and the *Western Sahara* case contain extensive discussion about the development of customary international law particularly ideas of *jus cogens* which include self determination and the prohibition against genocide. These advisory Opinions canvass issues of critical importance to the international community which can inform the debates in the Security Council or GA. One very significant advisory Opinion was the *Certain Expenses of the United Nations* case, where the court gave an Opinion on the legality of the extremely important phenomenon of peacekeeping. Although peacekeeping was not part of the original **UN Charter,** the court held that this had been a proper activity of the GA in pursuance of international peace and security.

Advisory Opinions are a unique and important activity in the ICJ and they do much to clarify the rules of public international law in addition to giving opinion on the proper activities of the organs of the UN.

 Examiner's tip

The student must refer to the important advisory Opinions in this answer but there is also scope to emphasize some and not others. Knowledge of how an advisory Opinion is initiated is critical as states cannot ask for advice from this court, only the United Nations system.

Question 3

One of the most complex parts of an ICJ contested case is the method of determining whether the court has jurisdiction.

With reference to ICJ jurisprudence, discuss the various bases of jurisdiction.

Commentary

A great portion of the jurisprudence of both the PCIJ and the ICJ deals with the complex issue of determining jurisdiction in the court. This answer needs to contain knowledge of the provisions in the **Statute of the International Court of Justice** on jurisdiction but also on the cases that have considered this issue.

As the ICJ is a court based on the consent of sovereign states, the way in which the court assumes jurisdiction over a dispute is a matter of considerable controversy. Several cases have ruled on various aspects of this issue and the student would be well rewarded by preparing a careful outline answer. For a discussion of jurisdictional issues, see Merrills (2005). A cautionary note: this question applies only to contested cases, and not advisory Opinions, which contain issues on jurisdiction as well.

Answer plan

- Discussion of the various provisions in the **Statute of the International Court of Justice** on jurisdiction in contested cases.
- Description of the 'optional clause' procedure.
- Application of the case law to the jurisdictional issues.

Suggested answer

The first aspect of jurisdiction is that there must be a legal dispute, defined in the ***Mavrommatis*** case as a '*disagreement over a point of law or fact, a conflict of legal view or of interests between two persons*'. In the ***Bosnia Genocide*** case, at the jurisdiction phase, it was held that for a legal dispute to arise it is sufficient for the respondent to an application before the court merely to deny the allegations made even if the jurisdiction of the court is challenged.

In the **Statute of the International Court of Justice** there are two separate bases of jurisdiction: the capacity to decide disputes between states and the capacity to give advisory Opinions. Only a state can be a party in a contentious case, the court does not provide in any respect for participation as parties by individuals.

As the statute is appended to the **UN Charter** all Member States are *ipso facto* parties but even non-members can be parties on conditions determined by the GA on recommendation of the Security Council. The condition for a non-member is that the state party files a declaration before the court accepting the jurisdiction and undertaking to comply in good faith with decisions of the court—for example West Germany agreed on such a basis before becoming a member of the UN.

Article 36(1) Statute of the International Court of Justice sets out in detail the basis for consent to jurisdiction in disputes between sovereign states. The provision establishes that the jurisdiction of the court includes all cases which the parties (states) refer to it and all matters specially provided for in the **UN Charter** or in treaties or conventions in force. States can refer a dispute by means of a special agreement called a *compris*, which will specify the terms of the dispute. Merrills states that a negotiation of a special agreement is the most common method of consent to the exercise of jurisdiction and he gives the examples of Indonesia and Malaysia in the ***Ligitan and Sipadan*** case and Botswana and Namibia in the ***Kasikili/Sedudu Island*** case. A case example cited by Shaw (2008) of finding an agreement to adjudicate was ***Corfu Channel (United Kingdom v Albania)***, in which consent was inferred from letters and declarations. The court relied on a letter sent by Albania to the court, even though it was not a special agreement. This case had also been referred by the Security Council but the court did not rule on that basis which separate Opinions dealt with and stated that the Security Council should not bring in a new way of compulsory jurisdiction.

Some treaties also provide for the ICJ to have jurisdiction with respect to questions that might arise from the interpretation and application of the agreements—examples include the **Genocide Convention**, the **Convention Against Racial Discrimination**, and the various conventions dealing with hijacking. For example, in the ***Bosnia Genocide*** case, the court founded its jurisdiction upon **Art. IX Genocide Convention**.

More complex is the second major basis of jurisdiction—the **Art. 36(2)**, optional clause provision. This provision states that states which are parties to the statute may declare that they recognize as compulsory and without special agreement the jurisdiction of the court in all legal disputes concerning:

1   the interpretation of a treaty;

2   any question of international law;

3   the existence of any fact which, if established, would constitute a breach of an international obligation; and

4   the nature or extent of the reparation to be made for the breach of an international obligation.

States can file unilateral declarations accepting the jurisdiction of the court deposited with the Secretary-General of the UN. Recent ICJ documents indicate that 66 states have filed declarations, which is a small number in relation to the international community of 192 states.

Article 36(3) contains a particular limitation on optional clauses—that the declarations may be made unconditionally or on condition of reciprocity on the part of several or certain states, or for a certain time. Brownlie (2008) discusses the complexity of the optional clause provision. It is based on the principles of reciprocity which is that the lowest common factor in the two declarations is the basis for jurisdiction and thus a respondent state can take advantage of a reservation or condition in the declaration of the applicant state. An example given in Harris (2010) is the **United Kingdom Declaration** which restricts jurisdiction and will not accept jurisdiction over disputes over other members of the Commonwealth (former colonies). Cases which discuss reciprocity are the *Interhandel* and *Norwegian Loans* cases which confirmed that both sides of the dispute can rely on each other's reservations as to jurisdiction.

The key case on this area and on jurisdiction generally as discussed by Shaw is the jurisdictional phase of the *Nicaragua* case. Nicaragua had declared in 1929 that it would accept the compulsory jurisdiction of the PCIJ, but had never ratified the instrument. The United States argued that therefore Nicaragua had never become a party to the court and could not rely on **Art. 36(5)** which provided that declarations made under **Art. 36 Statute of the Permanent Court of International Justice** and which are still in force shall be deemed, as between the parties to the present statute, to be acceptances of the compulsory jurisdiction of the ICJ. The court in a rather convoluted decision on jurisdiction held that the declaration was still in force and ratification of the ICJ statute by Nicaragua transformed the potential commitment into an effective one. This decision has been very controversial and the United States was particularly unhappy and did not participate in the rest of the case.

There is a final problem with jurisdiction and that is when courts refused to take jurisdiction due to the involvement of third-party states in contentious litigation. The key example is the *East Timor* case where the court refused to take jurisdiction in the case because of the absence of a key party, Indonesia, holding that the court will not act on matters affecting a third state without its consent. In the *East Timor* case, the court felt that it would have to rule on the lawfulness of Indonesia's conduct with regard to East Timor as a prerequisite for deciding upon Portugal's claims against Australia and that it would not be lawful to proceed without Indonesia which had not consented to the court's jurisdiction.

 Examiner's tip

This is a very complex area of practice in the International Court of Justice and the student can impress the examiner by even attempting the answer. However, if attempted, extensive reference to jurisdictional disputes in the court is essential. The ICJ jurisprudence in this area is extensive and a student must thoroughly review the leading cases on jurisdiction.

Question 4

Does the ICJ have the power to review legally the decisions of the UN Security Council?

Commentary

An interesting legal issue with respect to the practice of the ICJ is whether the court is a type of supreme court with power to review the decisions by other organs of the UN. This issue came to a head with the decision in the **Lockerbie (Libya v the United States and United Kingdom)** case. There have been several scholarly articles on this subject and the student could take a strong position either for or against the proposition.

Suggestions for sources are: Akande, 'The International Court of Justice and the Security Council: is there room for judicial control of decisions of the political organs of the United Nations?' (1997); Gowlland Debbas, 'The relationship between the International Court of Justice and the Security Council in light of the *Lockerbie* case' (1994); and Alvarez, 'Judging the Security Council' (1996). This answer necessitates reference to academic literature as well as to the court's ruling in the **Lockerbie** case.

Answer plan

- Describe the nature of the court with reference to the **Statute of the International Court of Justice**.
- Discuss the **Lockerbie** ruling and the **Tadić** jurisdiction decision in the ICTY.
- Propose an opinion on this issue.

Suggested answer

A particularly contentious issue with respect to the ICJ is the question whether it has the jurisdiction to review actions by the Security Council as some type of a supreme or constitutional court. This debate came to a head with the *Case Concerning Questions of Interpretation and Application of the Montreal Convention Arising out of the Aerial Incident at Lockerbie (Provisional Measures)*. In the case at the provisional measures stage the court was faced with the issue of examining the relative status of treaty obligations and binding decisions adopted by the Security Council. In its decision on the provisional measures requested by Libya, the court accepted that by virtue of **Art. 103 UN Charter** obligations under the Charter (including sanctions decisions) prevailed over treaties. The case was resolved on settlement between Libya and the other parties on the issues involved in the hijacking and the case was withdrawn from the court before a final decision.

However, there is a well-reasoned dissent by Judge Weeramantry at the provisional measures stage in which he argues that the court should have power to review the legality of Security Council actions. Although he accepted that the ICJ does not have review or appellate jurisdiction, it is charged with deciding in accordance with international law such disputes as are submitted to it. As a judicial organ, Judge Weeramantry argued that the court may have the duty to examine from a legal point of view matters which may also be before another principal organ. After examining the *travaux préparatoires* of the UN Charter he concluded that the history of the Charter corroborated the view that a clear limitation on the Security Council's powers was that these powers must be exercised in accordance with the well-established principles of international law. As Harris (2010) points out, this opinion could lead to a number of questions. Would it be open to the court to rule that the Security Council's interpretation of what might constitute a threat to the peace was incorrect as a matter of law? Could it go further and exercise a power of judicial review over the decision on the facts in a particular case as to whether there was a threat to the peace of an act of aggression? Or over a decision to adopt a particular response (economic sanctions, the establishment of a war crimes tribunal) to a threat to the peace?

In the *Tadić* jurisdiction case ((**1996**) **35 ILM 35**) the Appeals Chamber of the International Criminal Tribunal for Yugoslavia did review the legality of the existence of the tribunal. Although it supported the powers of the Security Council under **Chapter VII** to create the tribunal, it was the fact of its having conducted a review that seems to lend support to Judge Weeramantry's opinion.

These cases have generated academic commentary. Alvarez (1996) argues that there are two positions: the realists and the legalists. The realists believe that the World Court should stay out of the Security Council's way and the legalists argue that:

1   the court needs to be the last resort defender of the system's legitimacy;

2   the Charter is a constitution of limited enumerated powers under the rule of law;

3   the court is the one institution capable of so affirming; and

4   functional parallelism, which means there is not an institutional hierarchy but that the Security Council and the ICJ have complementary but distinct functions, one primarily political, the other legal, and each should operate to permit the other to fulfil its role.

While the Security Council has wide discretion, it cannot violate fundamental rules of international law. The last point by Alvarez seems to summarize accurately Judge Weeramantry's opinion.

Alvarez correctly seems to take a middle position between both extreme views. He argues that both Security Council and the ICJ have a role to play in international peace and security and they need to coexist in a state of inevitable and sometimes desirable tension. No one model of judicial review has been articulated by the ICJ, but aspects of review of the ICJ already exist and especially through the ICJ's advisory function which has been established for some time. Alvarez predicts that the ICJ as well as other national or international courts will be required to pass on legal issues that are decided by the Security Council. It may not be on the level of a US Supreme Court review but there may be a continuum of interpretive modes.

These points are still pertinent, as the debate currently exists on whether the measures imposed by the Security Council on terrorist organizations should comply with fundamental rules of public international law. In September of 2008 the European Court of Justice in the *Kadi* decision annulled the implementation within the European Community of the UN sanctions regime against al-Qaeda, the Taliban, and their associates. The main finding of the court was that the implementation of the sanctions had inadequately respected the rights of the parties concerned, in particular their right to be heard and their right to effective judicial review. It also found that the individual's right to property had been unreasonably restricted. This decision will no doubt generate much academic commentary, but Alvarez's prediction of involvement of other tribunals has certainly come to pass.

However, the current opinion has to be that the ICJ as established and by practice does not have the power to review decisions of the Security Council. Although the court can issue Opinions on issues of peace and security as it did in the ***Nicaragua***, ***Oil Platforms***, and ***Corfu Channel*** cases it cannot rule on the legality of Security Council resolutions dealing with the same issues.

 Examiner's tip

This question requires reference to academic opinion in addition to the case law. The student is welcome to take any position provided it is based on reasoned academic opinion. These cases are rare before the court and the key case, *Lockerbie*, needs to be reviewed for both its majority and dissenting opinions.

Further reading

Akande, D., 'The International Court of Justice and the Security Council: is there room for judicial control of decisions of the political organs of the United Nations?' (1997) 46 ICLQ 309.

Alvarez, J., 'Judging the Security Council' (1996) 90 AJIL 1.

Brownlie, I., *Principles of Public International Law*, 7th edn (Oxford: Oxford University Press, 2008).

Gowlland Debbas, V., 'The relationship between the International Court of Justice and the Security Council in light of the *Lockerbie* case' (1994) 88 AJIL 643.

Harris, D. J., *Cases and Materials on International Law*, 7th edn (London: Sweet & Maxwell, 2010).

Merrills, J. G., *International Dispute Settlement*, 4th edn (Cambridge: Cambridge University Press, 2005).

Shaw, M., *International Law*, 6th edn (Cambridge: Cambridge University Press, 2008).

13 Use of force by states—unilateral

Introduction

The use of force is normally taught in two sections, unilateral use of force and collective security (multilateral use of force), so there will be two separate chapters in this book covering these topics. Quite frequently there are two use of force questions in international law exams.

This first of two chapters will contain questions which discuss the prohibition on the use of force developed both in treaty and customary international law and the accepted and contested exceptions to that prohibition including self-defence, rescue of nationals, support for democracy, and humanitarian intervention.

Success in answering these questions will depend on four elements. The first element is knowledge of the provisions in the **UN Charter** dealing with the unilateral use of force: **Art. 2(4)** and **Art. 51**. In addition, the well-prepared student will have a good understanding of the historical background to the prohibition on the use of force as developed in the **Covenant of the League of Nations** and the Kellog–Briand Pact.

The second is comprehensive knowledge of the relevant but limited International Court of Justice (ICJ) case law in this area. These cases are: the *Corfu Channel, Nicaragua, Oil Platforms, Armed Activities in the Territory of the Congo* contentious cases and the *Legal Consequences of the Construction of a Wall in the Occupied Palestinian Territory*, and the *Legality of the Threat or Use of Nuclear Weapons* advisory Opinions.

The third element will be extensive knowledge of the academic literature on the subject and a key source in this area in addition to literally thousands of academic articles is Gray (2008). Another useful monograph is Franck (2002). A hint is always to search for recent articles on any subject you might be revising. An excellent journal to search is the *Journal of Conflict and Security Law* which specializes on the use of force.

The fourth element is knowledge of the case studies in this area which are outlined in the various international law texts and Gray (2008). I often advise my students that a thorough knowledge of the history of the twentieth century is essential in understanding the law on the use of force. Students must also keep up to date on current affairs by a thorough review of the media reports on conflicts between states. Two conflicts that resulted in international reports on the important issue of self-defence are the Gaza conflict and the Russia–Georgia conflict. The United States issues National Security Strategies which discuss their position on use of force, with the most recent one released in 2010.

A danger in these questions is that the student will want to engage in a political discussion of the various actions. This is a grave mistake as this area, as with all other areas of international law, can be subject to legal analysis. There is not a large amount of case law on this topic but an important element of customary international law is composed of state practice and discussion of that practice can constitute legal analysis.

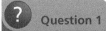 Question 1

The 2012 National Security Strategy for the United States released by Barack Obama fails to conclusively dismiss the Bush doctrine of 'pre-emptive self-defense'. Discuss.

Commentary

Since the attack on the Twin Towers on 11 September 2001, the area of self-defence has been under sustained analysis. The Bush doctrine of pre-emptive self-defence has triggered a great deal of academic debate and is not an accepted alteration to the law on self-defence. Nevertheless, it merits full academic discussion as the US National Security Strategy documents released in 2002 and 2006 include pre-emptive self-defence and the 2012 National Security Strategy fails to dismiss the doctrine.

This question necessitates a detailed discussion of the self-defence exception to the prohibition on the use of force as outlined in **Art. 51 UN Charter** and in customary international law. The major controversy concerns whether and at what stage self-defence can be exercised before an actual armed attack. This exercise of self-defence prior to an attack could be either anticipatory self-defence or pre-emptive self-defence. It is important to distinguish between these two concepts as pre-emptive self-defence could occur much earlier in the development of the conflict.

Besides the necessity to review the National Security Strategies and the standard textbooks, there are a number of academic articles on this topic. Three relevant articles are: Reisman and Armstrong (2006); Greenwood (2003); and Henderson (2010). Another interesting source is a 2006 article by Wilmshurst 'The Chatham House Principles of international law on the use of force in self-defence' which specifically addresses pre-emptive self-defence. As Henderson (2010) points out, the words pre-emptive, anticipatory, and preventive are used in different ways by different authors but in this answer it is probably only necessary to discuss the contrast between anticipatory self-defence and pre-emptive self-defence.

Answer plan

- Discuss the self-defence exception to the prohibition on the use of force.
- Introduce the controversy concerning anticipatory self-defence and pre-emptive self-defence.
- Distinguish between the possible legality of anticipatory self-defence and the lack of acceptance of legality of pre-emptive self-defence.
- Apply state practice to the issue of self-defence and draw conclusions about the legality of anticipatory self-defence.

 Suggested answer

The **UN Charter** prohibits in **Art. 2(4)** the use of force in a state's international relations subject to two exceptions: (a) where the Security Council has authorized the use of force to maintain or restore international peace and security under **Chap. VII UN Charter;** and (b) where a state is exercising its inherent right of individual or collective self-defence recognized by **Art. 51** of the Charter. Self-defence according to the *Nicaragua* case is an inherent customary law right which runs side by side with the provision of **Art. 51.** The Charter provision sets out that nothing in the Charter would impair the inherent right of individual or collective self-defence if an armed attack occurs against a member of the UN, until the Security Council has taken measures necessary to maintain international peace and security. Conditions in the article mandate that measures taken in the exercise of this right of self-defence 'shall' be immediately reported to the Security Council and shall not affect the authority and the responsibility of the Security Council to take any action it deems necessary.

The 2002 and 2006 US National Security Strategies (hereafter referred to as NSS) deal directly with the controversial issue of the meaning of an armed attack. Historically, the law and practice of self-defence dealt with such situations as: large-scale attacks by one state against another (such as the Falklands, Iraq–Kuwait); smaller-scale cross-border raids (such as Nicaragua); and government or terrorist activities injuring the nationals of another state (such as the US raids on Libya, or the Israeli rescue of its citizens in the Entebbe incident). The NSS seeks to broaden the notion of an armed attack to prevention of future attacks from terrorist groups or weapons of mass destruction. On 17 September 2002 the National Security Strategy included the statement that the United States would not hesitate to act pre-emptively against terrorists who attempt to gain or use weapons of mass destruction. Reisman and Armstrong (2006) expand on that statement and argue that the claim to pre-emptive self-defence is a claim to entitlement to use unilaterally high levels of violence to arrest an incipient development that is not yet operational or directly threatening, but that, if permitted to mature, could be seen by the potential pre-emptor as susceptible to neutralization only at a higher and possibly unacceptable cost to itself. In the 2006 NSS the claims are somewhat moderated as, although the strategy states that the place of pre-emption in the national security strategy remains the same, Reisman and Armstrong argue that the 2006 version places much more emphasis on alternatives to military pre-emption and reliance on multilateral solutions. Yet it keeps alive the debate on whether any type of military pre-emption is lawful. The 2012 Security Strategy does not address the issue of pre-emption and its discussion of '*jus ad bellum*' is confined to three paragraphs (p. 22) but as Henderson (2010) argues it does introduce a concept entitled 'necessary force' and the right to act unilaterally 'if necessary to defend our nation'. It certainly does not reject the Bush doctrine.

The concept of pre-emptive self-defence could be confused with the longstanding debate over the lawfulness of anticipatory self-defence dating from the *Caroline* case in the 1830s. This debate stems from two views of self-defence: one that suggested that self-defence was only to be exercised after an actual armed attack, and the other view that a state would have a right to act in self-defence in order to avert the threat of an imminent attack. In the *Caroline* case, Secretary Webster stated that self-defence could be used in advance of an armed attack if the necessity of self-defence was instant, overwhelming, leaving no choice of means, and no moment of deliberation. There have been disagreements among legal scholars about the lawfulness of anticipatory self-defence, although in terms of state practice, often cited is the Six Day War when Israel reacted to troops massing on its borders in advance of an actual armed attack. In this case the international community did not condemn this action; a consensus among states found that an attack was imminent. Another example given by Franck (2002) is the Cuban missile crisis where the United States imposed a naval quarantine on Cuba to force the removal of the Soviet missiles. Frank argues that the crisis revealed the support of the Western European and Western hemisphere states behind the US action. The third example is the Israeli attack on the Iraqi nuclear reactor at Osirak. In this case Israel was condemned by the international community, as there was no evidence of an imminent attack by Iraq. Frank would argue that these three examples illustrate that anticipatory self-defence could only be used in cases where an attack was probable and imminent.

Notwithstanding the international support of anticipatory self-defence under strict conditions, the NSS seek to push the limit of what has been called imminence towards a future threat. In fact the strategy is not clear about how early on an action in self-defence could be taken. The 2002 strategy argues that the United States must be prepared to stop rogue states and their terrorist clients before they are able to threaten or use weapons of mass destruction. As Reisman and Armstrong argue, pre-emptive self-defence differs from anticipatory self-defence in that those contemplating the latter can point to a palpable and imminent threat.

According to the Chatham House principles of international law on the use of force in self-defence, outlined in Wilmshurst (2006), to the extent that the doctrine of pre-emption encompasses a right to respond to threats that have not yet crystallized, such a doctrine has no basis in international law. According to these principles, the fatal flaw in reasoning is that the doctrine is dealing with threats that have not yet materialized so there is no possibility of an *ex post facto* judgment of lawfulness. This opinion is also strongly supported in the academic literature. Reisman and Armstrong argue that as one moves from an actual armed attack as the threshold of self-defence, to the palpable and imminent threat of attack, which is the threshold of anticipatory self-defence, and from there to the 'conjectural and contingent' threat of the mere possibility of an attack at some future time, which is the threshold of pre-emptive self-defence, the nature and quantum of evidence that can satisfy the burden of proof resting on the unilateralist becomes less and less defined and is often, 'extrapolative and speculative'. Greenwood (2003) does not support pre-emptive self-defence and argues that there is no right to take military action in self-defence against a threat that is not imminent.

On account of the weight of academic analysis against the concept, it can be concluded with certainty that pre-emptive self-defence is not a doctrine of public international law. It has not attracted acceptance in academic analysis nor in state practice. However, the doctrine of anticipatory self-defence has found academic acceptance and support in state practice and the key distinguishing element is the notion of imminence, a requirement not present in pre-emptive self-defence.

Examiner's tip

The key in this question is to carefully define the concepts of pre-emptive self-defence and anticipatory self-defence. It is vital to discuss the *Caroline* case and distinguish that situation from the discussions in the Bush doctrine. It is important to refer to the 2010 National Security Strategy and the Chatham House principles. The Henderson article is a concise summary of this issue and would be essential.

? Question 2

A group calling itself the Alliance has set up a group of training camps in the state of Chaotica. The state is in the middle of a civil war and does not have control over the portion of the territory that the Alliance is using. The Alliance declares a holy war on capitalist states and in the past few months has sent its members to bomb certain financial targets. During one successful attack, the state of Prospero's stock exchange was obliterated by a helicopter full of explosives flying into the building. Over 3,000 people were killed.

You are the legal adviser to the Foreign Ministry of the state of Minor Prosperity, the neighbour and close ally of Prospero. Advise your prime minister as to whether it is lawful to invade the state of Chaotica and install a new government which will not tolerate training camps on its soil.

Commentary

This problem question seeks to elicit discussion about some thorny issues in the law of self-defence. The first is whether the threshold of an armed attack is reached in the bombing of a building in another country. The second issue is the controversial one of self-defence against non-state actors and those states that harbour terrorist training camps. The third and equally complex issue is the crucial customary limitation on self-defence of necessity and proportionality. Is installing a new government a necessary and proportional use of self-defence?

The problem directly relates to the events surrounding the bombing of the World Trade Center and the Pentagon on 11 September 2001 and the subsequent invasion of Afghanistan and the removal of the Taliban regime. Although widely accepted at the time, subsequent academic analysis has raised doubts about the legality of the action. An excellent discussion of all these issues is contained in Gray (2008) and Franck (2002). Three relevant articles are: Byers, 'Terrorism, the use of force and international law after 11 September' (2002); Greenwood, 'International law and the pre-emptive use of force: Afghanistan, Al Qaida and Iraq' (2003); Cassese, 'Terrorism is also disrupting some crucial legal categories of international law' (2001).

 Answer plan

- Discuss whether the attack on the stock exchange constitutes an armed attack.
- Advise whether the state of Prospero can exercise the right of self-defence against the Alliance.
- Discuss whether it is lawful for Minor Prosperity to invade Chaotica.
- Analyse whether it is a proportionate and necessary response to the bombing of Prospero's stock exchange to install a new government in Chaotica.

 Suggested answer

As legal adviser to the state of Minor Prosperity, there are four separate aspects to the legal opinion on the international legality of the invasion of the state of Chaotica. All involve various aspects in the law of self-defence that have arisen since the attack on the World Trade Center and the Pentagon on 11 September 2001. After reviewing each in turn, I will render my opinion on whether it is lawful for Prospero to invade Chaotica and assist in the installation of a new government.

The first question is whether the attack on the stock exchange, which is very similar to the attack on the World Trade Center, is an armed attack. I would strongly argue that it is. As Greenwood (2003) argues, there is no doubt that terrorist acts by a state can constitute an armed attack and thereby justify a military response. His argument is supported by the UN General Assembly (GA) definition of aggression in 1974, which included certain types of terrorist activity committed by states. The ICJ, in the *Nicaragua* case in

1986, considered that covert military action by a state could be classified as an armed attack. The level of gravity concerning the attack on the stock market could certainly rise to that level.

The second issue is whether there is a right to take action against the Alliance. Greenwood also argues that it would be '*strange formalism*' that regarded the right to take military action against those who caused or threatened such actions as dependent upon whether or not their acts could be imputed to a state. He therefore concludes that self-defence could be exercised against terrorists themselves. He argues that the famous *Caroline* dispute supports such an interpretation as the sinking of the ship did not emanate from a state. It must be cautioned that this opinion is opposed by certain international lawyers such as Byers (2002) who argues that the right to use force against terrorists is not yet part of customary international law.

The third issue is the question of whether we can invade Chaotica who harboured the Alliance terrorist training camps. Byers argues two instances of state practice that go against the legality of such an action. In 1986, a terrorist bomb in a Berlin nightclub attributed to Libya killed a number of US soldiers. The United States responded by bombing Tripoli on the basis of self-defence against terrorist attacks. Byers argues that the claim was widely rejected by many states. The second example was the 1993 bombing by the United States of the headquarters of the Iraqi Secret Service in response to an assassination attempt made on George Bush, Sr. It claimed self-defence on the basis that the attack on the ex-president was tantamount to an attack on the United States itself. Again, Byers asserts that the claim received little support from other states. However, Cassese (2001) states that in a matter of a few days practically all states (all members of the Security Council plus members of NATO other than those sitting on the Security Council, plus all states that have not objected to resort to **Art. 51**) have come to assimilate a terrorist attack by a terrorist organization to an armed aggression by a state, entitling the victim state to resort to individual self-defence and third states to act in collective self-defence (at the request of the former state). It may well be that the attack on the World Trade Center and the reaction as encompassed in **Security Council Resolution 1368** confirming the right of self-defence in the wake of the terrorist attacks is evidence of instant customary international law. This is confirmed by Franck (2002) when he argues that it is becoming clear that a victim state may invoke **Art. 51** to take armed countermeasures against any territory harbouring, supporting, or tolerating activities which culminate in, or give rise to, terrorist attacks.

However, the fourth part of this opinion poses the most difficulty in supporting the legality of an armed response to Chaotica and installing a new legal regime. It is certainly customary international law as supported by the *Nicaragua* decision that any response in self-defence must be necessary and proportionate. Is it a necessary or proportionate response to install a new government in Chaotica, because they would or could not arrest the Alliance or dismantle their training camps? As Cassese argues the use of military force must be proportionate, and the purpose must be: (a) to detain the persons allegedly responsible for the crimes; and (b) to destroy military objectives, such as infrastructures, training bases, and similar facilities used by terrorists. The use of force in self-defence to Cassese must not be used to wipe out the Afghan leadership or destroy Afghan military installations and other military objectives that have nothing to do with the terrorist organizations, unless the Afghan central authorities show by words or deeds that they approve and endorse the action of terrorist organizations. The reason for this opinion is based in the judgment of the ICJ in *US Diplomatic and Consular Staff.* In that case the court held that the Iranian militants who had illegally occupied the US embassy and consular premises, once their action was approved and endorsed by the Iranian government, became 'agents' of the Iranian state, which therefore became internationally responsible for their action. According to Cassese, this would mean that the terrorists would have to be treated as state agents and the Afghan state itself would bear international responsibility for their actions, with the consequence that the state's political and military structures could become the legitimate target of US military action in self-defence. Furthermore, as soon as legitimate military objectives are destroyed, military action must cease. In the case of Chaotica this will be a high burden indeed as with the Taliban administration in Afghanistan there is no evidence that the Alliance was acting as agent of the government of Chaotica.

My legal opinion concludes that it is on this final condition of necessity and proportionality that the planned action of Minor Prosperity fails. It will almost certainly be lawful to attack the terrorist camps and *pursue* the terrorists, but to invade a country and install a new government seems an unnecessary and disproportionate use of self-defence.

 Examiner's tip

The student has to refer to the important jurisprudential debate in the *Nicaragua* case. Reference to the **Security Council Resolution 1373** post 9/11 is also necessary. An excellent summary of this issue can be found in Gray and reference to that text is essential.

? Question 3

You are the legal adviser to the foreign minister of the state of Narnia. You have just been told that one of your national airlines has been hijacked and your nationals are being held by a guerrilla group in the airport of the state of Upstart. The government of Upstart has not acted to assist your nationals and has allowed the guerrillas to hold them at the airport.

Assess the legality of a rescue operation mounted by the special forces of Narnia and advise your foreign minister.

Commentary

This question concentrates on one of the possible exceptions to the prohibition on the use of force—rescue of nationals abroad. Although certainly not included as an exception to the prohibition on the use of force in the Charter, there are particularly pertinent examples of state practice that can be discussed, which are the Entebbe incident where Israeli special forces rescued their nationals from a hijacked airliner in Uganda, the invasion of Panama, and the invasion of Grenada based on the danger to US nationals. There is also relevant international case law on this issue in the **United States Diplomatic and Consular Staff in Tehran (United States of America v Iran)** case.

Both Gray (2008) and Harris (2010) include protection of nationals in their discussion of the law of self-defence. Franck (2002) also has a chapter in his book on this issue. It is well worth accessing these publications in preparation of this answer. Harris also includes excerpts from the Security Council debate on the Entebbe incident.

Answer plan

- Define the use of force issues involved in this problem as the rescue of nationals abroad and address first whether the proposed action may offend the prohibition on the use of force.
- Propose the rescue of nationals as an exercise of self-defence.
- Examine the debate concerning the legality of this practice applying relevant state practice and case law.
- Conclude with your advice to the government of Narnia on the proposed action.

Suggested answer

As the legal adviser to the Narnian foreign minister, I have to determine whether a rescue of our nationals from the airport at Upstart is in compliance with international law. I will begin this analysis by examining **Art. 2(4) UN Charter** which prohibits the use of force in international relations and specifically against the territorial integrity and political independence of another state. An argument could be made that this type of force will not affect the territorial integrity or political independence of another state but I do not believe this argument will be successful, as the rescue will involve the use of force, violation of another country's airspace without permission, and possible casualties among Upstartian forces.

The second issue, then, is whether there is a specific exception in the prohibition on the use of force for rescue of nationals abroad. Gray (2008), Harris (2010), and Franck (2002) include protection of nationals in their discussion of the law of self-defence. Gray argues that it is less satisfactory to view this use of force as a customary international law right of intervention to protect nationals and based on the literature it seems that the state of Narnia should argue this as an exercise of self-defence. Therefore, we can then view the rescue of our nationals as part of our exercise of self-defence.

The next question for consideration is whether the customary law of self-defence (as it is not included in **Art. 51**) allows for rescue of nationals? Gray argues that the use of force to rescue nationals without the consent of a state is uncommon and has only been practised by a few states since the Second World War. The examples she gives are: Suez (1956), Lebanon (1958), Congo (1960), Dominican Republic (1965), in the Mayaguez incident (1975), Entebbe (1976), Iran (1980), Grenada (1983), and Panama (1989). According to Gray, all the states involved (primarily the United Kingdom, United States, and Israel) used self-defence as a partial justification for their action. These states interpret the Charter as allowing the forcible protection not only of a state's territory but also of its nationals abroad. Franck on the other hand argues that powerful states have long claimed a legal right to use force to protect citizens abroad but that the practice has continued even after the **Art. 2(4)** and **(7) UN Charter** prohibition on the use of force and interference in internal affairs.

Three of these examples of state practice merit specific review. The first is the rescue by the Israeli special service forces in 1976 of their citizens in Entebbe, Uganda who were held there by virtue of a pro-Palestinian hijacking of an Air France airbus flying from Israel to Paris. Harris includes sections of the Security Council debate on this issue which included the representative of Israel arguing that this method of self-defence was in accordance with international law. He relied particularly upon Bowett's seminal work (1958) and Brierly (1963) which included sections supporting rescue of nationals. However, Harris also includes the statement from the representative of Cameroon which condemns the action by Israel. Harris reports that a resolution condemning Israel was not adopted. Franck argues that it was clear that even in this instance there was no agreement as to whether a state might use force to protect its citizens' lives overseas in a situation where neither the host state nor the international system had been able to offer effective protection.

The second incident is the failed attempted rescue of their hostages by the United States in Iran. The United States justified its action in its report to the Security Council pursuant to **Art. 51** as being an exercise of its right of self-defence. The court in the *United States Diplomatic and Consular Staff in Tehran (United States of America v Iran)* case, although aware of the rescue attempt, did not make any comment with respect to the legality of the operation although separate opinions of Judges Morozov and Tarai concluded that the action was not justified by **Art. 51 UN Charter**.

The third example of state practice is two incidents to be considered together. Those were the United States' invasions of Grenada and Panama based on the United States' argument that its interventions were to protect its nationals. Gray indicates that the GA condemned the invasions of both Grenada and Panama, although she indicates that these were not unequivocal, as other justifications were offered for the use of force (for example, an invitation given by the Governor-General of Grenada). She also points out that the Security Council resolutions to condemn these actions were defeated. The complicating factor is that in both of these cases the interventions were also used to install a new government and not only to rescue the citizens of the United States. In the conclusion of their review of state practice both Gray and Harris point out the international community is divided over this issue.

However, Franck supports the practice when the facts and their political context support a pre-emptive or deterrent intervention on behalf of credibly endangered citizens abroad if the UN itself is incapable of acting. In this case the use of force by a state might be accepted as legitimate self-defence within the meaning of **Art. 51**. Gray argues that those who support the doctrine as furthering the purposes of the UN attempt to propose conditions under which this right might be exercised. These threshold conditions are derived from the United Kingdom in its intervention in the Suez crisis. These are: (a) whether there is an imminent threat of injury to nationals; (b) whether there is a failure or inability on the part of the territorial sovereign to protect the nationals in question; and (c) whether the measures of protection are strictly confined to the objective of protecting them against injury.

In conclusion I cannot advise the foreign minister that such an action is unequivocally legal. However, I would suggest that our claim for legality will be assisted by strict compliance with the conditions suggested by the United Kingdom in the Suez crisis and in circumstances where the UN fails to act. Our troops must confine themselves to rescuing our nationals only and not interfering in the political arrangements in Upstart. These conditions are also in accordance with the customary rules of self-defence of necessity and proportionality. We need only use such force as is necessary to rescue our citizens.

 Examiner's tip

The rescue of nationals could be a branch of self-defence or a right on its own. The marker will be looking for a discussion of both these viewpoints. Reference to an academic discussion of this issue is vital. It is also necessary to discuss the Entebbe and Tehran incidents.

 Question 4

The only permissible uses of force pursuant to the **UN Charter** are self-defence and collective security pursuant to **Chap. VII**.

Is this statement correct?

Commentary

This question gives the student the opportunity to discuss briefly the disputed exceptions to the prohibition on the use of force which are: reprisals; rescue of nationals abroad; humanitarian intervention; pro-democratic intervention; and intervention on consent. There are also self-defence issues, such as anticipatory self-defence and self-defence against non-state actors, but these are usually discussed within a question concerning the scope and ambit of self-defence and will not be canvassed here.

It has to be noted that in any use of force exam question each of these disputed areas might merit a question on its own. Primary sources for preparation are Gray (2008) and Harris (2010), and Franck (2002). However, the excellent student will also conduct a search of relevant articles, as each of the disputed areas has a host of monographs and articles written on the subject.

Answer plan

- Outline the **UN Charter** provisions on the use of force.
- Discuss the nature of the customary law on the use of force.
- Review the proposed exceptions to the prohibition.
- Conclude as to whether any of these exceptions are lawful.

Suggested answer

Article 2(4) UN Charter contains the general prohibition on the use of force. The article states that '*All Members shall refrain in their international relations from the threat or use of force against the territorial integrity or political independence of any state, or in any other manner inconsistent with the Purposes of the United Nations.*' The Charter sets out two exceptions to the prohibition on the use of force. The first is **Art. 51** on self-defence and the second is **Chap. VII** which provides for collective action pursuant to **Art. 39** which states that '*The Security Council shall determine the existence of any threat to the peace, breach of the peace, or act of aggression and shall make recommendations, or decide what measures shall be taken in accordance with Articles 41 and 42, to maintain or restore international peace and security.*' **Article 42** mandates that, should the Security Council consider that measures short of force provided for in **Art. 41** (often economic sanctions) to be inadequate, it may take such action by air, sea, or land forces as may be necessary to maintain or restore international peace and security.

In spite of these clearly set out prohibitions, states have argued other bases for the use of force. These include: reprisals; rescue of nationals abroad; unilateral humanitarian intervention; pro-democratic intervention; and intervention on consent. Each one will be examined and conclusions drawn with respect to their legality. The *Military and Paramilitary Activities in and Against Nicaragua (Nicaragua v United States of America)* decision established that the customary use of force can exist side by side with the Charter and therefore there could be the evolution of exceptions to the prohibition by the combination of state practice and *opinio juris*. It must be noted that reprisals, rescue of nationals abroad, pro-democratic intervention, and intervention by consent might all be part and parcel of a rather wide interpretation of the law of self-defence. Unilateral humanitarian intervention, on the other hand, is protection of persons that might not be your own nationals and therefore would not be part of self-defence. A justification in that case could be advancing the purposes of the UN in terms of protection of human rights. The method of analysis in each case must be an examination of the state practice and whether that practice is accepted to be lawful by the international community; only then can a new doctrine of the customary law on the use of force be accepted.

The first of these exceptions with long historical roots is reprisals. Gray (2008) asserts that reprisals are generally agreed to be unlawful. This prohibition is set out in paragraph one in the **Declaration on the Principles of Friendly Relations 1970,** which states that states have a duty to refrain from acts of reprisal involving the use of force. Another source of condemnation is **Security Council Resolution 188** in 1964 in response to the British attack on the Harib fort in Lebanon which condemned this action as a reprisal which was contrary to the purposes and principles of the UN. Notwithstanding the clear statements of illegality, the borderline between reprisals and self-defence is unclear. Bowett (1972) argued that there could be an accumulation of events of a series of guerrilla raids or terrorist attacks raising an expectation of further attacks. Responding by force may not be a reprisal but an action in self-defence. This is a continual argument of Israel in its response to Palestinian attacks. However, in spite of Bowett's view, many of the Israeli responses to Palestinian incursions and the US response of bombing Tripoli as a result of the Libyan bombing of a Berlin nightclub where US soldiers were located are generally considered to be unlawful reprisals.

The second exception to the prohibition on the use of force is the protection of nationals. As with reprisals, this exception might well be examined as a part of the law of self-defence. In the Entebbe incident in Uganda, Israel argued the right of a state to take military action to protect its nationals in mortal danger. In the case where the Security Council fails to act and the host state will not intervene can a country intervene to save its own people? See also the *US Diplomatic and Consular Staff* case where the United States justified its attempted rescue on the basis of self-defence. The court did not rule on the legality of the rescue attempt. However, Gray and Franck examine state practice and argue that there is no basis to argue that this is a clear exception to the prohibition on the use of force. It might only be lawful on certain conditions when the UN fails to respond to the incident and the host state is not taking any action to protect the citizens in imminent peril, such as the cases of Uganda and Iran.

The next exception is the disputed right of unilateral humanitarian intervention. This is the argument that force can be used without Security Council approval, in the event of the risk of massive abuses of human rights. The most famous recent example of this was the NATO campaign against Yugoslavia over Kosovo. There are several historical examples including: Indian intervention in Bangladesh (1971); Tanzania in Uganda (1979); Vietnam in Cambodia (1979); ECOWAS in Liberia (1996); United States and UK in Iraq (1991–2003); ECOWAS and the UK in Sierra Leone (1998–2002). Prior to the intervention in Kosovo, the UK Foreign Office Policy document stated that '*the best case that can be made in support of humanitarian intervention is that it cannot be said to be unambiguously illegal*'. When one views the debate subsequent to the intervention in Kosovo, it can be properly concluded that the world community is not unanimous in supporting unilateral humanitarian intervention although UN intervention with a Security Council resolution is accepted in spite of the **Art. 2(7)** provision of non-interference in internal affairs. The United Kingdom has now issued guidelines on unilateral humanitarian intervention and is the leading proponent of legality, but based on the analysis conducted by Gray and Franck, the practice cannot be said to be unambiguously legal. Surprisingly, the Russians argued humanitarian intervention when invading parts of Georgia but once again this was not judged as a legal justification for the use of force by the rest of the international community.

The fourth exception is pro-democratic intervention and intervention to promote self-determination. This again could be seen as a part of the law of self-defence as intervention would be to support a democratically elected regime from a *coup d'état*. Examples of state practice are the United States' invasions of Grenada and Panama. This supposed right to intervene is to support a people fighting an alien regime. In the **Friendly Relations Declaration** in 1970 there was an acknowledgement that a state might assist people fighting a war of national liberation but this seemed to be restricted to the colonial context. Once again the analysis of state practice, particularly relative to Grenada and Panama conducted by Gray, seems to establish that such a practice is not a lawful exception to the prohibition on the use of force.

Finally, there is intervention by invitation to support an existing government which is being attacked by rebel groups. This again would be a type of self-defence operation. Examples of state practice are the Grenada, Panama, Hungary, and Czechoslovakia interventions by the forces of the United States and the USSR. Doswald-Beck in 'The validity of military intervention by invitation of the government' (1985) argued that the problem with this type of intervention is that it has to be at the consent of the legitimate government, not a rebel group and the government has to have *de facto* control of the territory or most of it. Unlike the other examples given in this answer, this practice may well be lawful if the condition of an actual invitation by the existing government is met. The problem with the examples given of Grenada, Panama, Hungary, and Czechoslovakia is that the existing governments may not have given their consent to the intervention.

It can be seen by the given examples that there are controversial arguments of additional exceptions to the prohibition on the use of force to **Art. 51** and collective security. The critical focus has to be on the examples of state practice to see if the exception exists in customary international law. In these cases, only intervention by invitation seems to be unequivocally legal subject to certain conditions.

Examiner's tip

There must be equal discussion of all of these grounds of use of force. Students tend to get bogged down in humanitarian intervention, which has now been subsumed by the collective use of force in the responsibility to protect (see next chapter). A knowledge of the fact situations in which these uses of force have taken place is essential.

Further reading

Bowett, D., *Self-defence in International Law* (New York: Frederick A. Praeger, 1958).

Brierly, J. L., *The Law of Nations*, 6th edn (Oxford: Clarendon, 1963).

Byers, M., 'Terrorism, the use of force and international law after 11 September' (2002) 51 ICLQ 401.

Cassese, A., 'Terrorism is also disrupting some crucial legal categories of international law' (2001) 12 EJIL 993.

Doswald-Beck, L., 'The validity of military intervention by invitation of the government' (1985) 56 BYIL 189.

Franck, T., *Recourse to Force* (Cambridge: Cambridge University Press, 2002).

Gray, C., *International Law and the Use of Force*, 3rd edn (Oxford: Oxford University Press, 2008).

Greenwood, C., 'International law and the pre-emptive use of force: Afghanistan, Al Qaida and Iraq' (2003) 4 *San Diego Int'l L.J.* 7.

Harris, D. J., *Cases and Materials in International Law*, 7th edn (London: Sweet and Maxwell, 2010).

Henderson, C., 'The 2010 United States National Security Strategy and the Obama Doctrine of 'Necessary Force' (2010) 15 *Journal of Conflict and Security Law* 403.

Reisman, W. M. and Armstrong, A., 'The past and future of the claim of pre-emptive self-defense' (2006) 100 AJIL 525.

Wilmshurst, E., 'The Chatham House Principles of international law on the use of force in self-defence' (2006) 55 ICLQ 963.

Use of force by states—multilateral

Introduction

The questions in this second chapter on the use of force will focus on the collective security system for the maintenance of international peace and security which was established in the **UN Charter** in 1945. There are two important elements necessary for a successful answer to this type of question. The first is detailed knowledge of the provisions contained in **Chap. VII** of the Charter and the difficulties involved in implementation of these provisions. The second is a thorough knowledge of the examples of the use of collective security both before and after the end of the cold war. A very important modification in collective security has been the innovation of peacekeeping and a very important international decision deals with the power to introduce such an activity. This case is the advisory Opinion of 1961, the *Certain Expenses of the United Nations (Article 17, paragraph 2, of the Charter)* case.

This area has become very important as one of the key arguments about the legality of the war in Iraq in 2003 was that it may have been an exercise in collective security. A detailed knowledge of the various Security Council resolutions, the history of the conflict, and the opposing legal opinions, will be essential. There is also a body of literature that argues that the collective security system has suffered a fatal blow as a result of the deadlock over the Iraq war. The student must be cautious about launching into a political tirade over Iraq, as any question on this issue will demand legal analysis in addition to the knowledge of the political factors that went into the decision-making.

Particularly important in any question is an analytical discussion of the flaws in the system together with examples of collective security, since the advent of the Charter. It is clear that the use of the veto has hampered the use of collective security particularly during the cold war which is why peacekeeping was developed. This has also resulted in delegation of collective security actions to sovereign states, which was not contemplated in the Charter. However, an open question is whether the system has improved since the

1990s and an astute student will review *A More Secure World*, the report of the Secretary-General's High-Level Panel on Threats, Challenges, and Change. This report contains recommendations to improve the system of collective security in the wake of the war in Iraq.

A new and important area in collective security is the obligation of intervention to protect populations from massive abuses of human rights from their rulers; this was known as multilateral humanitarian intervention but since the 60th Anniversary Summit of the UN it is known as '*the responsibility to protect*'. There is one question in the chapter dealing with this particular area. Once again knowledge of the situations in which this has been used is particularly important as well as the current debates over such situations as Darfur, Burma, and Zimbabwe. Critically the intervention in Libya in the wake of the 'Arab Spring' is viewed to be a responsibility to protect action. The crisis in the United Nations over Syria however, is an indication that intervention in human rights catastrophes is by no means automatic. Therefore, the debate concerning the responsibility of the Security Council in these situations continues.

Question 1

Economic sanctions are an important weapon in the arsenal of collective security.
Do you agree or disagree with this statement?

Commentary

The purpose of this question is for the student to display knowledge of the gradations in collective security. This means that other methods short of the use of force are used to deal with nations which violate **Art. 2(4)** of the Charter. However, economic sanctions are only used under **Chap. VII** of the **UN Charter** if the **Art. 39** threshold is reached and the student must be aware of the debates concerning whether an act by a state constitutes a threat to international peace and security sufficient enough to warrant economic sanctions.

The student must also give examples of the use by the Security Council of economic sanctions and the ongoing debate as to their effectiveness. Two excellent examples of the use of economic sanctions that were of questionable value were sanctions against Saddam Hussein's Iraq after the First Gulf War and the sanctions against the Federal Republic of Yugoslavia. Shaw (2008) contains excellent detail about various sanctions regimes in his chapter on the UN. Excellent critical articles are: Reinisch, 'Developing human rights and humanitarian law accountability of the Security Council for the imposition of economic sanctions' (2001) and de Chazournes, 'Collective security and the economic interventionism of the UN—the need for a coherent and integrated approach' (2007).

Answer plan

- Describe the **Chap. VII UN Charter** on collective security.
- Discuss examples of economic sanctions in UN practice.
- Discuss the evolution from full sanctions to specifically targeted sanctions.
- Assess the effectiveness of economic sanctions.

Suggested answer

The UN system of collective security as set out in **Chap. VII** of the Charter is crafted to allow for an increase in level of measures to be taken against a state which engages in actions which constitute a threat or breach of international peace and security. Under **Art. 39 UN Charter,** the Security Council is charged with determining whether there is a threat to the peace, act of aggression, and breach of the peace. The Security Council, once that determination has been made, must decide upon measures to maintain or restore international peace and security. **Article 41** involves measures which are to be used which do not involve the use of armed force. The main measures under this article involve the use of economic sanctions and they have been adopted on several occasions. Only when these measures fail, can the Security Council authorize the use of force. It is important to note that once the Security Council agrees on sanctions pursuant to **Art. 103 UN Charter** all members must impose the sanctions. The provision states that in the event of a conflict between the obligations of the Members of the UN under the Charter and their obligations under any other international agreements, the obligations under the Charter shall prevail.

Prior the end of the cold war, there were two examples of economic sanctions. The first was the situation in Rhodesia. On 11 November 1965 the minority regime in Southern Rhodesia unilaterally declared independence intending to impose an apartheid regime similar to that of South Africa. At the request of Britain, the UN Security Council imposed economic sanctions against Rhodesia. **Resolution 232** adopted 16 December 1966 imposed economic sanctions on certain items and categorized the situation in Southern Rhodesia as a threat to international peace and security. In May of 1968 **Resolution 252** extended those sanctions to cover almost every aspect of economic life except for humanitarian relief. The economic sanctions were continued by various resolutions through the 1970s. The issue of Southern Rhodesia was finally settled in a constitutional conference in London in 1979 and the economic sanctions were lifted.

The second situation was South Africa. It took some time for the UN to agree upon sanctions against the apartheid regime. In 1977 **Resolution 418** introduced a complete arms embargo. There were several more Security Council resolutions over the years condemning the regime and calling for international action to end apartheid. However, unlike the action with respect to Rhodesia, the UN never imposed a complete economic embargo. **Resolution 569** in July of 1985 urged Member States not to invest in South Africa and to impose restriction on sports and cultural relations, but it did not impose mandatory economic sanctions. On 25 May 1994, the Security Council lifted the embargo and other measures against South Africa as a result of the democratic elections, which were monitored by the UN Observer Mission in South Africa.

Although both South Africa and Rhodesia abandoned their apartheid regimes, it is not clear whether this was as a result of the sanctions regimes. After the end of the cold war, there were many more examples of economic sanctions regimes but the debate rages as to whether these regimes are effective. There are two examples of post-cold war actions that were very unsuccessful. According to Reinisch (2001), the end of the cold war has led the Security Council to intensify its use of economic sanctions. Two prominent examples of failures of effectiveness were the sanctions imposed in the 1990s against the Federal Republic of Yugoslavia and the sanctions imposed on Iraq subsequent to its invasion of Kuwait. On 30 May 1992 in **Resolution 757** the Security Council imposed a wide range of sanctions against Yugoslavia. These sanctions were further tightened by a series of subsequent resolutions and were not finally lifted until after the Kosovo crisis in 2001. Iraq too had a series of sanctions resolutions beginning with Security Council **Resolution 661** which imposed a wide range of economic sanctions. Shaw (2008) concludes his examination of these sanctions regimes by concluding that the issue of the efficacy of sanctions remains open and it has to be noted that both these situations, unlike Rhodesia and South Africa, eventually resulted in an escalation of measures and the use of force.

Reinisch is also very critical of the use of economic sanctions arguing that they have contributed to the emergence of black markets, created huge profit-making opportunities for ruling elites, and have tended to hit the wrong targets—the population at large, instead of the regime. This was certainly the case with the sanctions in Iraq which led to the oil for food crisis and allegations of profiteering on the part of UN officials. In fact Reinisch argues that the economic sanctions in Iraq led to a humanitarian disaster. Shaw has argued in his text that this has resulted in a debate as to whether sanctions may be better focused and targeted or made smarter.

It can be seen that since these comprehensive sanctions regimes, sanctions have been more targeted and examples of this, according to de Chazournes (2007), are Sierra Leone and Liberia. In 1997 the Security Council imposed oil and arms embargoes as well as restrictions on travel for the military junta of Sierra Leone and in 2000 prohibited the direct or indirect import of diamonds from Sierra Leone. The same type of sanctions on the export of rough diamonds was also imposed on Liberia in 2001. The general tenor of this article as with Reinisch is that there is not yet a conclusion that these targeted sanctions will be any more successful or humanitarian than comprehensive sanctions. De Chazournes argues that the promotion and integration of a broader set of principles and rules of international economic law such as principles of fair competition, non-discrimination, or transparency, would help enhance the legitimacy of these sanctions actions of the UN Security Council.

There have been sanctions regimes imposed on both North Korea (2006) and Iran (2006) for their possible development of nuclear weapons. These sanctions were also targeted sanctions on trade in materials that could result in nuclear weapons and travel restrictions. The situation in North Korea has eased with an agreement to halve nuclear weapons development, but the situation in Iran continues.

It can therefore be concluded that at this point it is unclear whether or not economic sanctions imposed under **Art. 41** are an important or successful part of collective security. The success of both comprehensive and targeted economic sanctions is at best mixed and a lot more study is needed as to whether any type of sanctions regime can avoid the next level of severity—armed conflict—in the name of the international community.

 Examiner's tip

The examiner will want to see knowledge of the history of the use of sanctions beginning with Rhodesia. The distinction between comprehensive sanctions and smart sanctions is also critical. Academic discussion of sanctions regimes is plentiful and inclusion of some analysis is important for excellent results.

 Question 2

It has been argued by some international law and relations scholars that the lead-up to the war in Iraq (known as the Second Gulf War) sounded the death knell for the collective security system in the UN and that we returned to a system of power and hegemony. Even though several years have passed since the war, this remains the greatest crisis the United Nations has ever faced.

Comment on this statement and assess the legality of the action in Iraq in 2003.

 Commentary

An assessment of the legality of the invasion of Iraq necessitates knowledge of the existing system of collective security with its alterations given the cold war. It will also involve reading carefully the legal opinions justifying the war and those legal opinions that are against the war. A first step, however, is knowledge of the response of the Security Council to the Iraqi invasion of Kuwait in 1990, one of a handful of examples of the true use of collective security since the advent of the Charter. The second step is to understand the arguments for and against the legality of the invasion. An article presenting the opinion in favour of legality is Greenwood, 'International law and the pre-emptive use of force: Afghanistan, Al Qaida, and Iraq' (2003). Articles opposed are to be found in 'Agora' in the AJIL, particularly the comments by Falk *et al.* (2003).

Second, the student has to engage with the debate about the demise of the collective security system. An excellent article to read is Glennon, 'Why the Security Council failed' (2003). For a contrary view, see Wippman, 'The nine lives of Article 2(4)' (2007). This debate would allow the student to display analytical skills in assessing the reaction to the war in Iraq as either the death knell for collective security or its revitalization.

Answer plan

- Discuss the system of collective security.
- Review the elements of legal justification of the use of force in Iraq.
- Assess the impact of the war on the system of collective security.
- Propose your own view on the future of the UN system of collective security.

Suggested answer

Collective security pursuant to **Chap. VII** of the **UN Charter** is one of the two exceptions to the **Art. 2(4)** prohibition on the use of force. **Article 39** of **Chap. VII** states that the Security Council is to determine the existence of any threat to the peace, act of aggression, or breach of the peace and shall decide what measures to take in accordance with **Arts 41** and **42**. On 19 March 2003, after much debate in the Security Council, forces under the command of the United States with the support of the United Kingdom and other forces invaded Iraq without the benefit of a new Security Council resolution specifically authorizing the use of force.

The legal justification given by the United States and the United Kingdom on the invasion of Iraq was a revival argument. The revival of armed conflict argument dates from the 1990 invasion and occupation of Kuwait by Iraq. The Security Council condemned the invasion by **Security Council Resolution 660** and in a series of subsequent resolutions demanded that Iraq withdraw from Kuwait. When that did not happen, **Security Council Resolution 678** authorized Member States' cooperation with the government of Kuwait to use '*all necessary means to uphold and implement*' **Security Council Resolution 660** and to restore international peace and security. After the coalition forces successfully forced Iraqi troops out of Kuwait and by agreement with Iraq there was a ceasefire—**Security Council Resolution 687** was passed which contained many conditions, including almost complete disarmament.

The argument put forward by the United Kingdom was that the Security Council in previous resolutions particularly **Resolution 678,** had provided permission to the United States and its coalition partners to use force, even though there was not a current enabling resolution. Part and parcel of this justification was that there had been non-compliance with the ceasefire provisions set out in **Security Council Resolution 687** and that therefore the use of force authorization in **Resolution 678** was revived. This argument also relied on Security Council **Resolution 1441** which declared that '*Iraq has been, and remains in, material breach of its obligations under relevant resolutions, including resolution 687 (1991)*'. The requirements set out in **Resolution 687** were that all weapons of mass destruction were to be destroyed, removed, or rendered harmless. **Resolution 1441** stated that Iraq had not provided an accurate, full, final, and complete disclosure as required and had repeatedly obstructed immediate, unconditional, and unrestricted access to sites designated by the UN inspectors (UNSCOM).

The difficulty with this argument is that **Resolution 678** had been drafted specifically to authorize force to repel the Iraqi invasion of Kuwait and not to invade Iraq proper. At that time the coalition forces stopped short of conquering Iraq. **Resolution 1441** did not specifically authorize force and an attempt to obtain a specific resolution to do so had failed. Furthermore, a vast majority of states including France, Russia, and Germany had objected to such an action. An argument can be made that there must be a specific authorization to use force for a particular situation and this had not happened in this case. **Resolution 678** had not been clear enough to be a basis for a continuation of authorization to use force.

Academic opinion is divided over the issue of legality, although the bulk of opinion would seem to be against the justification. However, Greenwood in 'International law and the pre-emptive use of force: Afghanistan, Al Qaida, and Iraq' (2003) argued in favour of the legal justification on the basis that **Security Council Resolution 1441, para. 1** determination that Iraq was guilty of a continuing material breach of the conditions of **Resolution 687 (1991)** showed that the conditions for the revival of the authority to use force existed. The decision to grant Iraq a final opportunity to comply, however, together with the requirement that any failure on the part of Iraq to take that opportunity had to be reported to the Security Council for consideration under **para. 12 of Resolution 1441,** meant that **Resolution 1441** did not automatically revive the authorization of military action. He argued that the requirement in **para. 12 of Resolution 1441,** that the Security Council consider the matter, did not mean that no action could be taken under **Resolution 678** unless the Security Council decided on such a course. On the other hand, Stahn argues in his article 'Enforcement of the collective will after Iraq' (2003)—see Falk *et al.* (2003)—that the case against authorization of force under **Security Council Resolution 1441** was much more compelling and that even if **Resolution 1441** did revive the authorization under **Resolution 678,** it did not include a right to effect regime change.

Given the division in academic and public opinion the question arises as to whether this alleged unilateral action by the United States and the United Kingdom sounded the death knell for collective security. Glennon in 'Why the Security Council failed' argues that the Iraq crisis made clear that the '*grand experiment of the twentieth century—the attempt to impose binding international law on the use of force—has failed*'. He asserts that as Washington showed, nations need to consider not whether armed intervention abroad is legal, merely whether it is preferable to the alternatives. He further goes on to argue that the structure and rules of the UN Security Council really reflected the hopes of its founders, rather than the realities of the way that states work. One can take issue with this opinion of collective security and argue the reverse—that the reaction to the proposed use of force by the international community showed respect for the provisions of **Chap. VII**, as the argument was made that Iraq had not reached the threshold of a threat to international peace and security. Furthermore, the efforts by the United States and United Kingdom to argue international legality clearly demonstrate that they have regard to their international legal obligations. Borrowing the title of Wippman's article (2007), one can argue that **Art. 2(4)** indeed has nine lives. Wippman asserts that **Art. 2(4)** has displayed remarkable resilience, stubbornly refuses to die, and emerges stronger than before. He is correct that the core of the ban against the invasion, occupation, and eventual annexation of another state remains largely intact. In fact, if the open Security Council debates just prior to the war of Iraq taught us anything, it is how much the prohibition on the use of force meant to many members of the international community, who were unwilling to support the invasion of Iraq. There is currently an inquiry commissioned by the government of the United Kingdom, the Chilcot inquiry, that is also considering the legality of the invasion, and its conclusions are eagerly anticipated after testimony by two former Foreign Office legal advisers who both indicated that they did not believe the invasion was lawful.

The debate over Iraq and the subsequent invasion was not a '*dramatic rupture*' which ended '*the grand attempt to subject the use of force to the rule of law*', as Glennon has argued. Although the collective security system might have been badly wounded, its functioning since and the recommendations before the international community of states by international law academics and practitioners could go some way towards its recovery. The practice of collective security even by 2003 had improved tremendously, since the troublesome resolutions of 1990–1. During the 1990s, UN staff, academics, and indeed states, worked towards improving the system of international peace and security. Announcing a new world order in the early 1990s may have been premature, but announcing the demise of the UN was equally foolhardy. Glennon argues that the whole edifice has come crashing down but an examination of the totality and scope of **Chap. VII** and related Security Council resolutions since the Second Gulf War do not support this gloomy forecast.

The fact that the United States and the United Kingdom chose to return to the Security Council after the armed conflict with Iraq (as they had done in the **Kosovo** case) contradicts Glennon's statement. Glennon argues that the United States will likely confront pressures to curb its use of force which it must resist. This erroneous view is based on a claim that as the one remaining superpower, it is the United States' responsibility to maintain international peace and security. Examinations of the practice of the UN and the practice of states since the fall of the Berlin Wall reveal that the role of protection of international peace and security remains with the Security Council.

Examiner's tip

The successful student will be able to list and analyse the various Security Council resolutions involved in this crisis. An excellent student will also study the various reports about the Iraq crisis, particularly the Chilcot inquiry. Finally, the divided academic opinion necessitates quoting from both sides of the debate. The articles are plentiful—those mentioned are only a small selection.

Question 3

The state of Tallyho has been subject to a series of cross-border raids from insurgents hiding in the neighbouring state of Illyria. Tallyho sends in troops to Illyria to crush the insurgents. The matter is brought by Illyria to the UN Security Council. The Security Council is asked to intervene to restore international peace and security.

With reference to actual examples, discuss what measures the Security Council might take.

Commentary

This problem question enables the student to discuss the full range of measures that the UN Security Council can employ to deal with threats to international peace and security. It also compels the student to discuss the failings of collective security and the evolution of the use of peacekeeping. Students should make sure, however, that they address the specific facts of this problem.

There are numerous examples of UN peacekeeping efforts in various parts of the world. A recent action that began unilaterally was the UN involvement in maintaining the peace between Israel and Lebanon. This can be contrasted with the inability to deal with the situation between Russia and Georgia, as Russia has the veto on the Security Council.

Gray (2008) has a chapter in her book devoted to the UN and the use of force, which could be an excellent reference point. Harris (2010) also has a section in his chapter on use of force entitled 'Collective measures through the United Nations' which contains pertinent sections from Simma (ed.), *The Charter of the United Nations: a Commentary*. However, students should continually be reading the newspapers and monitoring the media for coverage of recent conflicts.

Answer plan

- Outline the Charter provisions on collective security and discuss the modifications in practice.
- Discuss the evolution from peacekeeping to peacemaking in UN practice.
- Provide specific examples of UN efforts in peacekeeping, including the Israel–Lebanon situation.
- Apply those provisions to this conflict.

Suggested answer

The UN Security Council has before it the armed conflict between the states of Tallyho and Illyria. There are two separate allegations: first, the cross-border raids originating from Illyria into the territory of Tallyho; and, second, the reaction of Tallyho sending troops into Illyria to crush the insurgency. The Security Council now has to decide on what measures to take to resolve this conflict.

Under **Chap. VII UN Charter**, the first threshold question under **Art. 39** is whether this situation constitutes a threat to the peace, breach of the peace, or act of aggression. According to Simma (2002, in Harris, 2010) **Art. 39** is a broad and indistinct concept and in practice the Security Council normally will not use breach of the peace or aggression but rather a threat to international peace and security. In this case the Security Council could determine that this situation is a threat to international peace and security. One of the problems with this determination is that there is a veto for the five permanent members of the Security Council. If one of the parties in the conflict is either one of the members or within their sphere of influence a situation might not get beyond the discussion stage. This is the case for example with the recent conflict between Georgia and Russia, where Russia would veto any resolution condemning its actions.

However, if such a veto does not occur, then the next step is the for the Security Council to make recommendations, or decide what measures shall be taken in accordance with **Arts 41** and **42** to maintain or restore international peace and security. **Article 41** enables the Security Council to decide on whether measures not involving the use of armed force are to be employed to given effect, and it may call upon Member States to apply such measures. These may include complete or partial interruption of economic relations and of rail, sea, air, postal, telegraphic, radio, and other means of communication, and the severance of diplomatic relations. The usual course is to impose economic sanctions, as has been done with Iraq, Yugoslavia, Liberia, Sierra Leone, Iran, and North Korea, to name a few. However, Shaw (2008) concludes his examination of various sanctions regimes by finding that the issue of the efficacy of sanctions remains open.

If this level of reaction fails, then under **Art. 42,** should the Security Council consider that the measures provided for in **Art. 41** would be inadequate or have proved to be inadequate, it may take such action by air, sea, or land forces as may be necessary to maintain or restore international peace and security. Such action may include demonstrations, blockade, and other operations by air, sea, or land forces of Member States. This stage is where there has been a substantial alteration in UN practice. **Article 43** provided for agreements between individual states and the UN on the forces that each state would agree to make available to the UN, and **Art. 6** provided that '*plans for the application of armed force shall be made by the Security Council with the assistance of the Military Staff Committee*', with **Art. 47** setting out the composition and functions of the Military Staff Committee. Regrettably, there are no standing forces and although the Military Staff Committee is constituted it does not act.

Due to the paralysis of the collective security system, an innovation introduced in the cold war has been the phenomenon of peacekeeping which is a likely possibility in this case. The only true collective security actions have been in Korea (when the Soviet Union walked out) and Iraq–Kuwait. The usual course is to persuade both parties to allow a peacekeeping operation into their territory to police a ceasefire between the parties. This has been done on many occasions, with examples including Cyprus, the Congo, and the Middle East. As Simma (2002, in Harris, 2010) declared, during the cold war, the innovative character of **Art. 42** had almost no impact.

However, as Simma points out, with the end of the cold war, there have been several operations with a more robust mandate which has represented an evolution from peacekeeping to peacemaking with peacekeepers being given more robust mandates to protect the civilian population from the consequences of violence. Examples of current peacemaking mandates are Darfur, Congo, and Burundi. Another example well worth referring to in this case is the example of the UN reaction to the recent conflict between Israel and Lebanon. **Security Council Resolution 1701** in August of 2006 was accepted by all parties to the conflict and, after determining that the situation was a threat to international peace and security, the resolution increased the number of the UN Interim Force in Lebanon (established in 1976) to 15,000 troops, with a mandate to take all necessary action in the area of the deployment of its forces to ensure that the area is not used for hostile activities of any kind and to resist by forceful means to prevent it from discharging its duties including humanitarian assistance and monitoring cessation of hostilities and a specific mandate to protect civilians. This resolution with its robust mandate could be a model for the resolution of the conflict between Illyria and Tallyho.

There is another important provision in **Art. 48** that the action required to carry out the decisions of the Security Council for the maintenance of international peace and security shall be taken by all the members of the UN or by some of them, as the Security Council shall determine. However, experience indicates that it is difficult to raise the troop numbers needed to keep the peace.

Finally, the two states might refuse to allow a robust peacekeeping mandate and it will be left to the Security Council to take the very rare step of an enforcement action, such as was the case of Iraq–Kuwait. If so, the consent of the states will not be necessary.

 Examiner's tip

This question demands thorough knowledge of **Chap. VII** of the Charter. It is particularly important to discuss those sections that have never been implemented such as the development of the United Nations armed forces. The excellent student will also discuss the innovations in peacekeeping.

Question 4

Has the system of collective security evolved to include a responsibility to protect?

Commentary

In its Sixtieth Anniversary Summit, the UN General Assembly adopted a statement supporting the *'responsibility to protect'*. This was based on three separate reports, all of which should be reviewed by the diligent student: *The Responsibility to Protect*; *A More Secure World*; and *In Larger Freedom* (all available online). There is very little international law literature on the subject, but a relevant article is Breau, 'The impact of the responsibility to protect on peacekeeping' (2006) and a new chapter in Evans (2010) by Zifcak entitled 'The responsibility to protect'. Information on the **Great Lakes Region Peace Process** can be accessed through the website of the International Humanitarian Law Project at the London School of Economics Department of Law. Students also should read literature on the intervention in Libya in 2011.

Answer plan

- Discuss the historical evolution of the responsibility to protect.
- Analyse the meaning of the concept and its impact on the practice of collective security.
- Give examples of UN practice in compliance with the doctrine, including the resolutions on Darfur and Libya and the **Great Lakes Region Peace Process**.

Suggested answer

One of the few positive results of the disappointing UN Sixtieth Anniversary Summit was its endorsement of the *'responsibility to protect'*. This means that the international community, through the UN, has a responsibility to use appropriate diplomatic, humanitarian, and other peaceful means, in accordance with **Chaps VI** and **VIII** of the Charter, to help protect populations from genocide, war crimes, ethnic cleansing, and crimes against humanity. In this context, states are prepared to take collective action, in a timely and decisive manner, through the Security Council, in accordance with the Charter, including **Chap. VII**, on a case-by-case basis and in cooperation with relevant regional organizations as appropriate, should peaceful means be inadequate and national authorities manifestly fail to protect their populations from genocide, war crimes, ethnic cleansing, and crimes against humanity.

The pivotal report on the responsibility to protect was authored by the International Commission on Intervention and State Sovereignty entitled *The Responsibility to Protect*, which emerged at the same time as the attack on the Twin Towers, then quickly faded into obscurity in the wake of the so-called war on terror. The report was not only concerned with intervention for human protection purposes but also with the whole area of peace and security.

An important innovation of the doctrine was the development of principles for military intervention in the responsibility-to-react phase. The first principle was the just cause threshold which stated that military intervention for human protection purposes is an exceptional and extraordinary measure. To be warranted, there must be serious and irreparable harm occurring to human beings, or imminently likely to occur, of the following kind: the criteria is for large-scale loss of life which is the product either of deliberate state action, or state neglect or inability to act, or a failed state situation; or large-scale 'ethnic cleansing', carried out by killing, forced expulsion, acts of terror, or rape.

All of these recommendations might never have emerged had it not been for the crisis in the Security Council generated over the lawfulness of the invasion of Iraq. The Secretary-General commissioned a High-Level Panel on Threats, Challenges, and Change which in its report entitled *A More Secure World* reviewed the whole range of collective security mechanisms, including peacekeeping. Gareth Evans, one of the co-chairs of the International Commission on Intervention and State Sovereignty, was also on the High-Level Panel. It was, therefore, no surprise that a large portion of the recommendations concerning peacekeeping were identical to those formulated three years earlier in *The Responsibility to Protect*. Again the focus was on the threat of civil violence, ethnic conflict, and genocide. The report argued that UN Secretariat officials had failed to provide the Security Council with early warning of the plans to kill thousands of Tutsis and moderate Hutus in Rwanda. In relation to Bosnia and Herzegovina, the report asserted that protection of humanitarian aid and peacekeeping had been substituted for political and military action to stop ethnic cleansing and genocide. Finally, the panel asserted that Security Council paralysis had led NATO (North Atlantic Treaty Organization) to bypass the UN in Kosovo. The only instance cited where the Security Council had worked together with national governments and regional actors to halt large-scale killing was in East Timor.

The report went on to endorse the view that there was a growing recognition that the issue was not a '*right to intervene*' but a '*responsibility to protect*' of *every* state in situations of '*mass murder and rape, ethnic cleansing by forcible expulsion and terror, and deliberate starvation and exposure to disease*'. If sovereign governments are unable or unwilling to protect their own citizens from these catastrophes, the international community should employ a continuum involving prevention, response to violence, and rebuilding shattered societies. The primary focus would be on the aspect of prevention by '*assisting the cessation of violence through mediation and other tools and the protection of people through such measures as the dispatch of humanitarian, human rights and police missions*'. Kofi Annan in his report *In Larger Freedom*, prepared for consideration by the Sixtieth Anniversary General Assembly, endorsed the recommendations in *A More Secure World* concerning the responsibility to protect and the peacekeeping recommendations.

This has now been confirmed in practice. In a resolution on civilians and armed conflict, the Security Council confirmed the responsibility to protect civilians from genocide, war crimes, ethnic cleansing, and crimes against humanity in **Resolution 1674** on the protection of civilians. This resolution could be taken to be further endorsement by the Security Council of the responsibility to protect. In the recent successful conclusion of the International Conference on the **Great Lakes Region Peace Process** there is included a protocol on non-aggression and mutual defence which includes a clause that Member States in this process agree that they have a responsibility to protect populations from genocide, war crimes, ethnic cleansing, crimes against humanity, and gross violations of human rights committed by, or within, a state. The decision of the Member States to exercise their responsibility to protect populations in this provision shall be taken collectively, with due procedural notice to the Peace and Security Council of the African Union and the Security Council of the UN.

There are two examples of United Nations practice in Sudan and Libya. Firstly, **Security Council Resolution 1769**, authorized the deployment of a 26,000-strong UN peacekeeping force to Darfur, Sudan: the first responsibility to protect action. A second example is the authorization of intervention in Libya. United Nations **Security Council Resolution 1973** allowed a multinational force to prevent the Gaddafi regime from overrunning Benghazi. The justification contained in the resolution was the protection of the civilian population of Libya.

These developments represent significant international and state practice (11 African states are members of the **Great Lakes Region Peace Process**) on this relatively new norm of the responsibility to protect. It could become an important plank of an international constitution requiring a structural framework for implementation. This is further supported by the evolution of peacekeeping into peace enforcement actions, with several recent operations containing mandates to use force to protect civilians.

One major setback has been the paralysis of the Security Council in Syria. China and Russia blocked any efforts for collective action in Syria. There is ample evidence of large-scale attacks on civilians but this might constitute proof that the responsibility to protect, to at least some of the powers on the Security Council, is not a legal obligation.

In conclusion, however, it must be pointed out that although this was a consensus resolution of the General Assembly, and there has been practice to support such a resolution, at best this could be said to be a developing doctrine of the law of armed conflict. It is clearly intended by the various reports to be action by the Security Council and not unilateral action on the part of individual states.

Examiner's tip

This is a fast moving and developing area and the student must keep up to date on the latest developments in the Security Council. Excellent students will be familiar with the various reports recommending the responsibility to protect, most particularly *A More Secure World*. Finally, the student must be aware of the consensus **General Assembly Resolution**.

Further reading

Breau, S., 'The impact of the responsibility to protect on peacekeeping' (2006) 11 *Journal of Conflict and Security Law* 429.

de Chazournes, L. B., 'Collective security and the economic interventionism of the UN—the need for a coherent and integrated approach' (2007) 10 *Journal of International Economic Law* 51.

Falk, R. A., 'What Future of the UN Charter System of War Prevention?' (2003) 97 AJIL 590.

Glennon, M., 'Why the Security Council failed' in *Foreign Affairs* May/June 2003.

Greenwood, C., 'International law and the pre-emptive use of force: Afghanistan, Al Qaida, and Iraq' (2003) 4 *San Diego Int'l L. J.* 7.

Harris, D. J., *Cases and Materials on International Law*, 7th edn (London: Sweet & Maxwell, 2010).

Reinisch, A., 'Developing human rights and humanitarian law accountability of the Security Council for the imposition of economic sanctions' (2001) 95 AJIL 851.

Shaw, M., *International Law*, 6th edn (Cambridge: Cambridge University Press, 2008).

Stahn, C., 'Enforcement of the Collective Will after Iraq' (2003) 97 AJIL 804.

Wippman, D., 'The nine lives of Article 2(4)' 16 *Minn, J. Int'l. Law* 387 (2007).

Yoo, J., 'International Law and the War in Iraq' (2003) 97 AJIL 563.

Zifcak, S., 'The Responsibility to Protect' Evans, M. (ed.), *International Law* 3rd edn (Cambridge University Press, 2010).

15 International human rights law

Introduction

The questions in this chapter call for a discussion of the various sources of international human rights law. Although there is often a separate human rights or an international human rights module available in some law schools, an introduction to public international law often canvasses this topic. As discussed in the questions for Chapter 2, international law does not derive its authority from any single codified document, rather from customary international law and a group of conventions (treaties) drafted since the Second World War by the now defunct Human Rights Commission. Within customary international law, human rights engages with the controversial topics of *jus cogens* and obligations *erga omnes* discussed in the second chapter of this book, as human rights are often argued to be peremptory norms. The first area of examination for this chapter is whether the body of treaty law that makes up the body of international human rights law constitutes an international bill of rights. A competent scholar of this area must therefore be aware of the debate concerning the hierarchy that exists within international human rights in order to discern what if any rights might be included in such a bill.

The second question in this chapter is an often asked question regarding the effectiveness of the monitoring system of human rights protection. One of the major controversies in human rights law is the patchy system of enforcement of human rights norms. This has led to a major restructuring of the United Nations human rights system and students will have to be aware of the UN reform process which began with the Sixtieth Anniversary Summit and the creation of the Human Rights Council.

The third topic for review in this chapter asks for analysis of the cultural relativism critique of human rights. Some have argued that many of the international treaties are written with a Western culture in mind. To this, a cultural relativist thesis has emerged, advancing that cultural differences allow for non-compliance with aspects of international treaties. This can be answered by the student by careful reference to the diverse literature on the subject.

Although international human rights law is usually only introduced during the general public international law course, of particular concern for students are the recent measures to combat terrorism, particularly the provisions with respect to detention and the tension between these measures and human rights. The excellent student will refer to the updated literature on this subject and an excellent general text on this topic is Helen Duffy, 'The War on Terror and the framework of international law' (2005).

There are literally thousands of articles on all four of these question areas and there are no limitations to the amount of research the student could do. However, an excellent source for a range of literature in each of these topics is Steiner *et al.* (2007).

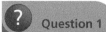 **Question 1**

A common term used to describe the totality of international human rights conventions in customary human rights law is the 'International Bill of Rights'.

Discuss which international instruments and customs might make up this bill of rights and discuss whether you agree or disagree with the existence of an international bill of rights.

 **Commentary**

This question calls for discussion of the general treaties that make up international human rights law and an analysis of whether there is any such thing as an 'International Bill of Rights'. The treaty regime includes the **International Covenant on Civil and Political Rights 1966 (ICCPR)**, and the **International Covenant on Economic, Social and Cultural Rights 1966 (ICESCR)**. Furthermore, there is a General Assembly resolution, the **Universal Declaration of Human Rights 1948 (UDHR)** that has become part of customary international law. The student must be aware of the variable enforcement mechanisms in each treaty, the rate of ratification of the treaties, and the difficulty in the reporting regime. Secondly, the question requires knowledge about the alleged hierarchy of human rights and whether indeed in the contested third generation of rights, they are really human rights at all. Finally, the question calls for a qualitative judgement as to whether the student believes the concept, and therefore can state which prevailing academic opinion is most persuasive.

A recent article strongly supporting the concept of an international bill of rights is Dugard, 'The influence of the Universal Declaration as law' (2010). This answer takes a position supporting the existence of such a bill of rights, but there could be an equally strong argument made for the reverse position and an interesting series of articles in vol. 19 of the *European Journal of International Law* marking the sixtieth anniversary of the **Universal Declaration of Human Rights** debates the issue of the existence of an international bill of rights.

- Describe the body of treaties and international instruments that make up a possible international bill of rights.
- Discuss the enforcement system for those human rights.
- Engage in a discussion of the hierarchy of human rights norms.
- Discuss the debate of this issue within the academic literature.
- Conclude as to whether a universal bill of rights exists.

Suggested answer

In order to discuss this issue the current treaty regime has to be the starting point. The **Vienna Declaration and Programme of Action 1993,** asserted that all human rights are indivisible from and interdependent of one another. As Steiner *et al.* (2007) argue, the two fundamental human rights treaties are the **International Covenant on Civil and Political Rights (ICCPR)** and the **International Covenant on Economic, Social and Cultural Rights (ICESCR).** They assert that together with the **Universal Declaration of Human Rights (UDHR)** these covenants, which came into force in 1976, form the **International Bill of Human Rights.** It must be noted that the **UDHR** was not a treaty but a 1948 General Assembly resolution; however it has been argued that the **UDHR** provisions are now part of customary international law. Ghandi (2006) indicates that the **UDHR** has been the bedrock of the efforts of the UN to legislate for an International Bill of Rights. There are other international treaties that can arguably be part of this treaty regime such as the **International Covenant on the Elimination of all forms of Racial Discrimination (1965),** the **International Covenant Against All Forms of Discrimination Against Women (1979),** the **International Covenant Against Torture and Other Cruel, Inhuman or Degrading Treatment or Punishment (1985),** and the **Convention on the Rights of the Child (1989)** (almost universally ratified). These conventions have attracted a high level of states parties and the rights enumerated could well be part and parcel of a bill of rights.

However, not all human rights are agreed to be part of the **Universal Bill of Human Rights.** Steiner *et al.* discuss the issue of generations of rights. The first generation of rights are the civil and political rights and the second generation are the economic and social rights. There is a third contested generation known as 'solidarity rights' which include among others the right to development, the right to peace, and the right to the environment. The third generation solidarity rights are not universally accepted by state practice or academic literature as binding or part of the universal bill of rights. Furthermore, there is a debate concerning enforceability of even the second generation of rights, as they are often argued to be political aspirations rather than enforceable rights.

As a result of the debate concerning generations of rights and in spite of the confident assertion of Ghandi, Steiner *et al.* not all academics are prepared to agree that the first and second generation of human rights as embodied in the **UDHR,** the **ICCPR,** and the **ICESCR** are part of a universal bill of rights. Franconi (1997) argues that the control machinery that guarantees actual observance and implementation of human rights in national legal systems remains unsatisfactory. He also indicates that at the international level the enforcement mechanism is limited to examining periodic national reports and that there is hardly any room for examining specific violations. It can be asserted that Franconi is being more negative than necessary due to the existence of the Optional Protocol to the ICCPR and the recently adopted similar protocol for the ICESCR, both of which provide for individual complaints. Recently, von Bernstorff (2008) argued that the **Universal Declaration of Human Rights** was politically and morally important rather than legally binding.

However, an examination of case law might contradict these assertions. In addition to numerous cases of enforcement of political and civil rights in international and domestic tribunals, there are examples within domestic legislation of enforcement of economic, social, and cultural rights. India reserved the right to enforce directly economic and social rights, and the Indian Supreme Court has heard economic and social cases. In *Olga Tellis v Bombay Municipal Corporation* the court considered the rights of pavement dwellers to be free from eviction and the Supreme Court has held in *Paschim Banga Khet Mazdoor Sabha v State of West Bengal* that the state's obligations to protect economic and social rights may include obligations to provide additional resources, for example to ensure essential healthcare services. South Africa also placed economic, social, and cultural rights in their constitution and the Supreme Court of South Africa has ruled on issues of enforcement of economic and social rights particularly in the *Grootboom* (housing rights), *Soobramoney* (health), and *Treatment Action Campaign* (medications) cases.

Therefore, one can support Dugard's argument that the **UDHR,** the **ICCPR,** and the **ICESCR** constitute a body of human rights law that gives substance to the rights enshrined in the human rights provisions, **Arts 55** and **56** of the **United Nations Charter.** As a consequence, their substantive principles are binding on all Member States of the United Nations under the Charter itself. It is this additional justification that gives credence to the notion that an international bill of rights exists and that the main provisions are legal rules binding on all states.

 Examiner's tip

The student could be penalized if the dates are not included in the treaties. Also it is important to keep up to date on the case law of enforcement of economic, social, and cultural rights. ESCR-net has a case law database that should be consulted prior to the examination and your lecturer may not be aware of the most recent case.

Question 2

The international system for the protection of human rights is based on the various human rights conventions agreed to by large numbers of states.

With referexnce to the enforcement mechanisms within one of these treaties, describe the system of human rights protection within the UN and assess its effectiveness.

Commentary

This question is on three levels. First, there must be evidence of understanding of the enforcement system of the eight major human rights treaties in force. Second, and crucially, the student must undertake a detailed analysis of the reporting and enforcement mechanisms of one of the treaties, and suggest possible solutions. Third, the student should address the apparent paradox that the treaties are broadly ratified but still human rights protection remains weak.

Keith's (1999) article and Mertus (2005) provide an excellent analysis of the current system of reporting and enforcement. Another source is Donnelly's 'International human rights: a regime analysis' (1986).

To test the veracity of the quotation, students must demonstrate the practical application of the theory of enforcement alongside one of the main human rights instruments. Taking the **ICCPR**, we can see, in the 42 years since it was open to ratification, the mixed effect it has had on state behaviour. More able candidates will demonstrate a deeper understanding of the subtleties of the processes of individual treaties, making frequent reference to provisions contained therein.

Students must then undertake a detailed critique of the implementation process and its success. A brief theoretical discussion as to the type of approach being used and the outcome it seeks to effect would be welcome. While detailed statistical data are not required, a broad understanding of the ratio of states that ratify to states that implement into national policy would be an excellent approach. Additionally, some suggestions, based on academic opinion as to the divergence of implementation would be helpful.

A total analysis would not be complete without a look at the suggestions for reform. Bowman's 'Towards a unified treaty body for monitoring compliance with UN human rights conventions? Legal mechanisms for treaty reform' (2007) looks at a single body for monitoring enforcement and implementation. While Special Rapporteur Katarina Tomaševski's *Report to Human Rights Commission* (2002) suggests a series of quantitative indicators to measure willingness of states to implement rights through an economic lens.

Answer plan

- Introductory discussion of the current human rights instruments, and understanding of their **UDHR** heritage.

- Discussion of the present system of enforcement, and demonstration that ratification and formal implementation into national policy are very different things.

- Analysis of the causes of lack of enforcement, be it either a weak reporting system or extra-legal factors.

- Critical analysis of one of the treaties and a critique of its reporting system.

Suggested answer

I shall take the **ICCPR** as the analytical backbone to assess the effectiveness of the enforcement mechanisms that exist within the seven major treaties (**ICESCR, ICCPR, International Convention on the Elimination of All Forms of Discrimination Against Women 1979, Convention Against Torture and Other Cruel, Inhuman and Degrading Treatment or Punishment 1984, Convention on the Rights of the Child 1989, International Convention on the Protection of the Rights of All Migrant Workers and Members of their Families 1990, Convention on the Rights of Disabled People 2006**) and propose avenues for reform. As Keith (1999) observes, the high levels of formal acceptance (over three-quarters of UN Member States) suggests substantial progress to high levels of human rights norms. Forsythe, however, in 'The United Nations and human rights, 1945–85' (1985) questions the effectiveness of treaties with inherently weak monitoring mechanisms and the provisions of which mainly serve socializing functions.

Forsythe sees the **UN Charter** as a *'constitution without a bill of rights'*; for it only briefly deals with the concept under its purposes, one of which is to *'promote and encourage respect for human rights and fundamental freedoms'*. For Steiner *et al.* (2007), this aspirations-based Charter led directly to the **UDHR** and in turn to the two principle human rights treaties, the **ICCPR** and the **ICESCR**. The **ICCPR** set up a committee of experts appointed to study reports from states on implementation, and has the power to make recommendations. The two primary implementation mechanisms are the reporting process and interstate complaints. **Article 40** requires states to submit reports, which are examined, and a response with recommendations is published. **Article 41** is a rarely used interstate complaints procedure. Additionally, the first Optional Protocol controversially allows direct petition, upon exhaustion of domestic remedies, to the Human Rights Committee (HRC).

International scholars have long questioned the wisdom of a self-assessed reporting system. For Robertson in 'The implementation system: international measures' (1981) the natural tendency for subjectivity to creep in via states completing their own reports is inevitable and makes a mockery of an objective process. Torkel Opsahl in 'The

Human Rights Committee' (1995) points to the multitude of tardy or non-compliant states. The HRC noted that at the time of Opsahl's article two-thirds of states were non-compliant. McGoldrick (1991) was more optimistic, however, citing that many states had improved their reports dramatically, and their punctuality had also improved, since their initial submissions. Robertson points to the heart of the problem with the current system, in that even in a true and punctual report, the committee has no power to compel change. Robertson is further unconvinced by **Art. 41** and the power to make inter-state complaints, describing it as a merely 'optional procedure'. McGoldrick criticizes the first Optional Protocol and the individual complaints procedure. Even given that many states have failed to ratify this protocol (notably the United States), there is no follow-up procedure and again no power to compel any change.

There are some positive comments, as Keith (1999) observes that the general acquies-cence to broader rights in the covenant has led to the creation of norms, and acts as a way of publicizing states that are lax on rights implementation. Finally, Keith notes the covenant and committee's ability to draw international attention to major human rights abuses in a way not seen before.

Although the seven major treaties operate in an almost identical fashion, each has their own separate institution. Bowman (2007) argues this to be a wasteful inefficiency, and suggests a single unified body for reporting would promote cooperation and that is precisely the mechanism that is being developed by the newly constituted Human Rights Council in adopting a single reporting mechanism.

Finally, it is necessary to review the system of complaints under the Optional Proto-col. The main difficulty is that many of the countries that have ratified the treaty did not do the same with the **Additional Protocol**. This means that many human rights com-plaints have no regional or international system of receiving complaints. Furthermore, the HRC can only issue views which are not enforceable. Nevertheless, the comments by Keith (1999) are equally applicable in that attention is drawn to major human rights abuses by these complaints and states generally respect the views that are issued. The system of views is also the same system utilized by the Committee on the Elimination of Racial Discrimination, the Committee Against Torture, and the Committee for the Elimination of Discrimination against Women.

In conclusion, the current treaty structure for rights protection has raised awareness of respective states' implementation, but has done little to promote rights enforcement. Until there are binding decisions, such as those issued by the European Court of Human Rights (ECtHR), the international enforcement system will be weak and ineffective.

 Examiner's tip

The student should be aware of the division of academic views on the effectiveness of human rights and reflect both view points. A knee-jerk reaction that enforcement of human rights does not happen would be a superficial answer and would not impress the marker.

Question 3

International standards of protection of human rights apply no matter what culture or national, religious, or ethnic group you belong to.

Discuss this statement.

Commentary

This question calls for an examination of the universality of human rights, and by extension a critical analysis of the cultural relativist argument.

Students will be aware that the seven major international human rights instruments draw their heritage from the **UDHR**, and are therefore imbued with a distinctly Western set of values. The question that needs to be resolved in answer to this statement is to what extent cultural, religious, or ethnic interpretations provide room for states to manoeuvre in implementing human rights norms.

The answer to this problem is the cultural relativism movement. Simply put, this advances a theory that cultural sensitivities allow for certain variance or non-compliance with provisions of international instruments, irrespective of international norms—see Orentlicher, 'Relativism and religion' (2001). However, for a challenge to relativism, see Breau, 'Human rights and cultural relativism: the false dichotomy' (2007) and Tilley, 'Cultural relativism, universalism, and the burden of proof' (1998).

The question is deeper than matters of mere definition, however, and therefore a critical analysis of the theory is needed. It is important for the student to maintain a position on this matter either for or against. This particular formulation takes issue with the cultural relativist position but an equally eloquent answer could support it.

Answer plan

- Introduction and definition of the cultural relativism argument.
- Relate the argument to the Western development of human rights.
- Critical analysis of the argument and conclusion using the argument of Tilley (1998) who analyses different facets of the cultural relativist argument.

Suggested answer

A major threat to the legitimacy and universality of human rights is the cultural relativist approach. Donnelly (1986) defines the term as a doctrine that holds that (at least some) cultural variations from human rights instruments are exempt from legitimate criticism by outsiders. The paradox to be reconciled is between the universality of moral judgements and the compelling relativist argument. This argument is particularly pertinent in the current context of a dispute over the universality of human rights in the different cultural contexts. Orentlicher (2001) debates the challenge that cultural relativism posed to the '*effectiveness and intellectual coherence of the human rights movement*'. She summarizes the relativist critique of human rights indicating that human rights are an expression, above all of Western values derived from the Enlightenment. She argues that those who advocate human rights ideas are at best misguided in their core claim that they embody universal values and that this is at worst cultural imperialism or moral hubris.

This is not the position that is maintained in this essay. One could equally argue that human rights are not just expressions of Western values, but, as a discipline, is inclusive of diverse cultural elements. One of the major outcomes of respect for human rights is the encouragement of diversity, including acceptance and respect for all cultures. Those who argue that human rights are solely derived from the Enlightenment, and thus do not respect other cultural contexts, do not recognize the diverse philosophical and spiritual underpinnings of human rights that stem from many cultural traditions. It is not an 'either or' proposition; both human rights and culture can coexist and thrive.

It can be asserted that the **UDHR** with its input in development from many nations can be applicable to all human beings as human rights and culture can actually complement and strengthen each other. Cultural relativism can stand for the principle that we should not judge the behaviour of others using the standards of our own culture, and that each culture should be analysed on its own terms. In fact the two concepts can be harmonized as human rights not only encompass respect for the individual but an understanding of the society in which that individual lives. This has been argued to be the cultural pluralist position as opposed to the relativist stance.

Tilley (1998) advances a persuasive critique of the concept. He first examines the position that the rightness of the deed is determined by the norms of the agent's culture; it has nothing to do with the origin or rationale of those norms. Tilley critiques this point on three grounds: (a) its impediment to progression; (b) the irrelevance of resolving ethical dispute by taking a poll; and (c) that it hinders moral reform of any kind. Using the salient arguments for relativism as a backbone to analysis, Tilley has set out a convincing critique of the doctrine. The triviality argument advances that morality is always right in every circumstance, and relies on subjective definitions. For example, 'kindness is always right' relies on the assumptions that kindness is universally the correct option, and on the definition of kindness, and therefore a relativist argument should triumph. Tilley advances that many statements, such as '*starting a nuclear war to demonstrate military might is wrong*' are universally accepted and that relativism cannot succeed.

He then examines the 'polygeny' argument which suggests that a standard of behaviour comes from social and cultural norms rather than any higher notions. Tilley is unconvinced, asserting that it only holds water if we parallel 'morality' as a set of precepts about marital customs, habits of dress, and so on. Once we recall that morality concerns such things as slavery and genocide, and not the broader Victorian conception of the term, the argument loses its appeal. There is a danger of over specifying the rights. Slavery and racism for example might be socially acceptable but would fall foul of the broader, more accepted premise to treat people with respect. Similarly the 'human sacrifice' argument fundamentally states that good and evil are culturally variable. Tilley counteracts this by asserting that such proponents fail to distinguish between blame and moral judgements; repeating the earlier point that some statements are universal—'genocide is not good', for example.

He also examines the 'research' argument which is the most common in favour of relativism. It asserts that cultures differ *radically* from one another; or rather that practices are *fundamentally* different. Tilley questions this argument and takes issue with the premise that cultures accept radically different morality. Perhaps the second most popular argument in relativism is the 'true for them' approach. This, Tilley argues, confuses justification for behaviour with truth.

A final argument is one of tolerance of others' beliefs and practices. Tilley expands this in 'Moral arguments for cultural relativism' (1999), arguing that it rests solely on the normative argument that we '*ought not to impose our morality on other cultures*'. Tilley refutes this by noting that the fact that if x practice conflicts with y, then international prohibition does not directly require our interference with x. Human rights protection does not impose a morality but a legally binding obligation to respect one another's rights and culture.

In conclusion, as Donnelly (1986) asserts, a radical universal or a radical relativism would allow for culture to be used as a shield for rights protection. It is therefore asserted that a strong universal doctrine with a weak level of relativism, similar to the margin of appreciation afforded by the European Commission for the implementation of its directives, would lead to greater implementation of international human rights instruments. Human rights can respect cultural diversity while insisting on the basic doctrine of the universal dignity of the person. Finally, Breau (2007) asserts that human rights standards dictate respect for language, dress, and religious practices. Those who seek to exploit the differences between cultures should travel around the globe and note the remarkable similarity of the hopes and aspirations of all for food, shelter, education, gainful employment and an active social, cultural, and religious life. All of these common goals would be established in an international bill of human rights.

 Examiner's tip

This answer requires the student to engage with academic literature as it is academics who have discussed the controversy over cultural relativism in detail. There are numerous articles on the topic and the student would be rewarded by an online database search.

Question 4

The state of Anglia is a party to the European Convention of Human Rights (ECHR) and the ICCPR. On account of a number of terrorist attacks which have occurred in the country, the state wishes to detain terrorist suspects without a judicial hearing for 42 days.

Discuss the treaty provisions affected and the procedure that Anglia must follow pursuant to its treaty obligations. Assess whether or not the state might be able to accomplish this measure and comply with its international law obligations.

 Commentary

This question concerns a very important issue in human rights law, particularly in light of the recent focus on anti-terrorism legislation, and that is the ability of a state to derogate from its obligations under human rights treaties. For an excellent analysis of **Art. 15** and derogation in other human rights treaties, see Higgins, 'Derogations under human rights treaties' (1976–7).

The problem question refers to the two key international and regional treaties and candidates would be expected to be familiar with their respective provisions pertaining to detention, and the applicable jurisprudence. More able students may question whether Anglia is a party to any optional protocols, namely the first **Optional Protocol** of the **ICCPR**, allowing for individual petition.

Students might wish to examine the principle of detention without trial on three main grounds in light of recent case law: (a) is the emergency threatening the life of the nation? (b) is the response proportionate? and (c) is the measure discriminatory in application? For an examination of the various responses to the attacks of 11 September 2001, see Katselli and Shah (2003). There have been a few instructive cases before the ECtHR in this field: *Brogan and others*, *Klass v Germany*, *Ireland v UK*; *and* in more recent times, the terrorism cases: *A (FC) and others*; *(X) FC and another v Secretary of State for the Home Department ('Belmarsh')*; see also *Chahal v UK*, *Lawless v Ireland*, the *Greek* case, and *R(S) v Chief Constable of the South Yorkshire Police*.

 Answer plan

- Outline of options for states in an emergency situation.
- Demonstration of knowledge of relevant article and optional protocols.
- Exposition of the law of detention without charge.
- Definition of the term 'promptly'.
- Conclusions as to the overall legality of 42 days *per se*.

Suggested answer

Detaining a suspect for 42 days without a judicial hearing seems to offend **Art. 5 of the European Convention on Human Rights (ECHR)** and **Art. 9(1) of the International Covenant on Civil and Political Rights (ICCPR)**. As the European Court of Human Rights (ECtHR) pointed out in *Moustaquim v Belgium*, states retain ultimate sovereignty over their territory. Therefore, following Higgins's (1976–7) reasoning, states may well derogate from the necessary provisions during an emergency. However, in order to derogate from the key provisions that mandate lawful review of detention, Anglia must comply with its international obligations. The key issues here are: (a) the compatibility of detention with judicial hearing with these international instruments; (b) the time limit before a judicial hearing; and (c) the legality of 42 days specifically.

The preliminary question is whether Anglia is a signatory of the first **Optional Protocol** of the **ICCPR**, which allows for individual petition to the Human Rights Commissioner (to which the United States is not a party). If not, detainees will have to rely on the antiquated enforcement procedures. This lack of ratification has led to a number of *'rights free zones'* as Koh observes in his article 'America's offshore refugee camps' (1994). However, in the case of citizens of Anglia, even if their country is not party to the Optional Protocol, the **ECHR** does allow a right of individual petition for 'victims' to the European Court of Human Rights once their domestic remedies have been exhausted.

The crucial question to be addressed is whether the principle of 'detention without judicial hearing' is ever compatible with **Art. 9(1) ICCPR** or **Art. 5 ECHR**. Gross demonstrates in 'Human rights, terrorism and the problem of administrative detention in Israel: does democracy have the right to hold terrorists as bargaining chips?' (2001) that one must determine whether the motivation of Anglia is to remove terrorists from the streets, or bring them quickly before a judicial hearing. While preventive detention is not explicitly prohibited in the **ICCPR**, it may fall within the prohibition on *'arbitrary arrest or detention'* contained in **Art. 9(1)**. The exception is where *'such procedures are established by law'*—as always, the answer is one of definition.

Article 7 ECHR, attempts to tackle arbitrariness through mandating that all detention has a recognized authority. In the instant case, however, it is clear that Anglia's legislator passed the 42 days' detention, and under this narrow interpretation *'arbitrary'* would be compliant with **Art. 9(1)**. Conversely, we may examine the adverb *'arbitrary'* under the wider, normative, lens. This would be that the arrest or detention was arbitrary if it were not just unlawful but also unjust, in accordance with a natural law of due process. The HRC in *Van Alphen v The Netherlands* 305/88 confirmed *'arbitrary'* to be equated against elements of inappropriateness, injustice, and lack of predictability. Similarly in *A v Australia* 560/1093 the committee demanded the term be assessed against *'inappropriateness and injustice'*. It is therefore submitted that the term is to be assessed against broader principles as delineated in the **UDHR** to *'protect individuals from despotic legislation and to establish that deprivations of liberty, such* *as occurred under the Nazi regime, are not consistent with human rights merely because they were prescribed by national law'*. It is further submitted therefore that preventive detention, as a motivation, is inconsistent with **Art. 9(1) ICCPR**.

It is necessary to examine next whether there can be a derogation from these provisions. The derogation provisions of **Art. 15 ECHR** talk of *'war or other public emergency threatening the life of the nation'*. As set out in *Lawless v Ireland* and by the European Commission on Human Rights in the *Greek* case, the threat must be *'actual or imminent'*. Additionally, the **Siracusa Principles on the Limitation and Derogations Provisions** in the **ICCPR** should be consulted. The case of *Ireland v UK* demonstrates that the threat is determined by the consequence, and that life of the nation is different to life of its individual citizens. Therefore one would have to ask whether the terrorist threat facing Anglia was of such magnitude that it threatened the life of the nation.

The general principle of proportionality must be adhered to when considering the legality of 42 days without judicial hearing. The UK Attorney-General in the *Belmarsh* case argued the court should follow the ECtHR's *'margin of appreciation'*, allowing states to vary somewhat from the provisions to accommodate state sensitivities. There are two problems with this cultural relativist approach. First, it is assumed that while granting a margin of appreciation, the measure (42 days) will achieve greater scrutiny in the domestic courts. Second, it is also assumed that the courts will intervene should the measure not accord enough weight to international or national rights. The utilitarian argument advanced by some that it might be permissible to infringe the rights of the few to safeguard the many, draws predictable criticism from Shestack (1988). It is asserted that the response of 42 days exceeds the general test of proportionality.

Finally, the measure must not be discriminatory in nature, and, as such, not offend **Art. 14 ECHR**. The test broadly deployed by the British courts is delineated in *R(S) v Chief Constable of the South Yorkshire Police*, broadly following the ECtHR formulation: (a) facts within the convention; (b) difference in treatment; (c) on proscribed grounds; (d) where comparators in analogous situation; and (e) was the measure objectively justifiable. Simply put, the measure must apply to all the citizens of Anglia, and not just a specific group.

We must also consider the timing itself. **Article 5(3) ECHR** mandates that detainees must be brought *'promptly'* before a judge or released. It is regarded as settled case law that the adverb *'promptly'* does not mean *'immediately'*, as the French term *'aussitôt'*, considered in *Ireland v UK*. That said, the court has never clearly stated the maximum time of detention acceptable under the convention, per *Brogan and others*. The HRC in its **Decision 2894/66** determined it permissible to detain a suspect for five days in exceptional circumstances; but in *Brogan* it was clear that this was an upper limit, not a starting point. It is therefore submitted that a detention of 42 days without appearance before a judge or formal charging is incompatible with **Art. 5(3) ECHR**.

In conclusion, the principle of detention under the convention is to punish criminality or accommodate practicality before judicial appearance. The principle of *habeas corpus* and natural justice must therefore apply, and a detention of 42 days without proof of wrongdoing is clearly inconsistent with international law.

Examiner's tip

The student is this case is aware that this country is a party to the **European Convention**. If the country is not a state party it would be important to say that the ECHR cases are persuasive and not binding. It also might be useful to include some domestic case law as many courts have considered detention in the context of detention and asylum seekers.

Further reading

von Bernstorff, J., 'The changing fortunes of the Universal Declaration of Human Rights: Genesis and symbolic dimensions of the turn to rights in international law' (2008) 19 EJIL 903.

Bowman, M., 'Toward a unified treaty body for monitoring compliance with UN Human Rights conventions?' (2007) 7(1) *Hum. Rts. L. Rev.* 225.

Breau, S., 'Human rights and cultural relativism: the false dichotomy', in J. Rehman and S. Breau (eds), *Religion, Human Rights and International Law* (Boston: Martinus Nijhoff, 2007).

Donnelly, J., 'International human rights: a regime analysis', International Organizations (1986) 40(3) *Journal of Peace Research* 599–642.

Duffy, H., *The War on Terror and the Framework of International Law* (New York: Cambridge University Press, 2005).

Dugard, J., 'The influence of the Universal Declaration as law', (2009) 24 *Maryland J. of International Law* 85–93.

Forsythe, D. P., 'The United Nations and human rights, 1945–85' (1985) 100(2) *Political Science Quarterly* 249.

Francesco, F., 'An international bill of rights: why it matters, how it can be used' (July 1997) 32 *Tex. Int'l L. J.* 471, 473.

Ghandi, S., 'The International Bill of Rights and the European Convention on Human Rights' (2006) 6 LIMUK 282.

Gross, E., 'Human rights, terrorism and the problem of administrative detention in Israel: does democracy have the right to hold terrorists as bargaining chips?' (2001) 18(3) *Arizona J. of International and Comparative Law* 721, 752.

Higgins, R., 'Derogations under human right treaties' (1976–7) 48(1) BYIL 281.

Katselli, E. and Shah, S., 'September 11 and the UK response' (2003) 52 ICLQ 245.

Keith, L., 'The United Nations ICCPR: does it make a difference in human rights behavior?' (1999) 36 *J. of Peace Research* 95.

Koh, H., 'America's offshore refugee camps' (1994) 29 *Richmond L. Rev.* 139.

McGoldrick, D., *Human Rights Committee: Its Role in the Development of the International Covenant on Civil and Political Rights* (New York: Oxford University Press, 1991).

Mertus, J., *The United Nations and Human Rights* (New York: Routledge, 2005).

Opsahl, T., 'The Human Rights Committee' (1992) in P. Alston (ed.), *The United Nations and Human Rights: a Critical Appraisal* (Oxford: Clarendon, 1992).

Orentlicher, D. F., 'Relativism and religion', in M. Ignatieff (ed.), *Human Rights as Politics and Idolatry* (Princeton: Princeton University Press, 2001).

Robertson, A. H., 'The implementation system: international measures', in L. Henkin (ed.), *The International Bill of Rights: the Covenant on Civil and Political Rights* (New York and Guildford: Columbia University Press, 1981).

Shestack, J., 'The jurisprudence of human rights', in T. Meron (ed.), *Human Rights in International Law: Legal and Policy Issues* (Oxford: Clarendon, 1988).

Steiner, H., Alston, P., and Goodman, R., *International Human Rights in Context: Law, Politics, Morals*, 3rd edn (Oxford: Oxford University Press, 2007).

Tilley, J., 'Cultural relativism, universalism, and the burden of proof' (1998) 27 *Millennium* 275.

Tilley, J., 'Moral arguments for cultural relativism' (1999) 17 *Neth. Q. Hum. Rts.* 36.

Tilley, J., 'Cultural relativism' (2000) 22 *Hum. Rts. Q.* 511.

16 International humanitarian law and international criminal law

Introduction

These two topics are often combined in an introductory fashion in the public international law course. As with many topics in public international law, this is a fast-developing area particularly with the rapidly increasing activity of the International Criminal Court (ICC) with its first judgment issued on 14 March 2012 in the **Lubanga** case and the continuing work by the International Criminal Tribunals for Rwanda and Yugoslavia (ICTR and ICTY). The cases often deal with issues of international humanitarian law and many international crimes concern violations of the laws and customs of war.

   In order to revise for this combined topic, it is necessary for the student to have a general knowledge about the treaties and customary laws that make up both topics. They are related, as serious violations of international humanitarian law can constitute international crimes. Most general international law textbooks have introductory chapters which discuss either or both areas. These questions will ask the student to discuss the definition of international humanitarian law and to display a general knowledge of the **1907 Hague Regulations** and the **1949 Geneva Conventions** and their **1977 Additional Protocols**. The student will also be required to answer questions on the nature of international criminal law which criminalizes violations of international human rights law and international humanitarian law. There will be a question in this chapter on the development of international criminal tribunals which requires knowledge of the **Rome Statute of the International Criminal Court**.

   It should be emphasized that these questions do not assume a thorough knowledge of these areas as they are normally studied in depth at a postgraduate level. Excellent additional sources for these areas are Cassese (2008) and Dinstein (2004). An additional important new reference is the International Committee of the Red Cross (ICRC)'s customary international humanitarian law study by Henckaerts and Doswald-Beck (2005). Two examples of the practical application of these rules are the UN Human Rights

Council report on the Gaza conflict (known colloquially as the Goldstone report) and the European Union report on the Russia–Georgia conflict.

These questions will only test introductory knowledge of these two important fields of international law but still require the student to be aware of the important international instruments and the major developments in both fields including some leading jurisprudence. For these topics on the syllabus, I urge my students to read the judgment of the International Military Tribunal (IMT) at Nuremberg, which often serves as an incentive for them to pursue postgraduate studies in these important topics.

 Question 1

With reference to treaties and customary international law, discuss the historical development of the rules of international humanitarian law.

 Commentary

This is a deceptively simple question needing organization and structure. This is the type of wide-open question that could lead to far too much detail and not enough analysis. It would be useful to refer to an introductory text in international law such as Shaw (2008) to determine the detail needed in a question such as this. It is important to describe the development of what is called Geneva law and Hague law.

It is also important to review the various international humanitarian law treaties. A good collection of these treaties is in Roberts and Guelff (2002). A good explanatory text is Dinstein (2010).

 Answer plan

- Discuss the earliest humanitarian law instruments.
- Describe the four **Geneva Conventions** and the status of their ratifications.
- Describe the two **Additional Protocols**.
- Analyse the role of customary international law.

 Suggested answer

Although the rules of the conduct of warfare have existed since ancient times, a series of treaties first codified the rules of war in the nineteenth century. As a consequence of the American Civil War, Henry Lieber developed a code of conduct for the Union army in 1863, the **Lieber Code**. In Europe the ICRC was founded by Henri Dunant who was horrified at the carnage he witnessed at the Battle of Solferino and the first **Geneva Convention for the Amelioration of the Condition of the Wounded in Armies of the Field** was adopted in 1864. In 1869 the **Declaration of St Petersburg** prohibited the use of small explosive or incendiary projectiles.

The next major developments in international humanitarian law were the Hague Conferences of 1899 and 1907 which developed the **Hague Regulations** which codified the principles of humanity in the conduct of armed conflict and developed the first rules of the law of occupation. The **1899 Hague Convention** contained the famous Martens clause, which stated that until a more complete code of the laws of war was issued the parties remained under the protection of the principles of international law which included the laws of humanity and the requirements of public conscience. Dinstein (2004) discusses the reference to the clause in the International Court of Justice (ICJ) advisory Opinion of 1996 on *Legality of the Threat or Use of Nuclear Weapons* to reveal the two cardinal principles of international humanitarian law. The first is the principle of distinction between combatants and civilians, in that states must never make civilians the object of attack or use weapons that are incapable of distinguishing between civilian and military targets. The second is that it is prohibited to cause unnecessary suffering to combatants. Dinstein states that this clause confirms customary international humanitarian law principles and also confirms the two requirements of principles of humanity and dictates of public conscience.

The **Hague Regulations 1907** are still in effect governing the law of occupation for those countries not parties to the **1977 Additional Protocol I** to the **Geneva Convention**. Two examples are the ongoing Israeli occupation of the Palestinian territories and the recent United States' occupation of Iraq.

A major treaty after the First World War was the **Geneva Protocol 1925 for the Prohibition of the Use in War of Asphyxiating, Poisonous or other Gases, and of Bacteriological Methods of Warfare**, a treaty prohibiting the first use of chemical and biological weapons. This was in response to the use of poison gas by both sides during that conflict. There were also updated Geneva conventions including the **1929 Convention Relative to the Treatment of Prisoners of War**; but this convention was not widely ratified before the Second World War and Russia and Japan were not parties to the treaty and thus neither respected these rules. Germany also took the position that it did not have to comply with the rules of the **Geneva Convention** with respect to its Russian prisoners and, as a result, millions of prisoners died.

After the horrors of the Second World War with 'carpet-bombing' of cities and the massive deportations of civilians in occupied territories the four **Geneva Conventions** were drafted in 1949. Most of the terms are now part of customary international law as the **Conventions** are now universally ratified. The first **Geneva Convention** deals with the protection of the wounded and sick on land, the second **Geneva Convention** contains provisions protecting the wounded and sick at sea. The third **Geneva Convention** contains detailed protections for prisoners of war in order to prevent the types of treatment meted out to allied soldiers by the Japanese during the Second World War.

The fourth **Geneva Convention** specifically contains protections for civilians including those in occupied territories.

General areas protected by international humanitarian law treaties are the protection of civilians, regulations that circumscribe the methods of warfare to prohibit arms, projectiles or materials calculated to cause unnecessary suffering (**Art. 22 Hague Regulations 1907**), and to regulate the development of new weaponry (**United Nations Conventional Weapons Convention**). **Article 3(a) Statute of the International Tribunal on War Crimes in Former Yugoslavia** criminalizes the employment of poisonous weapons or other weapons calculated to cause unnecessary suffering. The customary status of these prohibitions is confirmed in the ICJ's advisory Opinion on the *Legality of Threat or Use of Nuclear Weapons* that '*states must never make civilians the object of attack: and must consequently never use weapons that are incapable of distinguishing between civilian and military targets*' and that there is a prohibition against causing unnecessary suffering to combatants or to aggravate their suffering. The rule simply says that states do not have unlimited freedom of choice of means in the weapons that they use.

One of the other important aspects of international humanitarian law is the distinction between international and non-international armed conflict. **Common Art. 3** to all four **Geneva Conventions** provides protections for those who are not combatants within a non-international armed conflict. **Additional Protocol II** provides protections for both civilians and combatants in non-international armed conflict but it is still not widely ratified. However, the ICRC customary international humanitarian law study— see Henckaerts and Doswald-Beck (2005)—proposes that many of the rules contained in both **Additional Protocol I** and **Additional Protocol II** have customary status in both international and non-international armed conflict.

One of the interesting aspects of this area of international law is that, although states ratify the conventions, it is individuals who will be held criminally responsible for violations of international humanitarian law. Enforcement of this area of the law is based on domestic jurisdictions criminalizing violations of the rules of war and the obligations within the conventions of respect and ensures that nations must prosecute their armed forces if they violate these rules. It is certainly the case that most military manuals and codes of military justice throughout the world criminalize violations of the universally ratified four **Geneva Conventions**.

There are a number of other conventions with respect to weapons including the **United Nations Conventional Weapons Convention** with its numerous protocols describing weapons that would cause undue suffering. Furthermore, as Dinstein (2004) argues, some weapons can be employed in a manner that breaches the principles of distinction by being instruments of direct or indiscriminate attack against civilians. The issue in the determination of the legality of a weapon is whether the weapon is designed as in the words of the ruling of the advisory Opinion on the *Legality of the Threat or Use of Nuclear Weapons* as being 'incapable of distinguishing between civilians and military targets'. Weapons conventions seek to outlaw these types of weapons.

Finally, international humanitarian law continues to develop new treaty law with the **Ottawa Convention on the Prohibition of the Use, Stockpiling, Production and Transfer** of Anti-Personnel Mines and on Their Destruction 1997 and the **Convention on Cluster Munitions 2008**. Both of these treaties again seek to limit the effect of those weapons which will cause unnecessary suffering and are incapable of distinguishing between civilians and combatants. However, as with all conventions on international humanitarian law, they depend on the agreement of states and with respect to mines and cluster munitions some of the states that manufacture and use these weapons have indicated that they will not consent to the treaties.

 Examiner's tip

International humanitarian law has largely developed through a number of treaties. The examiner will want to ensure that the student has knowledge of both the Geneva and Hague laws and the newer weapons' laws.

 Question 2

In the state of Montague a group of rebels, the Capulets, has launched a series of attacks against the army of Montague and attacked military facilities. The Capulets have a military structure with a commanding officer. The Capulets now occupy the province of Romeo and the army of Montague is unable to enter the territory. Montague has signed the four **Geneva Conventions** but is not yet a party to the **Additional Protocols**, although its military manual indicates respect for most of the rules in the additional protocols. The rebel group, the Capulets, has filed a document with the Secretary-General of the UN that it will respect the applicable rules of war.

Discuss whether international humanitarian law applies to this situation and, if so, which rules of international humanitarian law apply.

 Commentary

This problem question seeks to elucidate knowledge of both treaty and customary international humanitarian law. The fact situation reveals a non-international armed conflict in a territory which has not ratified the **1977 Additional Protocols** to the **Geneva Conventions**. Notwithstanding that fact, it can be argued that the cardinal principles of customary international humanitarian law apply. It is essential to refer to a key case in international humanitarian law, the decision on jurisdiction of the Appeals Chamber of the International Criminal Tribunal for Yugoslavia, the *Tadić* decision **Case No. IT-94-1-AR-72, 105 ILR 453**.

Excellent source material for this answer would be the chapter in Shaw (2008) and Henckaerts and Doswald-Beck (2005), which is the study conducted by the ICRC on customary international humanitarian law. Another important source is Moir (2008).

 Answer plan

- Discuss the treaty rules that apply.
- Generally discuss customary international humanitarian law.
- Particularly apply the customary rules that might apply to non-international armed conflict.

 Suggested answer

In order for international humanitarian law to apply, any disturbance within a state must reach the threshold of an armed conflict. International humanitarian law has long considered the threshold of an armed conflict and the decision of the Appeals Chamber of the International Criminal Tribunal for Yugoslavia has done much to clarify the criteria. The Appeals Chamber in the *Tadić* jurisdiction decision decided that an armed conflict exists whenever there is a resort to armed force between states or protracted armed violence between governmental authorities and organized armed groups or between such groups within a state. In the case of Montague you have protracted armed violence on the territory of the state with an organized armed group. The threshold of an internal armed conflict seems to have been reached.

However, there is one further complication that should be addressed. **Common Art. 3**, common to all four **Geneva Conventions**, also gives criteria for its applicability. **Common Art. 3** is applicable to '*each Party to the conflict*' and this means there must be in existence at least two parties. It is not difficult to determine the existence of the armed forces of one of the parties—the state—but the non-state armed group is more difficult. Moir (2008) argues that the armed group has to have a certain level of organization and command structure, as well as the ability to implement international humanitarian law. The criteria contained in **Additional Protocol II 1977** to the **Geneva Conventions**—the Convention that governs internal armed conflict—is more stringent. In **Art. 1** the criteria includes all armed conflicts which take place in the territory of a high contracting party between its armed forces and dissident armed forces or other organized armed groups which, under responsible command, exercise such control over a part of its territory as to enable them to carry out sustained and concerted military operations and to implement the **Protocol**. The **Protocol** specifically states that it shall not apply to situations of internal disturbances and tensions, such as riots, isolated and sporadic acts of violence.

The two key factors were territorial control and the ability to carry out sustained and concerted military operations. An explanation is that **Additional Protocol II** was negotiated in an atmosphere of determining the least common denominator in a situation of infringement of state sovereignty. Therefore, the scope of application is much narrower than **Common Art. 3** but the Protocol specifically states that it develops and supplements **Common Art. 3** without modifying its existing conditions of application. The **Geneva Conventions** are now universally ratified conventions, whereas many countries are not party to **Additional Protocol II**, including Montague. The ICJ has declared that **Common Art. 3** represents customary international law in both international and non-international armed conflict *(Military and Paramilitary Activities in and against Nicaragua (Nicaragua v US), Merits)*.

As the Capulets seems to meet even the more stringent conditions of **Additional Protocol II**, we can safely argue that a non-international armed conflict exists in the territory of Montague.

However, the second issue is what rules of international humanitarian law apply. First, the Martens clause has formed a part of the laws of armed conflict since its first appearance in the preamble to the **1899 Hague Convention (II)** with respect to the laws and customs of war on land. It specifies that populations and belligerents remain under the protection of the principles of international law, including the laws of humanity and the requirements of public conscience. The primary focus then of international humanitarian law is to prevent human suffering for persons who were 'hors de combat' and civilians. A specific example of such protection is **Common Art. 3** to all four **1949 Geneva Conventions**. The protections for persons taking no active part in hostilities include prohibitions against violence to life and person, in particular murder of all kinds and torture; taking of hostages; outrages on personal dignity; and the passing of sentences and carrying out of executions without due process of a court. Finally, the wounded and sick shall be collected and cared for. This provision as part of four universally ratified treaties—the **Geneva Conventions**—can also constitute customary international law. It is binding on the government of Montague and on the Capulets.

In addition to these specific protections, and many more outlined in various treaties, the rules of *jus in bello* have evolved into three primary rules: necessity, distinction, and proportionality. It is accepted that human lives will be lost in an armed conflict but the primary goal is to limit the casualties to the actual belligerents. Armed conflict is to be directed against a state's military, not its civilians. Attacks are to be against military targets not civilian ones such as hospitals, schools, and churches. The recent report on the Gaza conflict, known as the Goldstone report, has confirmed the prohibitions against attacking these protected objects.

The first general principle is the rule of necessity which prohibits destructive or harmful acts that are unnecessary to secure a military advantage. Before any military action commences, it must be established that a direct military advantage will result. This is a primary rule of military targeting.

The second principle distinction requires that a belligerent distinguishes between civilian and military objectives and between civilians and combatants. **Article 48 Additional Protocol I** sets out the basic rule of distinction and mandates that the parties to the conflict shall at all times distinguish between the civilian population and combatants and between civilian objects and military objectives and accordingly shall direct their operations only against military objectives. Furthermore, **Art. 51(2) Additional Protocol I** prohibits '*acts or threats of violence the primary purpose of which is to spread terror among the civilian population are prohibited*'.

The third primary principle is the rule of proportionality. It means that in warfare: '*a belligerent may apply only that amount and kind of force necessary to defeat the enemy*'. The rule implies that the enemy should be defeated with a minimum loss of life or property. The use of any kind of force not required for the defeat of the enemy was prohibited. Even if a target was a military objective, it should be avoided if it might cause excessive civilian casualties. This principle is further supported in the advisory Opinion on *Nuclear Weapons* when it states '*respect for the environment is one of the elements that go to assessing whether an action is in conformity with the principles of necessity and proportionality*'.

These rules are also argued to be customary, as is evidenced by the ICRC's study on customary international humanitarian law—see Henckaerts and Doswald-Beck (2005). This influential study does much to clarify the rules of international humanitarian law in light of the fact that several countries have not ratified the more specific **1977 Additional Protocols I** and **II** to the **Geneva Conventions**. The first part, as may be expected, sets out the rules surrounding the three principles of distinction, proportionality, and necessity. All of these rules are argued in the ICRC study to be applicable in internal armed conflict, even though they are not specifically mentioned in the key treaties— either in **Common Art. 3** common to all four **Geneva Conventions** or in **Additional Protocol II**.

 Examiner's tip

The student in this problem question has to come to grips with the complex issue of customary humanitarian law. The study by the International Committee of the Red Cross has to be referred to in detail in this answer. The excellent answer will understand the primary customary rules applicable in non-international armed conflict.

 Question 3

One of the most significant developments in international law was the development of international criminal tribunals.

With reference to specific treaties and statutes, discuss the development of international criminal tribunals from the end of the Second World War to the present time.

 **Commentary**

This is a question designed to test your knowledge about the development of the institutions of international criminal law. Do not stray into a complete exposition of the crimes as that would form the subject of another question (see Question 4). It is important to know how these various tribunals were created, particularly the role of Security Council resolutions and treaties.

Cassese (2008) has an excellent chapter on the establishment of international criminal tribunals, but for the latest developments the well-prepared student will peruse the websites of the various tribunals and be aware of media reports of the various trials. For example, a major development in the ICTY has been the commencement of the trials of their two most wanted persons Radovan Karadžić and Ratko Mladić. Another major development is the first judgment issued by the International Criminal Court in March 2012 in the **Thomas Lubanga Dyilo** case which considered the issue of the recruitment and use of child soldiers in armed conflict.

 Answer plan

- Nuremberg and Tokyo tribunals.
- ICTY and ICTR.
- Special Courts for Sierra Leone and Cambodia.
- ICC.
- The Iraqi Special Tribunal.

 Suggested answer

As Cassese (2008) argues, the idea of an international criminal court bringing to justice individuals, including leading state officials, allegedly responsible for serious international crimes dates from the end of the First World War. The **Versailles Peace Treaty** contained in **Art. 27** a statement of responsibility of the German Emperor, Kaiser Wilhelm II, for the supreme offence against international morality and the sanctity of treaties and proposed the establishment of a tribunal to try him. This did not occur because of the protection that the Kaiser received from Holland. However, at the end of the Second World War, leaders of the Nazi and Japanese regimes were brought before the IMTs in Germany and Japan. An international conference on military trials held at London, which resulted in the **Nuremberg Charter,** set up the court to prosecute individuals for crimes against peace, war crimes, and crimes against humanity. With respect to Tokyo, General MacArthur, Supreme Commander of the Allied Powers in Japan, approved in an executive order the **Tokyo Charter** setting out the jurisdiction of the IMT for the Far East which also tried crimes against peace and humanity. These tribunals are criticized by Cassese as representing victors' justice over the defeated, as they were composed of judges and prosecutors from one side and not independent international courts proper, but judicial bodies acting as organs common to the appointing states.

Inspired by the efforts at international justice stemming from the end of the Second World War, the UN system, through the International Law Commission (ILC), attempted to establish a permanent criminal tribunal from 1947 but it was not successful until 1998. On account of the lack of political will, the 1953 draft Statute of an International Criminal Court was shelved. However, after the end of the cold war, there were remarkable developments in international criminal justice. In two areas of the world, civil conflict resulted in the establishment of 'ad hoc criminal tribunals'. First, the UN Security Council by **Resolution 827** set up the ICTY in 1993 and in 1994 by **Resolution 955** established the ICTR. Both resolutions had statutes of the tribunals appended to them which authorized trying individuals for genocide, crimes against humanity, and war crimes. This was an extraordinary development, as the Security Council interpreted its mandate of preserving peace and security as extending to the establishment of international criminal tribunals. The lawfulness of this action was confirmed by the ICJ in *Tadić*, a jurisdiction appeals decision in the ICTY.

Although these courts have been a strain financially on the UN system, they have successfully prosecuted several individuals for their crimes and they have done much to advance the court of international criminal justice. The tribunal in Rwanda has been able to try those most responsible for the genocide and clarify the law concerning the important crimes in the case of *Akayesu*. The ICTY has not been as successful in trying the leaders of the civil war and Slobodan Milošević died before his critical trial could be concluded. However, recently Radovan Karadžić, the leader of the Bosnian Serbs during the civil war, was brought to The Hague for trial and it is hoped that his trial will be concluded.

Further to these tribunals, the Security Council has considered situations in other places such as Sierra Leone, Cambodia, and East Timor. In each of these locations a hybrid international–national court has been established by treaty between the UN and the national governments. The Special Court for Sierra Leone has tried individuals responsible for that civil war and convicted the former President of Liberia, Charles Taylor for crimes against humanity and war crimes for his role in the civil war. In May 2012 the court sentenced him to 50 years in prison. The Cambodian court is called the Cambodian Extraordinary Chambers and is trying those still alive who were responsible for the Cambodian genocide. In East Timor the court is called the Special Panels for Serious Crimes. These last two courts are part of the judiciary of the national states, whereas the Special Court for Sierra Leone was as a result of an international agreement and was not part of the national judiciary. In East Timor and Kosovo it was the UN Interim Administration that passed regulations to set up these courts.

Cassese (2008) argues that using the national judiciary under some sort of international scrutiny might be advantageous, as it assuages the nationalistic demands of local authorities. It also includes the local officials in rendering justice, and involves the local population which might assist reconciliation. This might expedite trials and might contribute to the legal training of the local population. It remains to be seen if these lofty ambitions are realized, as the Special Court for Sierra Leone had suffered from underfunding and significant delays. The most high-profile accused person, Charles Taylor, was tried at The Hague (although the court is the Sierra Leone court) for security reasons.

However, the demand for international criminal justice for those countries that are unwilling or unable to try their international criminals grew in the 1990s, as did the interest in establishing a permanent institution. The growth of ad hoc and special tribunals provided an impetus for the development of the Statute for the International Criminal Court. The ILC produced a draft International Criminal Court Statute in 1993 and it was modified in 1994. A Preparatory Committee met between 1995 and 1998 to develop further the draft and prepare for an international conference which took place in Rome in 1998. As a result, at the Rome Conference in 1998 the **Statute for the International Criminal Court** was adopted by 120 votes to 7 but notably the United States objected to the court. However, the statute has been ratified by over 100 states and the court is now operational, with indictments having been issued in the situations of the Democratic Republic of Congo, Uganda, and Sudan. There has yet to be completed trials and it will remain to be seen how the court will contribute to international accountability for international crimes.

A final court to be discussed is the Iraqi Special Tribunal which, although it is an Iraqi court, the statute for which was drafted by international lawyers and there is international participation in the trials. The former dictator of Iraq, Saddam Hussein, was convicted and executed for crimes against humanity. This court is criticized for its aspect once again of victors' justice and the lack of consistent international participation. Some international lawyers, particularly British ones, could not participate because of the imposition of the death penalty, which is not present in any of the other courts.

All of these courts have in common that they try the most responsible for genocide, war crimes, and crimes against humanity. The jurisprudence developed by these courts assists in clarifying the elements of these various crimes and the evidence needed to convict those responsible. They are also developing a code of international criminal procedure which borrows elements from both the civilian and common law systems. An innovation with the ICC and the Special Court for Cambodia is the extensive involvement of the victims in the process.

 Examiner's tip

The essential source for this question is Cassese's seminal text on *International Criminal Law* (2008). The exceptional student will have read the text thoroughly and have an excellent grasp of the history of the development of international criminal tribunals. Do not forget the special courts in Sierra Leone and Cambodia.

Question 4

International criminal law prosecutes those who are charged with international crimes. What are those international crimes?

Commentary

This question is not straightforward. A major issue within international criminal justice was the dispute over the crimes of aggression which until the last review conference in June 2010 was not a crime under the **Rome Statute**. This is in spite of the fact that the Nuremberg Tribunal held Nazi leaders responsible for crimes against peace. The crime of aggression has now been adopted by the Review Conference but it will not be in effect until 2017 and only applicable under strict conditions.

Another complication is that the crime of genocide is relatively recent, having come into effect with the **1948 Genocide Convention**.

The student should refer to the **Charter of the International Military Tribunal at Nuremberg** and the **Statute of the International Criminal Court**. An excellent source for definitions of these crimes is Cassese (2008).

Answer plan

- Define genocide.
- Define crimes against humanity.
- Define war crimes and grave breaches.
- Define aggression and discuss the development of this crime under the **Statute of the ICC** with a particular emphasis on the review conference of 2010.

Suggested answer

The **Charter of the Nuremberg Tribunal**, established to try those German officials most responsible for the Second World War, in **Art. 6** set out the crimes for which it had jurisdiction. These were crimes against peace (aggression), crimes against humanity, and war crimes. Since that time, the major international crime developed is the crime of genocide. This answer will set out the elements of each crime and discuss the recent developments towards codification of the crime of aggression.

Genocide as set out in the **Genocide Convention 1948** is the intent to destroy in whole or part national, ethnical, racial, or religious groups by killing members of such groups, causing serious bodily or mental harm, deliberately inflicting conditions calculated to bring destruction, preventing births, and forcible transfer of children. This offence was not included in the Nuremberg IMT or in the Tokyo IMT. According to Cassese (2008), genocide only acquired autonomous significance as a specific crime when the UN General Assembly adopted the **Genocide Convention**. The Convention is important as it sets out a careful definition of the crimes, punishes other acts connected with genocide, such as conspiracy or complicity, and prohibits the crimes in either war or peace. There are flaws in the Convention, such as the fact that it does not embrace cultural genocide (destruction of a language and culture of a group) and does not encompass extermination of a group on political grounds. Only a few cases of genocide have been brought before national courts, the most important being the *Eichmann* case, where the defendant was tried for crimes against the Jewish people in Israel which incorporated the elements of genocide. However, the ICTY and ICTR have had successful convictions for genocide, notably the *Akayesu* decision in the ICTR and the *Krstić* case in the ICTY. The **Rome Statute** in Art. 6 includes the definition of genocide in the **Genocide Convention** and criminalizes the activity.

Cassese defines crimes against humanity as particularly odious offences in that they constitute a serious attack on human dignity or a grave humiliation or degradation of one or more human beings. These crimes are not isolated or sporadic events but are part either of a governmental policy, or of a widespread or systematic practice of atrocities tolerated, condoned, or acquiesced in by a government or a *de facto* authority. Crimes against humanity are crimes which involve murder, extermination, enslavement deportation, imprisonment, torture, rape, other sexual violence persecutions on religions, racial, political grounds, and other inhuman acts on a widespread or systematic basis. These crimes do not need a link to war—they can be prosecuted in either war or peace. In the Nuremberg Tribunal there needed to be a link with an armed conflict but, as Cassese points out, present customary law does not need such a requirement. An important factor of these crimes is that unlike war crimes that are linked to violations of international humanitarian law, crimes against humanity are widespread or systematic violations of international human rights law. The case law of the ICTY has done much to clarify the law of crimes against humanity, which include sexual violence against women. **Article 7 Rome Statute** includes rape, sexual slavery, enforced prostitution, forced pregnancy, enforced sterilization, or any other form of sexual violence of comparable gravity.

As Cassese asserts, war crimes are serious violations of the customary or treaty rules belonging to the corpus of the international humanitarian law of armed conflict. War crimes must have a nexus to armed conflict but can also occur in the course of a non-international or international armed conflict. War crimes can constitute grave breaches of the **Geneva Convention**, including wilful killing, torture, or inhuman treatment, extensive destruction of property, compelling prisoners of war to serve a hostile power, unlawful deportation or transfer of civilians and the taking hostage of civilians (**Art. 2 ICTY Statute**). War crimes can also include violations of the laws and customs of war including poisonous weapons, or weapons which cause unnecessary suffering, wanton destruction of cities, and so on, which are not justified by military necessity, attack of undefended locations, seizure/damage to religious, educational, charitable, historic, art, institutions, etc. and plunder of property. The scope and content of war crimes were canvassed in the decisions of the IMTs for Germany and Japan and have been further developed in the jurisprudence particularly of the ICTY. **Article 8 Statute of the International Criminal Court** has enumerated a long list of war crimes in both international and non-international armed conflict and these include both grave breaches and serious violations of international humanitarian law.

Finally, there is the crime of aggression. This is the violation of the prohibition against the use of force. It was included in the **Nuremberg Charter** but not incorporated into statutes of ad hoc tribunals or the **International Criminal Court Statute**. The elements of the offence in **Art. 6(a) International Military Tribunal Charter** are the planning, preparation, initiation or waging of a war of aggression, or a war in violation of international treaties, agreements or assurances or in the participation in a common plan or conspiracy for the accomplishment of any of the foregoing. The IMT defined this crime as the supreme international crime which in the IMT's view already existed in international law. The negotiations for the **ICC Statute** did not agree on a definition and only stated in **Article 5(2)** of the Statute that the court would exercise jurisdiction over the crime of aggression once a provision was adopted defining the crimes and setting out the conditions under which the court will exercise jurisdiction with respect to this crime. On 11 June 2010 the ICC review conference adopted a resolution amending the **Rome Statute** which included a definition of the crime of aggression and set out the conditions under which the court would exercise jurisdiction. The actual exercise of jurisdiction will be subject to a decision to be taken after 1 January 2017 by the same majority of states parties as is required for the adoption of an amendment to the Statute. The conference based the definition of the crime of aggression on **United Nations General Assembly resolution 3314 (XXIX)** of 14 December 1974, and in this context agreed to qualify as aggression, a crime committed by a political or military leader which, by its character, gravity and scale constituted a manifest violation of the Charter. As regards the court's exercise of jurisdiction, the conference agreed that a situation in which an act of aggression appeared to have occurred could be referred to the court by the Security Council, acting under **Chapter VII** of the **United Nations Charter**, irrespective of whether it involved states parties or non-states parties. However, in a critical proposal, while acknowledging the Security Council's role in determining the existence of an act of aggression, the conference agreed to authorize the prosecutor, in the absence of such determination, to initiate an investigation on his own initiative or upon request from a state party. In order to do so, however, the prosecutor would have to obtain prior authorization from the Pre-Trial Division of the court. Also, under these circumstances, the court would not have jurisdiction in respect to crimes of aggression committed on the territory of non-states parties or by their nationals or with regard to states parties that had declared that they did not accept the court's jurisdiction over the crime of aggression. If the crime of aggression is adopted the list of crimes first developed under the Nuremberg process will be complete.

Examiner's tip

A student may become confused in this answer between crimes against humanity and genocide. It is important to understand the distinction and the later development of genocide after the Nuremberg trials. If this is an essay question, access to the International Criminal Court's document on defining the elements of the various crimes would be essential.

Further reading

Cassese, A., *International Criminal Law*, 2nd edn (Oxford: Oxford University Press, 2008).

Dinstein, Y., *The Conduct of Hostilities under the Law of International Armed Conflict*, 2nd edn (Cambridge: Cambridge University Press, 2010).

Henckaerts, J. and Doswald-Beck, L., *Customary International Humanitarian Law*, vol. 1 (Cambridge: Cambridge University Press, 2005).

Moir, L., *The Law of Internal Armed Conflict*, 2nd edn (Cambridge: Cambridge University Press 2008).

Roberts, A. and Guelff, R., *Documents on the Laws of War* (Oxford: Oxford University Press, 2002).

Shaw, M., *International Law*, 6th edn (Cambridge: Cambridge University Press, 2008).

Report of the UN Fact-Finding Mission on the Gaza Conflict, United Nations Document A/HRC/12/48, 25 September 2009.

Independent International Fact-Finding Mission on the Conflict in Georgia, found at http://www.ceiig.ch/Report.html, Council of the European Union, September 2009.